Choice and Morality
in
Anthropological Perspective

Derek Freeman. Photograph taken by Monica Freeman in the mountain ranges south of Canberra.

Choice and Morality
in
Anthropological Perspective

Essays in Honor of Derek Freeman

Edited by

G. N. Appell and T. N. Madan

State University of New York Press

Published by
State University of New York Press, Albany

For information, address State University of New York
Press, State University Plaza, Albany, N.Y., 12246

10 9 8 7 6 5 4 3 2 1

Library of Congress Cataloging-in-Publication Data

Choice and morality in anthropological perspective.

Includes index.
1. Anthropological ethics.   2. Ethics—Cross-cultural
studies.   3. Choice (Psychology)—Cross-cultural studies.
4. Symbolic interactionism.   5. Freeman, Derek.
I. Freeman, Derek.   II. Appell, G. N.
III. Madan, T. N.
GN33.6.C48   1988   174'.9301   87-6534
ISBN 0-88706-606-2

Contents

Preface

This collection of essays on choice behavior and the moral order is by colleagues and former students of Professor Derek Freeman. It examines a critical dimension of human action from a variety of analytical perspectives. Professor Freeman has had a long and consuming interest in this field of inquiry, and he has made major contributions to the theory of choice making and the development of the interactionist paradigm.

This book is thus to honor Professor Freeman on his seventieth birthday. He is now Professor Emeritus of the Department of Anthropology, School of Pacific Studies at the Australian National University as well as Foundation Professor of Anthropology and Consultant on Samoan Studies at the University of Samoa. Professor Freeman, a stimulating teacher, an exceptionally gifted fieldworker, and an uncommonly innovative and seminal thinker, is as active as ever in extending the frontiers of anthropological thought with great strength of spirit and mind. We thus selected a theme for this volume that is representative of one of Freeman's major research interests—choice and the moral order—and it is hoped that these essays will help forward anthropological inquiry in a field of fundamental interest to him.

To those of us who have worked with him, Derek Freeman's contributions to anthropological thought are unparalleled. Freeman first became known for his pioneering researches on the Iban (1949–1951, 1957–1958, and 1976), from which he produced one of the finest ethnographic accounts of a people in Southeast Asia. But in addition, he has made important contributions to the study of human ethology, particularly in his analysis of choice behavior as critical to the development of the human ethogram, and to psychoanalytic anthropology. Freeman's field researches on Samoan culture and behavior, which began in 1940 and were interrupted by World War II and his Iban researches, have resulted in his refutation of Margaret Mead's account of Samoa, the first formal refutation in the history of anthropological inquiry.

vii

Freeman's insistence on the importance of choice in the growth of cultures and in the development of the ethogram of *homo sapiens*, his position that an interactionist paradigm is needed for anthropological inquiry, and his rejection of cultural relativism for a science that will evaluate cultural behavior in terms of its cognitive accuracy in mapping reality and its adaptive value, all testify to Derek Freeman as one of those outstanding scholars that cause a major shift in the direction of inquiry in their discipline.

During the last three decades, a large number of anthropologists have come into close contact with Professor Freeman as students or as professional colleagues. To many of us the most salient trait of Professor Freeman's character is his absolute insistence on intellectual integrity. Not only does he demand that we endeavor to make ethnography as accurate and comprehensive as possible, he also insists on an unswerving dedication to the scientific truth in the analysis and presentation of data. His moral outrage at shoddy or self-serving scientific work is well known, and he has told innumerable scholars about to set out on ethnographic fieldwork to make sure to "get it right." He, himself, is an outstanding ethnographer and takes infinite care with the collection, recording, and classification of field data.

These traits are all expressions of his vision of scientific inquiry as first and foremost moral action that demands unquestionable standards of conduct from all of us. The individual researcher is responsible for ensuring the trustworthiness and high quality of his work. Given such a stance, it is not surprising that his students have had to meet exacting standards in their fieldwork and in the writing of their dissertations. He has required comprehensiveness and depth in field data and lucidity in the presentation of the results. While some have found the pressure too heavy to bear, the great majority of us gratefully acknowledge the virtue and benefit of the intellectual discipline that Professor Freeman has taught us. Dr. Michael Jackson, a contributor to this volume, has written (personal communication): "I admired the methodical way he pursued his research interests, the scholarly thoroughness with which he wrote, and above all the passionate manner in which he studied his chosen subject ... What many have found dogmatic and self-assertive in his manner, I have construed as dedication, enthusiasm, and an unrelenting pursuit of the truth that underlies the conventional defenses we construct against it. He is one of the most uncomplacent men I have known."

While Professor Freeman has demanded the utmost in scholarly endeavor from his colleagues and students, he has on his side offered unstinting intellectual and moral support. He has been known to be as unsparing of himself as of his students in the care he takes to respond to an urgent query from a student in the field that requires library research and thought or in the effort he takes to read and respond to a field report or a draft of a dissertation.

Added to such intellectual support has been a keen sense of personal concern and caring. He has always been forthcoming with help in tackling personal problems, large or small, and offering carefully considered advice on them. He has followed with interest the professional careers of those who have worked with him and has kept in contact with them, discussing their work, as well as his own, in carefully written letters (often in longhand), and has exchanged offprints with them. He has also shared in their family joys and sorrows.

Another noteworthy trait in Professor Freeman's character is his deep sense of moral responsibility to espouse the cause of those, whether individuals or groups, whom he has believed to be the victims of caprice, prejudice, or persecution. At the same time he has been known to be generous and forgiving towards those who have wronged him. This rare quality was in evidence in the dignified manner in which he responded to the attacks on his work and personal integrity following the publication of his refutation, *Margaret Mead and Samoa.* He answered each point of criticism in the serious manner befitting a scholar and never returned abuse for abuse. Though Freeman presents a stern exterior, at heart he is a person of broad sympathy and gentle disposition.

A voracious reader, Freeman commands a wide-ranging scholarship in the fields of anthropology, sociology, biology, ethology, psychology, comparative religion, philosophy, literature, and the classics. He is also a fine literary craftsman and his writing is characterized by both the passion of conviction and the felicity of phrase—a rare combination.

In his thinking, Freeman has exhibited impressive intellectual daring. He has not hesitated to criticize his own earlier work when new intellectual perspectives have matured in his mind (for example, see the new Introduction to his *Report on the Iban* 1970a). This has kept him intellectually active all his life and bestowed on his published work a freshness and provocativeness that are very precious qualities. He has adhered firmly throughout his life to his view of anthropology as a comprehensive science of man and his works. His current efforts to construct an interactionist paradigm of human behavior is an expression of this same view.

Apart from being a scholar-thinker and a crusader for causes that move him, Professor Freeman has a cultivated aesthetic sensibility. He is interested in fine arts and music. It is incredible how his response to Indian classical or Japanese music is as sensitive as to Western classical or Australian folk music. His interest in nature is also noteworthy. Besides being a keen gardener, he has for years walked in the mountains and bush around Canberra, observed the behavior of wild animals and of those in sanctuaries and zoos, and explored the flora.

Derek Freeman's family, his wife, Monica, and their daughters, Jennifer and Hillary, are inseparable in the minds of all those who have had the privilege of being their friends. Monica Freeman has not only kept house for her husband but has also accompanied him on his many fieldwork trips to Sarawak and Samoa. She has helped in field observations and her artistic gifts—she is a sculptor of considerable refinement—have enriched his published work as the sketches in his *Iban Agriculture* illustrate so well. But the Freeman family is not confined to four persons—it includes their many friends all over the world.

G. N. A. and T. N. M.

Acknowledgments

We would like to express our appreciation to Clifford A. Sather for his continuing interest in the development of this festschrift and for his very thoughtful suggestions and valuable comments on it. We would also like to thank Robert K. Dentan for his useful comments on an earlier version of this festschrift. To Joan N. Bubier we owe our thanks for her hard work in the preparation of the manuscript and the index. And I, G. N. Appell, owe a special debt of thanks to my wife, Laura W. R. Appell, who has given me good advice and help in my share of the editing and preparation of the manuscript. She, as always, has been a constant support and indefatigable participant in our anthropological work. Peter Lawrence's encouragement and support is also deeply appreciated.

Contributors

G. N. Appell, Ph.D., Australian National University, is a Senior Research Associate, Department of Anthropology, Brandeis University. He has done fieldwork among the Dogrib Indians of the Northwest Territories of Canada, the Rungus Dusun of Sabah, Malaysia, and the Bulusu' of East Kalimantan, Indonesia. His publications include the edited volume of *The Societies of Borneo: Explorations in the Theory of Cognatic Social Structure* (American Anthropological Association, 1976); *Dilemmas and Ethical Conflicts in Anthropological Inquiry: A Case Book* (Crossroads Press, 1978); and the edited volume of *Modernization and the Emergence of a Landless Peasantry: Essays on the Integration of Peripheries to Socioeconomic Centers* (Studies in Third World Societies, 1985).

George Devereux was, until his recent death, Professor Emeritus, Ecole des Hautes en Sciences Sociales; Consultant in Ethnopsychiatry, Maison des Sciences de l'Homme, Paris. His publications include *Reality and Dream: Psychotherapy of a Plains Indian* (International Universities Press, 1951); *Mohave Ethnopsychiatry and Suicide: The Psychiatric Knowledge and the Psychic Disturbances of an Indian Tribe* (Bureau of American Ethnology, Bulletin No. 175, 1961); *From Anxiety to Method in the Behavioral Sciences* (Mouton, 1967); and *Ethnopsychoanalysis: Psychoanalysis and Anthropology as Complementary Frames of Reference* (University of California Press, 1978).

D. K. Feil, Ph.D., Australian National University, is Senior Lecturer in Anthropology, University of Sydney. He has done fieldwork among the Enga of the Papua New Guinea Highlands, on Normanby Island, Milne Bay, Papua New Guinea and more recently in Venice, Italy, on symbolism, politics, and history of Venetian public ceremonies and rituals. His publications include *Ways of Exchange* (Queensland University Press, 1984) and *The Evolution of Highland Papua New Guinea Societies* (Cambridge University Press, 1987).

Gilbert H. Herdt, Ph.D., Australian National University, is Associate Professor, Committee on Human Development and the College, University of Chicago. He has conducted fieldwork among the Sambia, Eastern Highlands Province, Papua New Guinea. His publications include *Guardians of the Flutes* (McGraw-Hill, 1981) and *Sambia: Ritual and Gender in New Guinea* (Holt, Rinehart and Winston, 1987).

Michael Jackson, Ph.D., University of Cambridge, has done fieldwork among the Kuranko of Northeastern Sierra Leone. His publications include three ethnographic monographs on the Kuranko, three volumes of poetry and a novel.

Peter Lawrence, Ph.D., University of Cambridge, is Professor Emeritus, Department of Anthropology, University of Sydney. He has undertaken fieldwork among the Garia and Ngaing peoples of the southern Madang Province, Papua New Guinea. His publications include *Road Belong Cargo* (Manchester and Melbourne University Presses, 1964) and *The Garia* (Melbourne and Manchester Presses, 1984).

T. N. Madan, Ph.D., Australian National University, is Professor of Sociology, Institute of Economic Growth, University of Delhi. His publications include *Family and Kinship: A Study of the Pandits of Rural Kashmir* (Asia Publishing Co., 1965); *Culture and Development* (Oxford University Press, 1983); an edited volume of *Way of Life: King, Householder, Renouncer: Essays in Honour of Louis Dumont* (Vikas, 1982); and *Encounter and Experience: Personal Accounts of Fieldwork*, which he coedited with Andre Beteille (Vikas and University Press of Hawaii, 1975).

Michael A. H. B. Walter, Ph.D., Australian National University, is Senior Research Fellow, Institute of Applied Social and Economic Research, Papua New Guinea. He has undertaken fieldwork among the Lauans of Vanua Balavu, eastern Fiji, and he has done research in Malaya, Singapore, and Papua New Guinea. His publications include "MB & ZS in East Fiji" (*Ethnology* 18); "Prudent Lechers" (*Bjidragen tot de Taal–, Land– en Volkenkunde* 134); "A $40,000 Question" (*JPS* 87); and "The Territorial and the Social" (*Ekistics* 45).

Michael W. Young, Ph.D., Australian National University, is Senior Fellow, Department of Anthropology, Research School of Pacific Studies, Australian National University. He has undertaken fieldwork among the Kalauna and Bwaidoka on Goodenough Island, Papua New Guinea, and he has also done research in Milne Bay (Papua New Guinea), Halmahera (Indonesia), and Epi Island, Vanunatu. Among his publications are *Fighting with Food* (Cambridge University Press, 1971), *The Ethnography of Malinowski*, which he edited (Routledge & Kegan Paul, 1979), and *Magicians of Manumanua* (California University Press, 1982).

PART I

Introduction

Derek Freeman:
Notes Toward an Intellectual
Biography[1]

G. N. Appell and T. N. Madan

Derek Freeman was born in Wellington, New Zealand, on August 16, 1916. Growing up there he developed a passion for exploring the bush and the mountains, which has not abated (Freeman 1983b:64).[2] This is characteristic of Freeman's deep involvement with the world and the great physical and mental energy with which he has approached anthropological inquiry, always with the hope that the use of science will improve the human condition. To understand the extent of the intellectual journey in which Freeman is engaged and the contributions both substantive and theoretical that he has made to anthropological inquiry and the human sciences, it would be best to start from the perspective of his present intellectual position and in his own words.

> The human species has reached a stage in its history where its sur-
> vival is being threatened both by antiquated customary moralities
> and by the unwise use of knowledge. This situation presents an
> immense challenge which, if it is to be met, will require the exten-
> sion of scientific understanding into human consciousness and
> action that reach beyond the determinisms of nature which have
> hitherto preoccupied scientists (Freeman 1983b:63).

Thus, his principal theoretical concern of recent years has been (Freeman 1983b:63):

> in contributing to the construction of an anthropological paradigm
> that takes cognizance of biological, cultural and environmental vari-
> ables, and their interaction, as also of the human capacity to solve
> problems by the making of wise choices. It is my hope that such a

paradigm will eventually lead to the emergence of an anthropology that will be both scientific and humanistic.

In 1934 Freeman became an undergraduate at Victoria University College of the University of New Zealand. He notes that had anthropology been taught there, he would certainly have chosen to study it. Instead he studied psychology and philosophy and took courses in education as well. During the years 1936–37, he also attended Wellington Training College for Teachers and was issued a Trained Teacher's Certificate of the New Zealand Education Department.

In 1938 Freeman became a member of Ernest Beaglehole's graduate seminar. Beaglehole, after completing a Ph.D. under Ginsberg at the University of London on the psychological basis of property, went on to study under Edward Sapir at Yale University and to do anthropological research among the Hopi, in Hawaii, and in Pukapuka before coming to Victoria University College. Under the influence of Beaglehole's teaching, Freeman began to envisage the possibility of doing anthropological fieldwork in Polynesia, although this was in conflict at the time with his devotion to mountaineering and exploration in the Southern Alps of New Zealand.

During these years at Victoria University College, Freeman also embarked on research on the socialization of children aged six to nine years in the schools of Wellington and became deeply impressed with the pervasiveness and power of social conditioning. In an article drawing on these researches entitled "Anatomy of Mind," published in 1938 in *Salient*, an organ of student opinion, he "declared 'the aims and desires which determine behavior' are all derived from 'the social environment'" (see Freeman 1983c:109). From 1938 onwards he was then very much an advocate of cultural determinism (see Freeman 1983c:109).

During this same period Freeman met Jiddu Krishnamurti, who was lecturing in New Zealand. This encounter with Krishnamurti's views on how one might liberate oneself from the mental shackles of social conditioning produced a new element in Freeman's thinking that was at odds with the then ruling doctrines of cultural and social anthropology. It was to remain a private reserve in his thinking until he began the systematic study of choice in human behavior over two decades later.

In 1939 the prospect of doing anthropological field research in Polynesia became real when Freeman obtained a position in the Education Department of Western Samoa. He arrived in Apia on the island of Upolu in April 1940. His first assignment was the teaching of children of the same age as those whose social conditioning he had studied in Wellington, so that he was able to continue this research in Samoa. He also learned the Samoan language in which he became qualified by government examination (see Freeman 1983c:171).

Among the books Freeman had with him were Franz Boas' *General*

Anthropology (1938) and Mead's *From the South Seas: Studies of Adolescence and Sex in Primitive Societies* (1939), which includes *Coming of Age in Samoa*. He also notes that his ruling aim, once he had gained sufficient command of the Samoan language, was to support Mead's already celebrated findings with researches of his own.

Freeman's teaching duties and vacation time were such that they enabled him to continue his study of anthropology and engage in field research. After two years of studying Samoan, by which time he had sufficient command of the language to converse in the company of chiefs with the punctilio that Samoan etiquette requires, he chose the settlement of Sa'anapu, consisting of four hundred individuals, for intensive research. He had previously visited Sa'anapu in 1942 during an archaeological survey of Seuao Cave, which was one of a number of archaeological investigations he carried out during the years 1941–43. During his visits there, he became friendly with a senior talking chief who had lost his youngest son after a sudden illness. This talking chief viewed Freeman's coming to live with him as reparation for his loss, and adopted him into his family (see Freeman 1983a:xiii–xiv).

In January 1943, when Freeman returned to Sa'anapu for an extended stay, its chiefs conferred on him one of their titles, that of *Logona-i-Taga* ("Heard at the Tree Felling"), which is the title of the heir apparent of the high chief of Sa'anapu. Having thus been accepted into the community to a degree unusual in fieldwork, Freeman was in an exceptionally favorable position to pursue his objective of making a study of the social structure of Sa'anapu.

Another major influence during these years was Dr. H. D. Skinner, Director of the Otago Museum in Dunedin, New Zealand. Under Skinner's guidance and advice, Freeman made a study of Samoan material culture and assembled a collection for the Otago Museum, where he became an Honorary Curator of Ethnology.

In November 1943, after having served since 1941 in the Local Defence Force of Western Samoa, Freeman left to join the Royal New Zealand Volunteer Naval Reserve, in which he became a Sub-Lieutenant. He served in landing ships in Europe and the Far East. In September and October 1945, when the landing ship to which he was attached was accepting the surrender of Japanese units on the west coast of Borneo, Freeman had his first encounter with pagan Iban tribesmen. This providential event aroused his interest in the remarkable Iban and eventually led to his study of Iban society, and from then on to a lifetime friendship with the Iban.

In October 1946, Freeman, having been awarded a Rehabilitation Bursary of the government of New Zealand, returned to England to join Professor Firth's seminar in the Department of Anthropology at the London School of.Economics and Political Science and to undertake two years of postgraduate study.

Between the end of his naval service and his postgraduate study in England, Freeman continued his study of Samoan history and culture, working on manuscript holdings in the Mitchell Library in Sydney and in the Turnbull Library in Wellington. In the summer of 1946 he spent five weeks back in Western Samoa as interpreter and guide to the author Robert Gibbings and in collecting additional data on Sa'anapu.

At the London School of Economics and Political Science, Freeman participated in seminars conducted by Professor Raymond Firth, Dr. Audrey I. Richards, and Dr. S. F. Nadel. In addition he took courses at University College, at the School of Oriental and African Studies and at the Institute of Archaeology.

During the years 1946–48, his principal research activity was the detailed study of all the manuscript resources on Samoa in the archives of the London Missionary Society. This provided invaluable data for his study of Samoan social structure and greatly extended his understanding of Samoan history and culture. The result of this research and of his fieldwork in Samoa was a thesis, written for the University of London under the supervision of Professor Raymond Firth, entitled *The Social Structure of a Samoan Village Community*, for which he was awarded an Academic Postgraduate Diploma in Anthropology in July 1948.

In 1947 Freeman made a study of the Polynesian collection of Trinity College, Dublin, the results of which were published in Freeman (1949). He also did considerable research in the Public Record Office, London, on the Peruvian labor trade in Polynesia of 1862–64. The notes of this research he later handed over to H. E. Maude when he found that he was also working on the same subject. He also spent some time at Lord Raglan's estate in Monmouthshire working through and classifying the papers of Professor A. M. Hocart, of which Lord Raglan was a trustee, and in arranging for the papers that referred to the South Pacific region to be lodged in the Turnbull Library.

In February 1947, Freeman gave a seminar at the Institute of Social Anthropology at Oxford University on Samoan social structure and then gave exactly the same paper two days later at a seminar of the Department of Anthropology at the London School of Economics. His notes on the reception of this paper are of considerable historical interest. At Oxford Dr. Meyer Fortes described the analysis as "exceedingly brilliant." But Professor Firth complained of "structure *ad nauseam*," and described the analysis as "pretentious" and "nonsense." Maurice Freedman, also a student at the time, called it "mere phantasy." From this time onwards Freeman was much influenced by the ideas and advice of Meyer Fortes, and when he left for research among the Iban in Sarawak in December 1948, he carried with him a copy of the page proofs of *The Web of Kinship Among the Tallensi*.

In August 1948, while on the way to Zermatt, Freeman met Monica Maitland of Hatchmere Wood, Cheshire. In November of that year they were married, and thus began a close partnership with Derek in all his fieldwork. Later, when Derek had established a research base in Borneo, Monica joined him and contributed to Iban research by her study of the beautiful Iban *ikat* weaving and its role in the economic, social, and ritual life of the Iban. This included several hundred scale drawings of weaving patterns as well as many drawings of daily life. Dr. Edmund Leach (1955:iv) writes of Monica's participation that Derek had with him on his Iban researches "a field assistant of quite exceptional qualifications . . ."

In 1947 Dr. Leach had undertaken a social economic survey of Sarawak on the request of the Governor to the Colonial Social Science Research Council. He had recommended eight different research projects be undertaken. Prominent among these was a study of the Iban. Freeman was offered the Iban project under the auspices of the Colonial Social Science Research Council. The objective of this research project was "a study of a traditionally based, stable, Iban community based on shifting dry rice cultivation and not subject to undue land shortage" (quoted in Freeman 1970a:xiii). Meticulously preparing himself for his researches prior to leaving England, which is characteristic of Freeman's approach to all scientific inquiry, he had begun to learn Malay, but after locating an Iban student in London at once undertook the direct study of the Iban language.

Freeman arrived in Sarawak in January 1949, to be joined in June by his wife, Monica. The main center of his field research was Rumah Nyala, an Iban longhouse community on the right bank of the Sungai Sut, the first major tributary of the Baleh above its confluence with the Batang Rejang. Much time was also spent living in Iban longhouses in other parts of the Baleh region as well as in making visits to Iban communities in the lower, middle, and upper Rejang, the Katibas, and Ngemah, all of the then Third Division of Sarawak.

In February 1951, the Freemans left Rumah Nyala, after two years of field research among the Iban of the Baleh. They then travelled to the Second Division to spend two months among the Iban in the Saribas region and to pay a short visit to the Iban of the Ulu Batang Ai. They set sail for England in June 1951, after a stay of almost thirty months.

On the invitation of Dr. Fortes, who had taken up the Chair of Social Anthropology at the University of Cambridge the year before, Freeman became a research student in the Faculty of Archaeology and Anthropology to write up his Iban materials under Professor Fortes' supervision. During the years 1951–53 Freeman wrote both his *Report on the Iban of Sarawak* (1955a; 2nd ed. 1970a) for the government of Sarawak and his Ph.D. dissertation entitled *Family and Kin Among the Iban of Sarawak* (1953). *Iban Agriculture* (1955b) is a version of the 1955a publication "in which the sections on social organization were much abridged and prominence was given to analysis of the shifting cultivation of hill rice" (1970a:v).

Freeman's *Iban Agriculture* is a superb piece of research. It is one of the best and most complete accounts of swidden agriculture that has yet been made. It pioneered in the use of quantitative data, both for the swidden economy and the Iban social organization.

Freeman notes that his objective in his dissertation was to describe the salient features of the cognatic social system of the Iban. The use of quantitative data was critical for establishing the dimensions of the principal regularities. He notes that one of the most significant of these regularities is expressed in the Iban system of filiation. "Iban filiation is of a special kind, for it may be either to an individual's mother's *bilek* [domestic family], or to an individual's father's bilek, but it cannot be to both at the same time. Moreover, in practice, both types of filiation occur to an approximately equal extent" (Freeman 1953:137). This system of filiation was of a kind hitherto unknown in the ethnographic literature, and Freeman devised the term "utrolateral" to refer to it (see Freeman 1955b, 1956b).

Freeman's analysis of Iban society has made a major contribution to the theory of cognatic social structure. His conclusion that the bilek is a perpetual corporate group (see Freeman 1955b, 1957a, 1960a) provided one solution to the problem of continuity in cognatic societies that theorists of unilineal societies had not been able to solve (see Appell 1976 for a discussion of this). His (1957a) study of the developmental cycle of the domestic family was ground breaking. It provided the basis for understanding the social dynamics of cognatic societies, and as a result it stimulated new and productive research. The creation of property through the economic activities of domestic family members and the rules for devolution of this property provide one of the major driving forces that shape the structure of cognatic societies. For those anthropologists who ignore this elemental point, their descriptions and analyses not only of Bornean societies but all cognatic societies are by comparison barren. Freeman's definitive statement on the kindred (1961a) appeared in 1961, for which he won the Curl Bequest Prize.

In sum, Freeman dispelled much of the conceptual confusion over the nature of cognatic societies, and in so doing laid the modern foundation for the study of cognatic social structure. Thus, Derek Freeman with his study of Iban society initiated a new and productive era in the study of cognatic societies, and his research has served as a paradigm to those working in Borneo and elsewhere.

Freeman notes that the cognatic system of the Iban is based on the operation of choice, but in his dissertation, given the then ruling emphasis within British social anthropology, he did not explore the phenomenon of choice as such but rather analyzed its structural consequences by the use of quantitative methods. Were he to embark on a restudy of the Iban family system, he writes, he would proceed rather differently, giving much more attention to choice *per se* and to its determinants in specific situations.

When he did revisit Borneo in 1976, he gave especial attention to the phenomenon of choice in Iban life (Freeman 1981a:58). Thus he eloquently describes Iban society in the following terms in the concluding pages of *Some Reflections on the Nature of Iban Society*, which was written in response to an ill-founded challenge to Freeman's finding (Freeman 1955b:10) that Iban society was "classless and egalitarian":

> Such a people, I suggest, with a social organization based on the kindred, . . . that encouraged the emergence of individual talent and creativity, . . . and in which participation in group activities was *by choice* rather than prescription, is of the greatest anthropological interest and human value.
>
> Almost three centuries ago . . . John Locke wrote movingly of mankind being, by nature in
>
> > a state of perfect freedom to order their actions and dispose of their possessions and persons, as they think fit, within the bounds of the law of nature; without asking leave, or depending upon the will of any other man . . . a state also of equality, wherein all the power and jurisdiction is reciprocal, no one having more than another . . .
>
> When recognizable approximations to this state of equality and freedom do occur in the anthropological record, as in the traditional society of the pagan Iban, this, I would claim, deserves the attention of all those ethologists, anthropologists, philosophers and humanists for whom Locke's engaging vision of human possibility remains fraught with significance for the understanding, and the future, of our emergent species [1981a:50–51].

Freeman also notes that he gave undue emphasis in his University of London thesis of 1948 on the Samoan family system to the notion that it was unilineal. He has since concluded that there is a definite incidence of choice in a system that is "optative with an emphasis on agnation" (Freeman 1983a:121). Thus, Freeman now considers that in his Samoan researches and particularly in his Iban researches the recognition of choice has been a "kind of slow fuse" in his anthropological thinking, which finally assumed full significance in his writings of the 1970s (Freeman 1986b:19).

In the Preface of the new edition of *Report on the Iban of Sarawak*

(1970), he indicates other ways in which his perspective on anthropological inquiry has changed:

> My approach to the observation and analysis of ethnographical facts has changed a good deal in recent years; for example, in the interpretation of kinship behaviour I would now give much more attention to its ambivalent emotional basis. Again, my analysis, in 1951–3, of Iban political leadership was, I now discern, couched too much in structural terms, and gives insufficient attention to the processes of dominance behaviour as such, which, at the period, were but little understood by anthropologists [Freeman 1970a:v].

Freeman was admitted to the degree of Doctor of Philosophy by the University of Cambridge in October 1953. He returned to New Zealand early in 1954 to take up a Visiting Lectureship at the University of Otago.

Dr. S. F. Nadel, whose student Freeman had been at the London School of Economics and Political Science, became the Foundation Professor of Anthropology at the Australian National University in 1950. In 1954 he wrote Freeman, inviting him to apply for a position in his department. Later that year Freeman was appointed to a Senior Fellowship in the Department of Anthropology and Sociology at the Australian National University. He took up residence in Canberra in February 1955.

Professor Nadel died suddenly in January 1956, only 53 years of age, at "the height of his powers and promise" (Fortes 1957:xvi). Freeman wrote in his obituary of Nadel that he was one of social anthropology's "most brilliant figures," and he described him in terms that shed light on and reflect Freeman's own character and intellect. Of Nadel's many qualities, Freeman wrote, three deserved special mention:

> First, there was the scientific spirit which so animated all his activities ... Second, there was his absolute integrity and his constant regard for ethical principle ... Third, and most difficult of all to describe was [his] remarkable lambency of mind ... Whatever the subject being discussed or the problem under inquiry, Nadel's original and discerning mind could always be expected to illuminate it [Freeman 1956a:10].

After Nadel's death, Freeman for a time became acting head of the department, and took action which led to the founding of the Australian Branch of the Association of Social Anthropologists, which later became the Australian Anthropological Society.

In August 1957, J. A. Barnes was appointed Professor to succeed S. F. Nadel, and Freeman was promoted to the position of Reader, or as it later became, Professorial Fellow.

The last half of the 1950s was a highly productive period for Freeman. In November 1957, he attended the ninth Pacific Science Congress in Bangkok to participate in a symposium on "Social Structure in Southeast Asia," convened by G. P. Murdock, the proceedings of which were published in 1960 by the Wenner–Gren Foundation for Anthropological Research. This brought into focus the status of research on cognatic societies and indicated what needed to be done. Freeman's contribution was the "Iban of Western Borneo." At the conclusion of the Congress, Freeman did further field research among the Iban from December 1957, to March 1958.

His seminal essay on "The Family System of the Iban of Borneo" was published in 1957 and in 1961 his paper "On the Concept of the Kindred." During this period he also coedited, with Professor W. R. Geddes, *Anthropology in the South Seas: Essays presented to H. D. Skinner* (1959) in which he contributed "Henry Devenish Skinner: A Memoir" and "The Joe Gimlet or Siovili Cult: An Episode in the Religious History of Early Samoa."

Then came the period of July 1960, to March 1961, which formed a major watershed in the development of Freeman's anthropological interests and theoretical perspective. Up to this point he had been working, as he explains, within the confines of the Boasian assumptions of American cultural anthropology, to which he had been exposed during his studies in New Zealand, and the Durkheimian assumptions of British social anthropology. The sources for his discontent with past paradigms were several.

First, there was the unresolved problem of the explanation of a notable Iban symbolic act, which he later described as follows:

> The climax of the remarkable allegory central to the Iban cult of head-hunting which, as it is chanted by bards is acted out by aspirant head-hunters, is a rite known as ... "to cut into pieces." In this part of the allegory a graphic description is given of the ritual splitting of a trophy head ... by Lang Singalang Burong, the Iban god of war. Lang achieves this feat (which actually symbolizes the actual beheading of an enemy) with one swift blow of his sword, and from the head which he has split open there pours forth seed which when sown grows into a human crop—as did the dragon's teeth strewn by Cadmus on the plain of Boeotia [Freeman 1979a:234].

This seed spilled forth includes all manner of seed but most prominently the seed of the sacred rice of the Iban. The question of why a trophy head should contain seed was, up until this period, an enigma to Freeman. "I could find no answer to it in the literature of anthropology, nor were my Iban informants of any great help" (Freeman 1979a:234).

This, and numerous other questions concerning the dreams of the Iban and their ritual behavior, remained quite unanswered.

Thus, by the late 1950s Freeman was becoming increasing dissatisfied with the inability of the methods of social anthropology to deal with such major features of social phenomena. His dissatisfaction applied particularly to the doctrine of levels which sought to establish a methodological barrier between social anthropology and most of the other behavioral sciences, in particular the emerging discipline of human ethology. In 1960 Professor Max Gluckman visited the Department of Anthropology and Sociology at the Australian National University, and during his stay he read a series of papers that were later published as *Closed Systems and Open Minds*. On July 22, 1960, Gluckman read a paper by V. W. Turner entitled "Symbols in Ndembu Ritual," which became a chapter in that book. One sentence in particular became stuck in Freeman's mental gullet on this (for him) momentous occasion: "Where psycho-analysts disagree, by what criterion can the hapless social anthropologist judge between their interpretations, in a field of enquiry in which he has neither received systematic training nor obtained thorough practical experience?" (Turner 1964:38).

Two months later Freeman wrote to Fortes about how deeply Turner's quandary had engaged him and how he had concluded that the only way for the hapless social anthropologist to escape from this quandary was to acquire for himself systematic training in psychoanalysis.

This then was Freeman's state of mind when in February 1961, he was asked by the Vice-Chancellor of The Australian National University to make an alteration in his plans for study leave in Indonesia and Southeast Asia and go directly to Kuching to investigate a serious difference that had been precipitated by the Curator of the Sarawak Museum with a research scholar in Freeman's department. Freeman found himself in the center of a complicated social situation in which he was able to study firsthand a whole series of deep psychological processes. He writes that for one who had reached his state of mind about the significance of psychological and behavioral variables for anthropological enquiry, this was an educational experience of a most fundamental kind, and led to what he has described as a "cognitive abreaction." He suddenly saw human behavior in a new light.

So momentous was this experience, he writes, that he returned to Canberra rather than continue on his study leave and in March 1961, began systematic reading in the fields of ethology, evolutionary biology, primatology, the neurosciences, psychology and genetics, all of which from his changed perspective he judged to be relevant to the development of a unified science of anthropology. He wrote in a letter to Meyer Fortes, dated 19 October 1962:

My approach to the science of man is now very much that of the natural historian . . . I now attach, for example, great importance to the study of human evolution, during the course of which the natures that we now have were laid down. I am now convinced that anthropology, if it is to become the science of man, must be biologically based—we must begin with the human animal, and never let him slip from our sight when studying social systems.

Freeman wrote similarly in his review (1962b) of Leach's *Rethinking Anthropology*:

For me, then, Leach's stimulating rethinking of anthropological issues poses the fundamental question of what anthropology should be about. In recent decades British anthropology has increasingly been concerned with enquiry on a single level of analysis. In so doing it has ceased to be 'the science of man' and has become little more than the science of man's customary behaviour. This, in my view, is a retreat from the historic task of anthropology. The time has come, I would suggest, when we ought to turn to rethinking even more basic issues; and, for my part, I would hope that during the decades that lie ahead there will emerge a unified science of man, that will concern itself in an integrated way not only with the social customs of man, but also with his psychological and historical nature and all other relevant aspects of his being in the world [Freeman 1962b:125–26].

Freeman's adoption of a naturalistic approach to human behavior also meant an abandonment of cultural relativism (see Freeman 1962c):

. . . in my view it is an erroneous dogma that seriously hinders the proper understanding of human cultures and of the affects which result for those who have become fully conditioned to them.
To assert, as Herskovits does, that behaviour is normal because it is set in a cultural mould, is to say no more than it is shared and accepted by the members of the culture concerned, but dereistic thinking and irrational behaviour are not one wit the less dereistic because they happen to be shared and accepted. Indeed, as a study of religious cults shows, the fact that a delusion is shared commonly results in an intensification of affect for the individual participant rather than any diminution [Freeman 1962c:272–73].

Freeman enlarged on this view in a 1964 communication to the Inaugural Congress of the Australian and New Zealand College of Psychiatrists posing the question of whether a culture can either in whole or in part be diagnosed as abnormal or maladapted in a psychiatric sense

(Freeman 1965b:65). He concluded that the science of anthropology "must evolve ways in which human behaviour—of whatever culture—can be scientifically and normatively evaluated, this being an essential step towards the discovery (to use the words of Bidney) of 'universal principles of cultural dynamics and concrete rational norms capable of universal realization'" (Freeman 1965b:67). He thus argued that the discoveries of the science of psychiatry are of the greatest relevance. As an example he referred to one of the criteria that appears in most definitions of mental health: superior reality perception. And he quoted Money-Kyrle to the effect that a man's beliefs "'do not have a relative degree of truth measured by their approximation to the prevalent beliefs of his own or some other culture arbitrarily chosen as a frame of reference. They have an absolute degree of truth measured by their approximation to the facts which alone can prove or disprove them.'" He concluded with a statement that also represents his approach to the evaluation of cultural facts: "In other words, the neurotic is not only emotionally sick—he is cognitively wrong" (Freeman 1965b:67). That is, cultural behaviors can be evaluated in terms of their truth value, which, since these behaviors are "functionally related to man's phylogenetically given nature and the outcome of the evolutional process," (1967c:133) must also be seen in terms of their adaptive value. The further development of Freeman's thinking on this approach to the valuation of cultures is presented in his major study of human nature and culture (1970b) and in his research on the nature of choice behavior.

From 1961 onwards Freeman also gave central importance in his approach to the problems of anthropology to the ideas of Karl Popper. In his review of Sahlins's *Social Stratification in Polynesia,* he wrote, "indeed, one expects to find the author attempting to invalidate his hypothesis the better to test it" (Freeman 1961b:148). In a further comment on Sahlins's book, he stated (Freeman 1962a) that this comment alluded to Popper's basic point about the falsification of hypotheses. But the fruition of Freeman's use of the Popperian approach was to come in his *Margaret Mead and Samoa: The Making and Unmaking of an Anthropological Myth* (1983).

In October 1962, Freeman read papers on Iban shamanism, Iban headhunting, and Iban dreams to members of the Melbourne Institute of Psycho-Analysis. Soon after this he arranged to spend a year at the London Institute of Psycho-Analysis where he attended lectures and seminar courses and underwent personal analysis. While in London he also attended seminars at the Hampstead Child Therapy Clinic, of which Anna Freud was the Director, and seminars at the Tavistock Clinic by Dr. John Bowlby and others.

Freeman's second main objective during his study leave in Europe was to improve his knowledge of ethology and to undertake research on infra-human primates with a view of applying as an anthropologist the methods and insights of ethology to the study of human behavior. During this period he delivered a paper entitled "Human Aggression in Anthropological Perspective" at a symposium on the "Natural History of Aggression" organized by the Institute of Biology and held at the British Museum of Natural History (Freeman 1964a). At this symposium he met and became friendly with Professor Konrad Lorenz, who guided him in his study of ethology. During this period he visited the Max-Planck-Institut für Verhaltensphysiologie in Seewiesen to confer with Professor Lorenz, Dr. I. Eibl-Eibesfeldt, and others. He visited the Ethology Laboratory of the Uffculme Clinic in Birmingham for discussions with Dr. M. R. A. Chance and Dr. E. C. Grant, and conferred with Professor N. Tinbergen during a visit to the University of Oxford. During this period he also undertook observational research on primate behavior at the Zoological Society of London.

These activities were intended to broaden Freeman's anthropological understanding in preparation for further fieldwork in Samoa. In July 1964, Dr. and Mrs. Freeman travelled back to Australia by sea. It was during this voyage that he read once again after many years Mead's *Coming of Age in Samoa*. Freeman realized that if he were to return to Samoa it would be incumbent upon him, in the course of his other researches, to reexamine and test the evidence on which Dr. Mead in 1928 based her conclusion that biological variables are of no significance in the etiology of adolescent behavior, evidence of which he was decidedly skeptical as a result of his own Samoan researches.

In November 1964, Mead visited the Research School of Pacific Studies at the Australian National University and Freeman met with her. During the course of this meeting Freeman communicated to her details of the evidence that had led him seriously to doubt certain aspects of her account of Samoan behavior and culture. He also informed her that he intended to undertake further fieldwork in Samoa and eventually publish a critique of the conclusions she had reached in *Coming of Age in Samoa*.

During this period of preparation for returning to Samoa, Freeman wrote a series of psychoanalytically informed papers (Freeman 1967a, 1967b, 1968). In his paper, "Totem and Taboo: A Reappraisal," he argued that there was no adequate anthropological or ethological evidence to support Freud's theory of the "primal deed" as critical for the development of the Oedipus complex; and further that Freud's theory rested on Lamarckian assumptions about the inheritance of psychical dispositions, for which there is no scientific basis. Further, he linked the theory advanced by Freud in *Totem and Taboo* to Freud's profound ambivalence of feeling toward his own father as evinced in his dreams and other aspects of his behavior.

Freeman wrote that to his astonishment, this paper, when read to a conference of the Australian Society of Psychoanalysts in 1965, provoked a markedly emotional response. Although (as Freeman notes) his paper was based on Popperian principles and had the aim of making psychoanalysis more scientific by the elimination of error, the substantive evidence he had presented was summarily rejected as dangerously heretical and he was pointedly ostracized. Freeman concluded from this unnerving but instructive happening that to some of its adherents psychoanalysis was very much a belief system in which doctrine was accepted merely on authority, this being a state of mind inimical to the advancement of scientific understanding.

In 1965 he prepared a position paper to justify in scientific terms the approach that he was proposing to make in his study of human behavior during the course of his researches in Samoa. He made the crucially important point that "There is ... no disjunction between nature and culture as Lévi-Strauss and some other anthropologists, with their Durkheimian assumptions, have been led to suppose" (Freeman 1966:337). Thus, he argued for the relevance of the findings of ethology, primatology, and evolutionary anthropology to the study and explanation of human behavior (1966:339):

> What the evolutionary evidence ... means is that socially inherited customs (in Durkheim's sense) must have gradually evolved from the phylogenetically given behavioural repertoire of the hominids. Furthermore, these customs which, as Durkheim indicates, are preponderantly concerned with the constraint of individuals, are clearly adaptational innovations for dealing with the pre-existing emotional and behaviour proclivities of human beings.
> *It follows that social customs to be understood adequately need to be related to the behavioural impulses in reference to which they have been evolved and in apposition to which they survive as shared modes of socially inherited adaptation.*

He then argued (1966:339–40) that this "leads to the important point that social rules are best studied 'in the breach', either incipient or actual, for in these situations the observer is presented with evidence of the behavioural proclivity against which the rule is a defence. The great importance of ethology ... is that it provides the investigator with methods of studying directly the interrelations between customary and impulsive behaviour...."

Freeman's innovative approach met with opposition in the Department of Anthropology and Sociology at the Australian National University. He writes (Freeman 1983c:171–72): "It is of historical interest that at that time my interest in human ethology was viewed by some senior colleagues as highly heretical, and that I encountered much obscurantist opposition.

For example, I was told by the Acting Head of the Department of Anthropology and Sociology ... at The Australian National University, in which at that time I was a Reader in Anthropology, that 'the study of behaviour' had nothing to do with anthropology, which was concerned only with 'social institutions', and I was threatened with foreclosure of funds to continue my researches in Samoa, both in human ethology and on the findings of Margaret Mead."

Nevertheless, Freeman persevered and was able to initiate his new Samoan researches, arriving with his wife and two daughters in Samoa at the end of December 1965. He remained there until early January 1968. As his research progressed it became apparent to Freeman that Mead's conclusions were indeed seriously inadequate, and he extended his investigations from Sa'anapu to Manu'a, the main location of Mead's Samoan researches.

On his return to Canberra, Freeman began to investigate the historical background of the Boasian school of American cultural anthropology. He writes that it became apparent to him that the conclusion reached by Mead in *Coming of Age in Samoa* in 1928 was pivotal to the development and acceptance in the United States of the doctrine of cultural determinism. Further, as he explored the origins of the ideas of Franz Boas, it became evident to him that he would have to extend his investigations into the interaction of biological and anthropological ideas from the time of Darwin onwards. These historical investigations occupied Freeman for a decade or more and as a byproduct resulted in his 1974 paper comparing the evolutionary theories of Darwin and Spencer, and particularly the Lamarckian basis of Spencer's evolutionary doctrine.

In a 1969 lecture, Freeman (1970b) criticized the insufficiencies of cultural anthropology and argued for the adoption of an interactionist paradigm in anthropological inquiry that would give "recognition to genetical and environmental feedback and interaction both in the ontogeny of individual organisms and in the phylogeny of breeding populations" (Freeman 1970b:68). Such an interactionist paradigm, he argued, would give rise to a unified science of man and his behavior. (See also Freeman 1971 for further reference to the interactionist paradigm.)

In this 1969 lecture he also discussed the nature and function of human values. "This human capacity to exercise preferences," he argued, "has gradually emerged in the course of human evolution in close conjunction with the capacity to symbolize," and we are thus confronted with "the phenomenon of human values, for values are a function of the capacity to exercise preferences, and so, ineluctably become a part of the subject matter of evolutionary anthropology ..." (Freeman 1970b:71–72). Freeman then asked what were the prospects for a science of human values.

He answered that "First, it will be necessary to transcend the inane doctrine of cultural relativism which denies even the possibility of any broadly-based evaluation of human choices, by asserting, as it does, that differing forms of cultural behaviour or shared preference, are normal *sui generis*, and so cannot be compared in biogenetic or other terms" (Freeman 1970b:72). But how to evaluate a system of values? Freeman argues (1970b:73):

> From [the] natural characteristics of populations of living things, we are able to derive the fundamental principle of *adaptive diversity*, and it is this principle, I would suggest, that must guide any science of human values, for it provides us with the soundest of biological foundations—*the positive evaluation of diversity whenever it is adaptive*—this being the value inherent in evolution by natural selection and so, in the life process itself.

It was at about this time that Freeman began systematic study of the human capacity to make choices.

It is of some historical interest at this point to review Freeman's analysis of his Samoan data during this period in terms of the light it throws on certain aspects of the Freeman-Mead controversy, which arose on the publication of his unprecedented formal refutation of Mead's account of Samoan culture and behavior (Freeman 1983a). The charge has been made against Freeman that he deliberately waited until Mead died to make public his refutation of her Samoan conclusions, a charge which is largely irrelevant to the truth value of this refutation. Nevertheless, it is important to review briefly Freeman's work on his Samoan data during this period to lay this false charge to rest.

In May 1968, just a few months after his return from Samoa, he presented a paper in Canberra at a conference of the Australian Branch of the Association of Social Anthropologists entitled "On the Believing of as Many as Six Impossible Things Before Breakfast: An Analysis of the Consequences of Cathecting Assumptions in Cultural and Social Anthropology." This paper publicly presented empirical evidence to show that Mead's account of Samoa was in numerous ways in error. Furthermore, when Freeman in 1967, while still in Samoa, learnt that the Bernice P. Bishop Museum was about to publish a new edition of Dr. Mead's *Social Organization of Manu'a* (1930), he wrote the then director informing him that this edition contained numerous literal errors in the Samoan language. He found, however, that when the new edition appeared in 1969 his warnings had been completely ignored. Consequently, he prepared a paper entitled "Social Organization of Manu'a (1930 and 1969) by Margaret Mead: Some Errata." This was sent to the *American Anthropologist* in 1971, but was rejected. It was then published in the *Journal of the*

Polynesian Society in 1972. A footnote to this paper stated: "In this communication I have dealt only with certain of the literal errors in Samoan which are to be found in *Social Organization of Manu'a*. I am, however, preparing for publication a general appraisal of Margaret Mead's anthropological writings on Samoa" (Freeman 1972:74).

By 1971 Freeman had completed a draft which summarized the contents of the book he was proposing to write. This was sent to Holt, Rinehart and Winston in New York. The negative responses to this outline by anonymous reviewers made Freeman realize that he would have to do much more research if he were to attain his objective of writing a convincing refutation of Mead's conclusion.

In October 1972, Freeman was appointed to the Chair of Anthropology in the Department of Anthropology and Sociology of the Research School of Pacific Studies at the Australian National University. In March 1973, the department reverted to its original title of Department of Anthropology. Freeman's time during the next several years was spent in reconstructing the department which during this time grew from three to twelve members. He established a Human Ethology Laboratory in the department. In 1973 he was elected a Fellow of the Academy of the Social Sciences in Australia, from which, for personal reasons, he has since resigned.

In May 1973, Freeman met Albert Barunga, an elder of the Worora tribe of the Kimberley region of Northwestern Australia. Barunga lived for some months with the Freemans in Canberra and this friendship led to an investigation by Freeman of the housing needs and general welfare of Barunga's home community of Mowanjum. During the course of this close friendship, which lasted until Barunga's death in 1976, Freeman did considerable research on the history and culture of the Worora, including the annotation of an extensive photographic record of the Worora made by the Rev. J. B. R. Love from 1927 to 1940. All of these materials and field notes are now lodged with the Australian Institute of Aboriginal Studies in Canberra.

Freeman had begun his study of attachment behavior in human infants in Samoa during the years of 1966–67. His researches in human ethology during the early 1970s were mainly centered on this topic, the results of which appear in his refutation of Mead's Samoan materials and in Freeman (1974b).

During the 1970s Freeman was also able to maintain an active interest in Iban studies by supervising three research scholars in his department who undertook extensive Iban research for their Ph.D. dissertations: Michael Heppell, Motomitsu Uchibori, and James Jemut Masing, himself an Iban.

During May to August 1976, Freeman visited Sarawak, Sabah, Brunei, Malaya, Singapore, Java, and Bali. In Sarawak he spent some time in each

of the long-house communities he had studied during the years 1949–
51 and 1957–58. He writes that at a long-house in the Sungai Melinau
he was fortunate in being able to attend the final initiation of a female
manang, or shaman, the commencement of whose vocation he had
witnessed in 1949. He also visited various Iban communities in the Second
Division of Sarawak and in Brunei.

In 1975 E. O. Wilson's *Sociobiology: The New Synthesis* was published. Freeman notes that while in 1975, as well as now in 1987, his view
is that it is of utmost importance that anthropologists recognize and incorporate in their theories all those biological mechanisms that have been
scientifically shown to be relevant to the understanding of human behavior;
he also holds that this acceptance is in no way incompatible with the full
recognition of the learned behavior and symbolic systems by which human
populations have long been characterized and which depend on the transmission of information by exogenetic means. When he discovered, in
studying the text of *Sociobiology* in 1976, that Wilson had failed to take
adequate account of these exogenetic mechanisms, and in particular the
human capacity to make choices, he turned to further research on the
anthropology of choice.

In December 1976, he completed a paper entitled "Towards an
Anthropology Both Scientific and Humanistic" (Freeman 1978b). In this
paper he argued that in attempting to escape the clutches of a deterministic biology, Boas, Kroeber, and others had invented a theory of culture
which was comparably confining. He pointed out that these two deterministic ideologies were still very much with us. On the one hand, in
addition to cultural anthropologists, there were the structuralists who viewed
human beings as the creatures of structures they are powerless to change;
and on the other hand there were those for whom virtually all human
behavior is phylogenetically determined. He made the crucial point that
neither of these forms of determinism can deal with the origin of culture
or with its evolution, in sum with change, and called for a paradigm giving
recognition to awareness and choice, capacities which are dependent on
human biology. His argument included the view that the "emergence of
systems of social control has largely been a response to the proclivity that
human individuals have for making choices that are judged to be unde-
sirable by their fellows. The human propensity to take up possibility, I
would argue, is very much a biologically-given characteristic which cultural
and social systems, with varying success, attempt to contain." Also, "When
it is realized that all values are a function of the capacity to make choices,
the misconceptions to be found in cultures are seen to be cognitive
choices made in the absence of adequate understanding ... It follows ...
that a scientific anthropology must make a fallibilist approach to cultural
values, just as experimental science does to knowledge."[3]

In 1976 Freeman completed "Choice, Value and the Solution of Human Problems" (Freeman 1983b). In this paper he dealt with the emergent capacity of human beings to solve problems by choice. He argued that "human cultures are complex sets of alternatives which, having been chosen at some time in the past, have become fixed and repetitive in their form. Frequently, these traditional alternatives incorporate misconceptions and involve consequences of a humanly deleterious kind. The major problem of our age then is to develop the knowledge and techniques that will enable the members of human societies to eliminate values and habits which scientific enquiry reveals to be deleterious" (Freeman 1983b:64). Moreover, as science is itself a value system, this means we can "practice science only if we value truth by actively seeking to eliminate error from our theories" (Freeman 1983b:64).

In 1977 Freeman participated in the "Werner-Reimers-Stiftung Colloquium on Human Ethology" held at Bad Homburg in West Germany. His proposal to have the biology of choice included in the agenda was declined by its organizing committee, and he notes that some of the participants who sought to apply biological concepts directly to cultural processes in the general discussion exhibited quite minimal understanding of exogenetic mechanisms. Freeman's paper (1979b) was entitled "Functional Aspects of Aggression, Fear and Attachment in Anthropological Perspective."

Freeman also visited Sir Karl Popper in November 1977. In 1973 he had sent Popper a copy of his draft manuscript of 1971 containing an account of the refutation of Mead's Samoan conclusions on which he was working and in which Popper had shown keen interest, describing it as "an immensely important piece of work." This visit enabled Freeman to discuss with Popper various aspects of his proposed refutation.

In May 1978, Freeman presented to a seminar at the Research School of Pacific Studies a paper entitled "Sweet Analytics 'Tis Thou Hast Ravished Me': A Critical Appreciation of the Sexual Values and Behaviour of the Samoans of Western Polynesia." This was the first draft of Chapter Sixteen in his book (1983a). In August 1978, after it had been revised, Freeman wrote Mead asking if she would like to see this paper informing her that it was highly critical. An assistant replied in September that Mead had been ill and that if she had the opportunity to read and comment on the manuscript Freeman would be notified. Freeman heard nothing more before Mead's death in November 1978 (see Freeman 1983c:112).

Freeman writes that Mead's "unexpected death had an immediate bearing on the work on which I was engaged, for it was obvious that the publication of my refutation would have to be deferred for some years." He turned to other topics. In 1978 he was invited by Ashley Montagu to prepare, for a volume he was editing, a critique of E. O. Wilson's views on the relationship between sociobiology and anthropology (see Freeman 1980). Freeman states that this was a topic of great interest that was moreover related to that aspect of his refutation concerned with the relation between biology and anthropology during the decade or so before the commencement of Mead's Samoan researches.

In this article Freeman (1980) argued that sociobiological theory when applied to human populations was irremediably deficient because of the nongenetically determined behaviors, to be found in all human populations, which are an expression of the human capacity to make choices. As a result human behavior cannot possibly be explained by sociobiological theory alone.

In his presidential address to the anthropology, archaeology, and linguistics section of the 49th Congress of the Australian and New Zealand Association for the Advancement of Science in January 1979, Freeman reviewed the development of his thinking on choice behavior (Freeman 1981b). In the course of this address he decried the conceptual polarization that has occurred in the human sciences in which there are both those who attempt to explain behavior and human nature in terms of biology alone and those who view culture as unlinked to biology. His thesis was that a most fundamental linkage is to be found in human choice behavior which is both intrinsic to human biology and to the formation of cultures.

On June 26, 1981, Freeman completed the first draft of *On Coming of Age in Samoa: The Analysis of an Anthropological Myth*, which was later to become *Margaret Mead and Samoa: The Making and Unmaking of an Anthropological Myth*. On September 13, 1981, accompanied by his wife, he flew to Samoa with a copy of this manuscript to carry out further inquiries and to have the text of the refutation checked by Samoan scholars (see Freeman 1983a:xiv–xv, 1983c:112). During this visit Freeman was successful for the first time in gaining access to the archives of the High Court of American Samoa to record crucially significant documentary evidence from the 1920s. In October, he flew on to Honolulu to carry out further research at the Bernice P. Bishop Museum, particularly in the field notebooks of the Maori ethnologist Peter H. Buck, who was in Samoa during the late 1920s. This vitally significant evidence from Samoa and from Buck's field notebooks was added to the final draft of the manuscript in late October 1981 (see Freeman 1983c:112).

On January 1, 1982, Freeman became Emeritus Professor of the Australian National University and a Visiting Fellow in its Research School of Pacific Studies, and during the rest of that year was occupied with seeing his refutation through the press.

On January 26, 1983, Freeman was telephoned from New York by Edwin McDowell of the *New York Times*. Unbeknownst to Freeman,

McDowell had been given by Harvard University Press an advance copy of the book, now titled *Margaret Mead and Samoa: The Making and Unmaking of an Anthropological Myth*. An article written by McDowell on Freeman's refutation then appeared on Monday, January 31, 1983, on the front page of the *New York Times*. This created an immense stir and was published in abbreviated form in newspapers throughout the world. As a result, by February Freeman's refutation had become a *cause célèbre* by a planned publicity coup in which Freeman himself had no hand (see also Freeman 1984c for a prepublication history of his book).

Freeman's scholarly refutation of Margaret Mead's *Coming of Age in Samoa* is a form of scientific critique unprecedented in anthropological inquiry. For various reasons it has provoked a storm of controversy and criticism, to which Freeman has replied in 1983c, and in a number of other publications. Many of us who view anthropology as a scientific and scholarly discipline have been shaken to our intellectual foundations by the response Freeman's book has received in American anthropology. The attempts to silence him, to deprive him of the right of adequate reply to published criticism, the failure to weigh the issues critically and put them to Popperian test, the conscious and unconscious misreading of his argument including denial of the facts on which it is based, and the attempts to divert attention from his refutation by *ad hominem* attacks have astounded many of us. We find these reactions counterproductive in a discipline that is supposed to be seeking for the truth. For all those skilled in social analysis and willing to turn this analysis upon their own social lives, such reactions are the reactions of a belief system that is out of touch with the real world and unresponsive to change.

Perhaps the best, succinct evaluation of the emotional response to Freeman's refutation was made by John Merson (1985:86): "The shift to a new paradigm, as science historian Thomas Kuhn argues, involves a revolution, usually as emotionally bloody as a military coup in some banana republic."

Perhaps then, it will transpire that Freeman's refutation will become a landmark, portending a significant, paradigmatic shift in the theoretical perspective of anthropological inquiry and a change in attitude toward research marked by a demand for more rigorous, long-term field studies. His refutation has already cast new light on the nature of anthropological inquiry and is stimulating the development of more productive theory. Thus, it clearly illustrates the importance of the elimination of error for anthropological as for all scientific inquiry, and demonstrates that constant checking for bias is crucial in social research and that the stating of one's results in a form that can be subjected to falsification procedures is scientifically imperative.

However, the history of the controversy will not be reviewed in depth

here. The literature that it has generated is enormous, and Freeman himself is reviewing it and analyzing the irrational reaction to his refutation in
a book tentatively titled *When Prophecy Failed: Reflections on the Controversy Over Margaret Mead and Samoa*. He writes (Freeman 1986b)
that the whole sequence of events is poignantly reminiscent of that
recounted by Festinger, Riecken and Schachter in their classic *When
Prophecy Fails* (1956).

One hopes that the controversy will then be resolved so that Freeman
can return to his anthropologically important study of choice behavior,
and to his seminal proposition that (1983c:64): "In that a wise and free
choice is a creative act determined at the moment it is exercised, it will
be necessary to develop a scientific paradigm able to accommodate choice
as an independent variable."

It is fitting to end this account with three quotations. It was Meyer
Fortes' view that Derek Freeman, whom he knew well, had (as he put it
in a letter of 1972): ". . . a gift of selfless devotion to the search for answers."

Finally, there are two almost contemporaneous quotations that Freeman frequently uses and which nicely reflect both his own character and
his Popperian approach to scientific inquiry. Franz Boas in his Diary on
23 December 1883 wrote:

All that man can do for humanity is to further the truth, whether it
be sweet or bitter . . .

And, as Charles Darwin had noted a few years earlier, in 1879:

to kill an error is as good a service as, and sometimes even better
than, the establishment of a new truth or fact.

Notes

1. The sources for this appreciation include a personal communication entitled
"Some Notes on the Development of My Anthropological Interests" that Derek
Freeman prepared in response to a request for more biographic information,
personal conversations, letters, and his published articles.
2. All references to the publications of Derek Freeman can be found in the
section, "Selected Bibliography of Derek Freeman."
3. These two quotes are taken from pages 15 and 16 respectively of a duplicated
version of the text as the published version was not available at the time of
preparation of this review.

References

Appell, G. N.
1976 Introduction. The Direction of Research in Borneo: Its Past Contribution to the Anthropological Theory and Its Relevance for the Future. In *The Societies of Borneo: Explorations in the Theory of Cognatic Social Structure.* Special Publication 6. Washington: American Anthropological Association.

Nadel, S. F.
1957 *The Theory of Social Structure.* Glencoe: Free Press.

Leach, E. R.
1955 Forward. In *Iban Agriculture: A Report on the Shifting Cultivation of Hill Rice by the Iban of Sarawak* by Derek Freeman. London: Her Majesty's Stationery Office.

Merson, John
1985 Whose Life Is It, Anyway? Review of *Neither Justice nor Reason* by Marc Gumbert and *Margaret Mead and Samoa* by Derek Freeman. *Look and Listen*, January, p. 86.

Turner, V. W.
1964 Symbols in Ndembu Ritual. In *Closed Systems and Open Minds: The Limits of Naivety in Social Anthropology,* edited by Max Gluckman. Chicago: Aldine.

Selected Bibliography of Derek Freeman

Freeman, Derek

1938 Anatomy of Mind. *Salient* (Victoria University College) 6 September:3.

1943 The Seuao Cave. *Journal of the Polynesian Society* 52:101–9.

1944a The Falemaunga Caves. *Journal of the Polynesian Society* 53:86–106.

1944b The Vailele Earthmounds. *Journal of the Polynesian Society* 53:145–62.

1944c 'O Le Fale o Le fe'e. *Journal of the Polynesian Society* 53:121–44.

1947 The Tradition of Sanalala: Some Notes on Samoan Folk-Lore. *Journal of the Polynesian Society* 56:295–317.

1948 The Social Structure of a Samoan Village Community. Thesis for the Academic Postgraduate Diploma in Anthropology, University of London.

1949 The Polynesian Collection of Trinity College, Dublin and the National Museum of Ireland. *Journal of the Polynesian Society* 58:1–18.

1953 Family and Kin Among the Iban of Sarawak. Ph.D. Thesis, University of Cambridge.

1955a *Report on the Iban of Sarawak*. Kuching: Sarawak Government Printing Office. (Second Edition with a new Preface 1970.)

1955b *Iban Agriculture: A Report on the Shifting Cultivation of Hill Rice by the Iban of Sarawak*. London: Her Majesty's Stationery Office.

1956a Siegfried Frederick Nadel, 1903–1956. *Oceania* 27:1–11.

1956b 'Utrolateral' and 'Utrolocal.' *Man* 56:87–88.

1957a The Family System of the Iban of Borneo. In *The Developmental Cycle in Domestic Groups*, edited by Jack Goody. Cambridge Papers in Social Anthropology, No. 1. Cambridge: Cambridge University Press.

28   G. N. Appell

1957b Iban Pottery. *Sarawak Museum Journal* 8:151–76.

1959a The Joe Gimlet or Siovili Cult. In *Anthropology in the South Seas: Essays Presented to H. D. Skinner*, edited by J. D. Freeman and W. R. Geddes. New Plymouth, New Zealand: Thomas Avery.

1959b Henry Devenish Skinner: A Memoir. In *Anthropology in the South Seas: Essays Presented to H. D. Skinner*, edited by J. D. Freeman and W. R. Geddes. New Plymouth, New Zealand: Thomas Avery.

1960a The Iban of Western Borneo. In *Social Structure in Southeast Asia*, edited by G. Murdock. Viking Fund Publications in Anthropology 29:65–87.

1960b A Note on the *Gawai Kenyalang*, or Hornbill Ritual of the Iban of Sarawak. In *The Birds of Borneo* (first edition) by Bertram E. Smythies. (Second edition, 1968.) Edinburgh: Oliver and Boyd.

1960c Iban Augury. In *The Birds of Borneo* (first edition) by Bertram E. Smythies. (Second edition, 1968.) Edinburgh: Oliver and Boyd. (Reprinted in *Bijdragen tot de Taal-, Land- en Volkenkunde* 117:141–67, 1961.)

1961a On the Concept of the Kindred. The Curl Bequest Prize Essay 1960. *Journal of the Royal Anthropological Institute* 91:192–220.

1961b Review of Social Stratification in Polynesia by Marshall D. Sahlins. *Man* 61:146–48.

1962a Environment and Culture in Polynesia. *Man* 62:24–25.

1962b Review of *Rethinking Anthropology* by E. R. Leach. *Man* 62:125–26.

1962c Review of *Trance in Bali* by Jane Belo. *Journal of Polynesian Society* 71:270–73.

1964a Human Aggression in Anthropological Perspective. In *The Natural History of Aggression*, edited by J. D. Carthy and F. J. Ebling. London: Academic Press.

1964b Some Observations on Kinship and Political Authority in Samoa. *American Anthropologist* 66:553–68.

1965a Samoa: A Matter of Emphasis. *American Anthropologist* 67:1534–37.

1965b Anthropology, Psychiatry and the Doctrine of Cultural Relativism. *Man* 65:65–67.

1966 Social Anthropology and the Scientific Study of Human Behaviour. *Man* N.S. 1:330–42.

1967a Totem and Taboo: A Reappraisal. *The Psychoanalytical Study of Society* 4:9–33.

1967b Shaman and Incubus. *Psychoanalytic Study of Society* 4:315–44.

1967c A Matter of Values. *Man* 2:132–33.

1968   Thunder, Blood and the Nicknaming of God's Creatures. *The Psychoanalytic Quarterly* 37:353–99.

1970a   *Report on the Iban.* New Edition. London School of Economics Monograph on Social Anthropology No. 41. London: Athlone Press.

1970b   Human Nature and Culture. In *Man and the New Biology*, edited by R. O. Slatyer et al. Canberra: The Australian National University Press. (Reprinted in The Bobbs-Merrill Reprint Series in Anthropology A–488.)

1971   Aggression: Instinct or Symptom? *Australian and New Zealand Journal of Psychiatry* 5:66–73.

1972   Social Organization of Manu'a (1930 and 1960), by Margaret Mead: Some Errata. *Journal of the Polynesian Society* 81:70–78. (Reprinted in *Ethical Dilemmas in Anthropological Inquiry: A Case Book* by G. N. Appell. Waltham: Crossroads Press, 1972.)

1974a   The Evolutionary Theories of Charles Darwin and Herbert Spencer. *Current Anthropology* 15:211–21.

1974b   Kinship, Attachment Behaviour and the Primary Bond. In *The Character of Kinship*, edited by J. Goody. Cambridge: Cambridge University Press.

1974c   A Report on Mawanjum Community with Special Reference to Its Housing Needs. Presented to the Aboriginal Housing Panel, Canberra.

1975   The Iban of Sarawak and Their Religion: A Review Article. *Sarawak Museum Journal* 23:275–78.

1977   On Sociobiology and Anthropology. *Canberra Anthropology* 1:24–32.

1978a   'A Happening Frightening to Both Ghosts and Men': A Case Study for Western Samoa. In *The Changing Pacific: Essays in Honour of H. E. Maude*, edited by N. Gunson. Melbourne: Oxford University Press.

1978b   Towards an Anthropology Both Scientific and Humanistic. *Canberra Anthropology* 1, 3:44–69.

1979a   Severed Heads that Germinate. In *Fantasy and Symbol*, edited by R. H. Hook. London: Academic Press.

1979b   Functional Aspects of Aggression, Fear and Attachment in Anthropological Perspectives. In *Human Ethology: Claims and Limits of a New Discipline*, edited by M. von Cranach et al. Cambridge: Cambridge University Press.

1980   Sociobiology: The 'Antidiscipline' of Anthropology. In *Sociobiology Examined*, edited by A. Montagu. New York: Oxford University Press.

1981a   Some Reflections on the Nature of Iban Society. Occasional Paper of the Department of Anthropology, Research School of Pacific Studies, The Australian National University, Canberra.

1981b The Anthropology of Choice. *Canberra Anthropology* 4:82–100.

1983a *Margaret Mead and Samoa: The Making and Unmaking of an Anthropological Myth*. Cambridge: Harvard University Press.

1983b Choice, Values and the Solution of Human Problems. In *Environment and Population: Problems of Adaptation*, edited by John B. Calhoun. New York; Praeger.

1983c Inductivism and the Test of Truth: A Rejoinder to Lowell D. Holmes and Others. In *Fact and Context in Ethnography: The Samoa Controversy*, edited by Gregory Acciaioli. Special Volume. *Canberra Anthropology* 6:101–92.

1984a The Burthen of a Mystery; Review Article on Bradd Shore's *Sala'ilua: A Samoan Mystery. Oceania* 54:247–54.

1984b "O Rose thou art sick!": A Rejoinder to Weiner, Schwartz, Holmes, Shore, and Silverman. *American Anthropologist* 86:400–5.

1984c Samoa and Margaret Mead: A rejoinder to Paula Brown Glick and Rosemary Firth. *RAIN* No. 60:6–8.

1985a Response to Reyman and Hammond. *American Anthropologist* 87:394–95.

1985b A Reply to Ember's Reflections on the Freeman-Mead Controversy. *American Anthropologist* 87:910–17.

1986a Rejoinder to Patience and Smith. *American Anthropologist* 88:162–67.

1986b Some Notes on the Development of My Anthropological Interests. Personal Communication.

1987   Letter to the Editor. *The American Scholar* Winter:157–59.

Introduction to the Essays
G. N. Appell

To what degree is human behavior a product of cultural constraints or of biological constraints? How bound is man by tradition? How free is he to choose and create both himself and his social world? While these issues of determinism and freedom have long been a concern of philosophers (see Hook 1958 for an assessment), anthropologists, with a few notable exceptions, have tended to ignore the relevance of these for theory building and field methods. Yet this issue is critical for anthropological inquiry if the proper questions are to be posed and genuine explanations for human behavior advanced.

Malinowski considered this issue in his little noticed book, *Freedom and Civilization* (1944), and found freedom to be defined and molded by culture. Dorothy Lee in a series of articles (1959, 1963) also dealt with the problem of freedom and cultural constraint, and reached a similar conclusion.

Evans-Pritchard (1964; orig. 1950) rejected sociological determinism as a procedure for studying sociocultural phenomena. He argued that it aimed "at proving that man is an automaton and at discovering the sociological laws in terms of which of his actions, ideas, and beliefs can be explained and in the light of which they can be planned and controlled" (1964:154). He argued (1964:152) that social anthropology is, instead, one of the humanities and like historiography "is interested in design rather than process, and that it therefore seeks patterns and not scientific laws and interprets rather than explains." (See Hatch 1973 for a discussion of Evans-Pritchard's position.) In his ethnography, however, Evans-Pritchard did not address the problem of where cultural determinism ends and free will begins.

But it was Bidney, trained as both philosopher and anthropologist, who became most deeply involved with the issue of freedom and determinism (Bidney 1953, 1963a, 1963b). He maintained that "human freedom and causal determinism are quite compatible and that no irreconcilable

31

conflict is involved" (1953:124). In his article "The Varieties of Human Freedom," Bidney further elucidated his typology of forms of freedom, distinguishing between the fact of freedom and the value of freedom. He concluded (1963a:34) that "human culture is the product of man's potentialities for freedom of creativity and freedom of choice. Once achieved, a given historical system of culture functions to determine and condition the behavior of its adherents, while opening up new horizons of possibility and choice not otherwise available. There is a polarity in the relations of freedom and determinism in the life of culture, such that cultural law is grounded in human freedom of consent and culture in turn may be utilized to promote freedom of action."

While Bidney has cleared away much of the confusion in the concept of freedom, we are left with several awkward problems. How do we move from the level of general discussion to the concrete level of empirical investigations? How do we distinguish the boundary between choice and determinism in a particular social situation? What theories, concepts and methods are required to define this boundary and isolate the phenomena divided by it? Or is not this contrast between freedom and determinism a falsely drawn distinction producing arguments that are misjoined? Would not, as is argued in this book, an interactionist paradigm be more productive in which freedom and determinism are in a dialectical relationship, being both constraint and opportunity?

Bidney is furthermore unclear to what degree sociocultural phenomena are subject to nomothetic procedures or require ideographic methods by their very nature. Some anthropologists argue that anthropology is essentially an ideographic discipline; it can only provide description and interpretation of cultural phenomena. This position should not be confused with the modern attack on methodological collectivism, the proponents of which argue that sociocultural systems can be described and explained only as a function of individual choices. For these proponents of opportunism still work within a nomothetic frame (see Appell 1980b, 1981, and Appell in this volume for a critical appraisal of this position and its failure to deal adequately with sociocultural phenomena).

Thus, many anthropologists proceed with the belief that sociocultural anthropology can become a nomothetic discipline, that human behavior can be ultimately explained, not just merely understood. This assumes that "science and scientific understanding has a potentially completable system" (Robinson 1976:200). But is free will amenable to scientific inquiry? What happens to human freedom if human behavior is found to be largely or fully determined? Will human freedom turn out to be only illusory?

The pan-human experience of this is otherwise. Human beings not only have the capacity for choice, but the opportunity to exercise it. Otherwise the idea of accident, moral responsibility, and punishment, again pan-human experiences, would be meaningless. Thus, one of the goals of anthropological inquiry clearly should be to investigate across the range of human societies the nature of this freedom to choose in order to better define the limits of human freedom and human possibility. This volume is directed towards that goal.

As many anthropologists work within a conceptual frame of cultural determinism, they overlook those realms of the social system in which choice behavior occurs, as in the opportunity structure, and ignore those processes that lead to social change. It is ironic that many of those who subscribe to the doctrine of cultural determinism with regard to the subjects of their inquiry nevertheless act as if it does not apply to their own social life. They take a nondeterminist position, ignoring their own cultural constraints, and expect that their behavior and that of others within their immediate social frame will be based on free choice, which is informed by enlightened reason or scientific knowledge (see Appell 1973; Bidney 1963a:33).

Thus, the relation of choice to culture and social structure has been a persistent problem to anthropological theory building. Anthropological inquiry has always been concerned with certain kinds of choice, such as marital residence, marriage partners. But this concern has never been integrated into a satisfactory theory of social behavior that encompasses both the constraints and freedom that we all experience (*pace* Firth 1954, 1955). Instead, anthropological explanation and concepts seem to have focused on determinism and ignored choice.

In opposition to this, as we have mentioned, there arose in the 1960s and 1970s a group of poststructuralists who argued that the social structure of a society is the product of the analyst's methods and does not reflect social reality. Instead social forms are the product of innumerable choices. (See Appell 1980, 1981, and in this volume for a critical discussion of this position.) Nevertheless, those who have taken this position and viewed society as the product of strategic interactions have not frontally attacked the problem posed by the doctrine of cultural determinism.

Cultural determinism has many referents in anthropological inquiry. Two of these are important for the discussion here. In the first sense, cultural determinism means that the behavior of a society's members are contingent upon and constrained by their cultural conditioning. Proponents of this school, as we have noted, tend to downplay choice behavior, and therefore, they have not been too successful in dealing with the processes of internal change and the redesign of a society by the actions of its members.

In the second sense, cultural determinism is used to contrast with biological determinism. This position arose in response to the paramount currents of thought in the first quarter of this century that explained behavior as a product of genetic endowment. (See Freeman 1983 for an insightful discussion of this.) In this sense of cultural determinism, human biology is perceived to be of no importance in explaining sociocultural behavior.

Freeman in a series of publications (1970, 1973, 1979, 1983) has pointed out that the doctrine of cultural determinism is inadequate on the one hand for its failure to consider the nature of choice behavior, which is a crucial element in the human ethogram; and on the other hand for ignoring the biological drives and constraints that form the ground for human behavior. He thus argues for an interactionist paradigm in which choice behavior is fundamental, being intrinsic both to our biology and basic to the formation of cultures—for cultures are the accumulation of socially sanctioned past choices. However, the greater the freedom to choose, the greater the scope for good or bad choices and the greater the need for ethics, rules, and laws for defining prohibited alternatives.

Freeman argues that choice systems can be evaluated on the basis of their adaptive value. However, what still has to be incorporated into a theory of choice behavior is a method of costing choice. Each choice has its costs, economically and ultimately biologically. The closer the choices move to the boundaries of the human ethogram, the more costly these choices become—socially, psychologically, and physiologically (see Appell 1984). Thus, the challenge to anthropological inquiry is to develop concepts for dealing with the cost/benefit of choice behavior that go beyond economics and incorporate the change in the adaptation load that the choice precipitates on the chooser and the social group of which he is a member.

Choice is constrained but not fully determined by the system of morality in which the choice is made. Appell, in his contribution to this volume, attempts a reconciliation of this problem in the relationship of social structure to choice behavior. He argues that if the social structure is conceived as consisting of that aspect of the moral order that we term the jural system, it not only constrains human behavior, it also delineates a field of opportunity for choice. This field may be termed the "opportunity structure." The social structure controls choices by public disincentives, or punishments. The opportunity structure channels choices by rewards. But choices in the opportunity structure are still somewhat constrained by that aspect of the moral order we refer to as "ethics" (see Appell 1980a). There is also a contrastructure, which consists of behaviors which are forbidden by the jural order but which nevertheless may be chosen by certain members of the society. Thus, the jural order not only defines what choices are acceptable, but also what choices are not acceptable.

There is another order of choice behavior that goes beyond the confines of the sociocultural system. This is the realm of what Freeman calls "radical choice." These are choices which may be made by madmen or charismatic leaders. The very conception of these choices are not delineated by the individual's sociocultural system, and they can lead to radical social change. Ethnography largely ignores this aspect of human behavior.

The more usual type of internal change arises as a result of human action that tests the boundaries of the social structure, the opportunity structure, and the contrastructure. Success in such testing changes both the boundaries and the interrelationship of the three subsystems. For society is an emergent phenomenon, arising from the choices that are or are not made. Again these processes have not received sufficient attention in anthropological inquiry.

In this volume Devereux explores the cultural rules lying behind choice behavior. He demonstrates how error can arise in interpreting choice behavior on the basis of surface criteria since identical outcomes can be the product of different sets of assumptions held by the choosers.

Lawrence, in his study of the historical antecedents of methodological collectivism in British anthropology, addresses the issue of how social anthropology became the prisoner of its own concepts of group behavior and failed to come to terms with the individual actor and the problem of choice, which has distorted ethnographic reality.

Feil contrasts two forms of gift exchange in Papua New Guinea. In one system the emphasis has developed on the transaction itself, and therefore is being modified and eroded by social change. The other system, the *tee* system, is focused more on the social relationship established and the moral order of this relationship than the goods exchanged. It also appears to be more resistant to change. Feil points out that the tee system is the most important institution in Enga society in which choice of relationship prevails. It is this factor of choice of trading partner with its associated moral order which pertains between partners that makes this institution resistant to the logic of modern economic thinking.

Young examines the nature of ambivalence in the father–son relationship in a Goodenough Island society to elucidate the point that any adequate explanation of human behavior requires an interactionist paradigm in which the interaction of biological, environmental, and cultural factors is fully considered. Following Freeman, he argues that ambivalence arises from the biologically defined nature of dominance behavior combined with the development of attachment behavior to the mother, which tends to be transferred in some degree to all subsequent relationships. Young, making a contribution to the psychoanalytic understanding of ambivalence, demonstrates how this ambivalence can be constrained or exacerbated by the moral order of society. A social structure that involves patrilineal descent will tend to intensify the natural ambivalence that exists between fathers and sons. He examines two cases of the expression of this ambivalence at that critical juncture of a father's death when a son must choose an appropriate response. He shows how its cultural expression threatens critical food exchanges but at the same time fuels some of the society's most creative achievements. He then draws parallels with the responses chosen by those in his case studies with those exhibited by Freud on his own father's death. Young's contribution provides clear evidence of the productivity of the interactionist paradigm. He concludes that an interactionist paradigm is the crux of a modern anthropology, neither mentalistic nor behavioralistic, that would explore the relationship between what is given and what is possible for man, while admitting his capacity to invent (or "choose") himself.

Madan explores the nature of the choice environment through the analysis of the mother–son relationship in Hindu society as revealed in a work of fiction. And he shows how adult choice behavior is a resolution of the conflicts that stem from the ambivalence of the mother–son bond, the constraints on choice by the moral order, the opportunities that arise in individual life experiences, and the accumulated karma of past choices. Madan uses his material not only to define more clearly the dimensions of the choice environment and the relationship that choice has to the moral order, but also to show how the accumulation of choices contributes to the construction of one's character and the kind of social relations one builds.

Herdt in looking at the ethnographer's choices raises the question of how an ethnographer achieves "knowledge" of another culture and transmits it. In analyzing the progress of his own fieldwork in New Guinea, he points out that the choices made in the field as to what to investigate and what to ignore, as well as in the writing of an ethnography, have an intimate affect on the resulting product. But his conclusions go beyond delineating the need for a reflexive ethnography. He raises the critical question of how an ethnographer can present the texture of experienced life in a society. For it involves the interplay of individual experience with the choices one makes, and the cultural and situational constraints that guide these choices as well as the expression of the meaning that each intersect of constraint and freedom has as it reverberates in one's emotional and expressive life. How then do ethnographers transform this multi-layered experience into words, substituting a text for the original perception and sensation?

In the controversy over scientific versus interpretative inquiry, Appell's position is that of methodological determinism (see Kaplan 1964:124). That is, it is critical for the development of anthropological inquiry to proceed as if it could be a nomothetic study, even if there are realms of sociocultural phenomena which may never be capable of full explanation.

For there are still major areas of sociocultural behavior that are amenable to scientific procedures, and we should push back the frontiers of knowledge as far as they can go to determine where the boundary lies between the nomothetic and ideographic study of human behavior. Herdt, Madan and Jackson in their contributions pose the problem of the limitations to understanding of a scientific anthropology. They argue for an anthropology with a strong ideographic component and demonstrate what insights can be achieved by this method, without necessarily ruling out the usefulness of the other approach for certain purposes.

Jackson's view is that man is not the sum of the conditions that bear upon him, and the critical task of anthropology is to fathom the relationship between what is given and what is chosen, between destiny and decision. Thus, the basic problem is to find a way to reconcile the nomothetic and the ideographic conceptions of behavior. He argues that both perspectives are necessary, as existence is a dialectic interplay between the impersonal and given forces that define the conditions of existence and individual projects and choices which not only reveal these prior conditions but surpass them. Jackson finds this view, which has its basis in Sartre's work, similar to the view found in many West African cosmologies, and he delineates these philosophical parallels in investigating the dialectic between destiny and decision in several societies.

Walter in his contribution returns to the problem of the biological constraints on choice behavior. To what degree is religious behavior the product of the accumulation of free choices in the past and to what degree is it the product of our biological givens interacting with the social environment and influencing what is chosen? Walter examines the nature of fetal development and parturition to determine what biological models are available for man from which to choose for use as symbols of rebirth in initiation rituals. As a result of these biological givens, he shows why certain common forms of symbolic expression have been chosen in a variety of cultures.

This volume is thus a contribution to the ethnography and theory of choice. This field of anthropological inquiry is still in its infancy. However, we will eventually have a better conception of the dimensions of choice behavior and its relation to the moral order. We will then be able to answer more fully many of the questions addressed in this volume. There are methodological questions such as: Is the study of choice behavior amenable to a deterministic approach or will it always require the methods of interpretation and understanding (also see Bridgman 1958:155; von Wright 1971)? Can methods be developed in the ideographic approach that will produce warranted knowledge?

There are also questions fundamental to the growth of the social sciences that need answering. To what degree is human behavior constrained or determined by the conditions of infancy and enculturation? Under what conditions and to what degree does the individual have the power and freedom to create and mold his own social world? Where does the boundary lie between voluntary and involuntary acts? Do all societies recognize the moral significance of voluntary and involuntary acts and include excusing conditions in their jural systems (also see Beardsley 1958 and Hart 1958)? To what degree can we overcome our past conditioning to construct our own character and be responsible for our choices and actions? To what degree are we prisoners of our past choices? Do we have the capacity and freedom to make original and creative choices? If we do, for what purpose this freedom?

References

Appell, G. N.
1973   The Distinction Between Ethnography and Ethnology and Other Issues in Cognitive Structuralism. *Bijdragen tot de Taal–, Land– en Volkenkunde* 129:1–56.

1980a Talking Ethics: The Uses of Moral Rhetoric and the Function of Ethical Principles. In *Ethical Problems of Fieldwork*, edited by Joan Cassell and Murray L. Wax. *Social Problems* 27, 3:350–57.

1980b Epistemological Issues in Anthropological Inquiry: Social Structuralism, Cognitive Structuralism, Synthetic Structuralism and Opportunism. Part 1. *Canberra Anthropology* 3, 2:1–27.

1981   Epistemological Issues in Anthropological Inquiry: Social Structuralism, Cognitive Structuralism, Synthetic Structuralism and Opportunism. Part 2. *Canberra Anthropology* 4, 1:1–22.

1984   Freeman's Refutation of Mead's *Coming of Age in Samoa*: The Implications for Anthropological Inquiry. *Eastern Anthropologist* 37:183–214.

Bidney, David
1953   *Theoretical Anthropology*. New York: Columbia University Press.

1963a The Varieties of Human Freedom. In *The Concept of Freedom and Anthropology*, edited by David Bidney. The Hague: Mouton.

Bidney, David (ed.)
1963b *The Concept of Freedom and Anthropology*. The Hague: Mouton.

Beardsley, Elizabeth Lane
1958 "Excusing Conditions" and Moral Responsibility. In *Determinism and Freedom in the Age of Modern Science*, edited by Sidney Hook. New York: Collier Macmillan.

Bridgman, Percy W.
1958 Determinism in Modern Science. In *Determinism and Freedom in the Age of Modern Science*, edited by Sidney Hook. New York: Collier Macmillan.

Evans-Pritchard, E. E.
1964 (orig. 1950) *Social Anthropology and Other Essays*. Paperback Edition. Glencoe: Free Press of Glencoe.

Firth, Raymond
1954 Social Organization and Social Change. *Journal of the Royal Anthropological Institute* 84:1–20.

1955 Some Principles of Social Organization. *Journal of the Royal Anthropological Institute* 85:1–18.

Freeman, Derek
1970 Human Nature and Culture. In *Man and the New Biology*, edited by R. O. Slatyer et al. Canberra: The Australian National University Press. (Reprinted in The Bobbs-Merrill Reprint Series In Anthropology A–488).

1973 Kinship, Attachment Behavior and the Primary Bond. In *The Character of Kinship*, edited by J. Goody. Cambridge: Cambridge University Press.

1979 Functional Aspects of Aggression, Fear and Attachment in Anthropological Perspective. In *Human Ethology: Claims and Limits of a New Discipline*, edited by M. von Cranach et al. Cambridge: Cambridge University Press.

1983 *Margaret Mead and Samoa: The Making and Unmaking of an Anthropological Myth*. Cambridge: Harvard University Press.

Hart, H. L. A.
1958 Legal Responsibility and Excuses. In *Determinism and Freedom in the Age of Modern Science*. New York: Collier Macmillan.

Hatch, Alvin
1973 *Theories of Man and Culture*. New York: Columbia University Press.

Hook, Sidney (ed.)
1958 *Determinism and Freedom in the Age of Modern Science*. New York: Collier Macmillan.

Kaplan, Abraham
1964 *The Conduct of Inquiry: Methodology for Behavioral Science*. San Francisco: Chandler.

Lee, Dorothy
1959 *Freedom and Culture*. New York: Prentice-Hall.

1963 Freedom and Social Constraint. In *The Concept of Freedom and Anthropology*, edited by David Bidney. The Hague: Mouton.

Malinowski, Bronislaw
1944 *Freedom and Civilization*. New York.

Robinson, Guy
1976 Nature and Necessity. In *Impressions of Empiricism*, edited by Godfrey Vesley. New York: St. Martin's Press.

von Wright, Georg Henrik
1971 *Explanation and Understanding*. Ithaca: Cornell University Press.

PART II

Theoretical Constructs, Meaning, and the Analysis of Choice Behavior

1

Emergent Structuralism: The Design of an Inquiry System to Delineate the Production and Reduction of Social Forms

G. N. APPELL

What part does choice play in the building of cultures? To explore this question I am going to discuss three epistemological issues:[1] (1) the controversy over actor-centered approaches versus institutional approaches to social anthropological inquiry; (2) the origin of social forms; and (3) the design of an inquiry system to discover these social forms so that the cultural contamination of data is minimized. These three issues are intertwined, and it will be impossible to discuss one without consideration of the others. But their resolution is central to the growth of Derek Freeman's paradigm on the anthropology of choice.

To illustrate my arguments, I shall use data from fieldwork among the Rungus. But as space is limited, I will focus on the theoretical aspects of my argument rather than on Rungus ethnography. Much of the relevant ethnography I have discussed elsewhere (see Appell 1976b, 1978). However, to set the stage for my theoretical discussion, let me briefly review the salient aspects of Rungus society.

The Rungus are a people of northern Borneo. They have a bilateral kinship system with no corporate descent groups. The major social units are the domestic family, the long-house, and the village. The modal domestic family structure is that of husband and wife and their children. The village usually includes several long-houses. It holds residual rights over its territory, and the cultivation of land in swiddens is restricted to those domestic families resident in the village.

The Debate Over Social Structuralism and Opportunism[2]

How is choice behavior related to the concept of social structure? Social structuralism has been faulted for failing to deal adequately with this dimension of social action (see Appell 1980, 1981). Thus Firth in 1954 wrote: "Here is our great problem as anthropologists—to translate the acts of individuals into the regularities of social process" (reprinted in 1964:46). Leach (1957:137) delineated the controversy as between those "who stress the importance of the ideal order conceived as a system of jural relationships and those who see behavior as the outcome of competitive individual self-interest," suggesting that Malinowski's concept of institution might perhaps provide a bridge between these two approaches. Then Leach in 1960 (see also 1961) took the position that "social structures are sometimes best regarded as the statistical outcome of multiple individual choices rather than a direct reflection of jural rules" (1960:124).

As the debate has grown, so too has there developed a polarization of views, which Garbett (1970:215) summarized as follows: "Broadly, those who adopt the institutional approach lay stress on the enduring framework of institutions which constrains individual behaviour; while those who adopt an actor-oriented approach, lay stress on the flux and change of day-to-day life and give central importance to the individual who, as manipulator and innovator, creates, in varying degrees, the social world around him."

In recent years there has been increasing emphasis in social anthropological inquiry on the individual as actor as shown in the development and use of decision models, social exchange theory, network analysis, situational analysis, and so forth. The social reality that these approaches are attempting to delineate I would like to refer to here as the "opportunity structure."

Not all writers have taken a polarized position on these issues. Some who have focused on the actor-centered approach, such as Mitchell (1971) and van Velson (1967), do not deny the importance of the structural domain. However, the fundamental point made by Firth in his 1954 article (reprinted in 1964) that social organization is complementary to social structure has tended to be overlooked.

The Opportunity Structure and the Contrastructure

If social structure is conceived of as representing the jural order, as soon as you have a social structure, so also must you have a structure of opportunity; and as soon as there exists an opportunity structure, so must you have a social structure; for the system of options available to the individual to manipulate and create his social world are provided by the social structure. Thus, Leach's later position (1960, 1961) was essentially in error for without matter there can be no antimatter; without structure there can be no decisions; but without decisions there can be also no structure.

This relationship between social structure, i.e., the system of presumptive and proscriptive constraints, and the opportunity structure is put, I believe, extremely well by Dorothy Lee:

> The clarity of the structure within which I find myself—that is, the "social constraint"—not only frees me from the interference of others, but actually makes it possible for me to act, that is, it furnishes me with the conditions of freedom. . . . when I am involved in this life, when I live in dialogue with this structure, I experience it as a condition of freedom. It makes it possible for me to proceed in what would otherwise be a confusing jungle; it makes it possible for me to function [Lee 1963:62–63].

In other words, without structure there is no opportunity; there is no basis on which to create or change one's social world.

The further criticism that social structuralism does not deal with rule-breaking and rule-manipulating may be applicable to the practice of social structuralism, but this is not inherent in the theoretical construct itself, or at least should not be. For it is the structure itself that provides the paths, the techniques, the very conception of doing what you are enjoined from doing. This domain might be called the contrastructure.[3]

EMERGENT STRUCTURALISM

The post-structuralists have argued that the actual structure of a society arises from the decisions that are made, from the social transactions and exchanges that are engaged in, and from the constant negotiations over the social order that occur. In one sense the post-structuralists are right. A social structure, viewed as the moral and jural order, always has the capacity for self-transformation, and in some societies this is a more rapidly occurring phenomenon than in others. But this is not what the post-structuralists mean. Their view is that social forms are generated by the sum total of decisions and transactions. It is here that they are involved in fundamental error, for this view is only a partial one of the social universe.

Decision-making and transactions by themselves do not generate all social forms. Certainly they do not generate the social forms of the social structure, although the occupants of these forms may indeed enter these roles by choice. Instead individual choice and transactions are relevant only to the opportunity structure. For to bring new social forms from the opportunity structure into the realm of the social structure requires a second level order of event, a reflexive event by the members of the society scanning their own opportunity structure and deciding that social structural change is in order. These new forms are then encoded into the social structure by a legitimizing act or relegated to the contrastructure as deviance by a representative body of members. Let me give an example.

The Rungus village territory is stated to include all the area in which the village members customarily cut their swiddens. This area is ritually closed off for a short period every decade or so when a ceremony is held to increase the fertility of the village (see Appell 1976b). Originally these village boundaries were not closely defined but were indicated only in a general way. However, a more precise definition of them became necessary as pressure on the village's resources increased.

Thus, some time late in the nineteenth century in the village where our field station was located, the headman discovered that members of a neighboring village had crossed over the watershed dividing his village from theirs and had cut their swiddens in an area that his village claimed. The headman and some of his followers set fire to the swiddens after the undergrowth had been cut but before the large trees had been felled, thus effectively preventing the intruders from using their swiddens. No challenge to this act was made, largely it is stated, because it was impossible to identify who had started the fires, and the intruders withdrew.

During the period of office of the succeeding headman, some members from a neighboring village built a long-house within the village territory without his permission as headman. After several years of argument over this intrusion, the headman told the intruders that they should either join onto his long-house or leave. The intruders finally did leave, and the headmen of the two villages involved reaffirmed that the boundary between their villages ran along the crest of hills dividing the watersheds of the two villages. They concluded that swiddens could not be further cut in each other's territory without the permission of the relevant village headman, thus explicitly affirming the evolving jural definition of the village that had been indicated by the acts of the headmen in dealing with those who were testing the boundaries.

The next headman found that the territory of his village had been intruded upon by members of still another village, and he got together with their headman and formalized a boundary between these two villages along the divide of hills. He publicly stated that any subsequent violation of the boundary would force him to sue for a gong as a fine. This was a new sanction, arising under the pressure of the emerging situation and represented a further refinement in the village's jural powers.

Thus, the multiple decisions of individual Rungus domestic families in response to population pressure upon the land to exploit the opportunity provided by ambiguous territorial and jural boundaries began to produce a change in social behavior. The change in the opportunity system was quickly perceived as a threat to the potential interests of others, and action was taken to protect these interests. As these actions were evaluated as legitimate and thus brought into the jural system as precedents to deal with other disputes of the same nature, a more evolved definition of the jural personality of the Rungus village began to emerge.[4]

In sum, changes in the opportunity system as a result of multiple decisions and transactions of individuals in competitive self-interest do occur and produce different social modes and at time social forms. But these are not transformed into a change in the social structure until they have been evaluated, given legitimacy, and backed up by appropriate sanctions. Similarly under like pressures of competitive self-interest, rules are brought into the negotiating arena, and as a result change may occur in these. But social systems are not continually in the process of change in all domains. Not all the rules of the social structure are simultaneously in the negotiating arena, and for those that are, it is important to distinguish whether it is the rule itself or its application that is being negotiated. Whatever, the empirical question is always which of the rules are perceived as being negotiable and which are not and under which conditions.

Thus, for the ethnographer, in order to elucidate the nature of the interrelationship between the opportunity structure and the social structure, the problem is to collect data on the processes by which changes in quantity are recognized and transformed into qualitative changes, processes by which emergent social modes in the opportunity system are legitimized and transformed into new social forms in the social structure. Of equal importance is the process which leads to the deregulation of social forms, removing social forms from the purview of the social structure to the opportunity structure.

The Design of an Inquiry System for Social Forms

However, before the theory of emergent structuralism can develop, clear procedures must be devised to distinguish the boundary of the social structure of a society from its opportunity structure. Is a discovered social form in the domain of the social structure or in the opportunity structure? Unfortunately social anthropology has not yet designed a system of inquiry for social forms in the domain of social structure that will clearly distinguish these forms from those in the opportunity structure. This is best illustrated by the problem of corporate descent groups. The analyst using the present conceptual tools may claim that a social form of the opportunity structure is instead a form in the social structure (see Appell 1973, 1983a, 1983b). This stems from what I have termed the cultural contamination of data by the observer's ideological and methodological position (see Appell, 1980, 1981).

While anthropology has always been concerned with the potentiality of cultural contamination of judgments and conclusions, little effort has been systematically devoted to resolving this problem with the exception of the work of the cognitive structuralists (see Appell 1973). Instead the solution to the problem has been largely relegated to the personal training of the observer. Anthropology thus had failed to deal with the problem that models and concepts derived from inquiry in one sociocultural system may carry cultural contamination from that system and cannot be productively used for the study of other systems (see Appell 1976a). Barnes (1962) pointed this out with regard to African models in the highlands of New Guinea. But little attention has been directed specifically to the epistemological question of how to design an inquiry system that would eliminate the problem of cultural contamination. This problem is compounded by the failure of anthropology to develop explicit observational procedures whereby investigators can move with some common basis from theoretical constructs to observables and back again.

Thus the goal here is to design an inquiry system for social forms that includes a methodology that eliminates the cultural contamination of data, that explicitly includes observational procedures for the theoretical constructs, and that is applicable to sociocultural domains that are not trivial.

In designing such an inquiry system, it would be useful to analyze those inquiry systems already in use that have been particularly productive.

MODELS FOR AN INQUIRY SYSTEM

Structural Linguistics

Structural linguistics has frequently been used as a model for the investigation of other anthropological domains. However, the claims for this model have been, in my opinion, overly enthusiastic (see Appell 1973, 1980, 1981). Certainly action systems are not equivalent to language.[5] Those who claim so much for the linguistic model have confused the content of that system of inquiry with its underlying theoretical assumptions and methodological procedures. In fact, seldom is its theory and methodology adequately analyzed.

The goals of a phonemic analysis is to isolate the functioning distinctions found in a specific language. The phonetic grid delineates the range of potential speech sounds that can be found in human societies. The analyst, using this grid, begins with a phonetic transcription and moves to a phonemic rendering of the language by certain prescribed procedures.

Underlying this is the assumption of an abstract analytical system that is composed of formal entities, that is without cultural content, and that includes the necessary relations between these entities.[6] That is, the linguist assumes that all languages "have," or can be described with, the concept of phonemes and that these have a characteristic interrelationship.

Let me now extrapolate this to apply to other sociocultural domains.

For any particular sociocultural domain of interest, etic grids need to be constructed. These grids should incorporate the range of possible distinctions to be found in all human societies, and as such they are essentially an inventory of ethnographic data. However, etic grids differ from other cultural inventories. They are constructed from system-specific discriminations found in the range of world cultures and should exclude material derived from the use of tools of analysis that carry any cultural contamination, which would distort the shape of these discriminations.

Before we describe how this is accomplished, it is important to note that the grid items may be of two types: universal items or particular items. A universal item appears in all cultures; a particular item pertains to one or more cultural systems and is not a discrimination to be found in the full range of societies. Thus, while all the items in an etic grid are not necessarily universal, the grid itself is applicable to all societies as part of the inquiry system for the identification of system-specific discriminations.

The etic grid must be distinguished from what I have called an abstract analytical system. Such a system, like the theory of phonemic systems, is composed of abstract analytical entities, or formal entities, that are found universally in all sociocultural systems along with a characteristic structure of interrelationships. Such entities and their relationships are devoid of any substantive content. They carry no cultural burden from any sociocultural system beyond that of why the question was posed in the first place. They form in a sense a theory of how a sociocultural domain is structured. While they carry no cultural content, they should include the observational procedures whereby the content of any particular sociocultural system can be discovered and described. Let us use this procedure for the analysis of property systems.

AN INQUIRY SYSTEM FOR DELINEATING SOCIAL FORMS WITH RESPECT TO PROPERTY RELATIONS[7]

As I have argued, a social form can be the product of the analyst's techniques. Such spurious social forms are thus not reflective of the society's cultural contours, and therefore they are not functioning entities of the specific society. Functioning entities are distinctive features of a society, and I have termed any such functioning entity as a "social isolate." Social isolates may be persons, networks, corporate social groupings, aggregates, collectivities, and so forth (see Appell 1983b, 1984), and may occur in the social structure, the opportunity structure, and the contrastructure.

The social isolate forms the fundamental social unit of our analysis. It is closely equivalent to the phoneme in a metatheory of linguistics, but we still have to cast it into the framework of an abstract analytical system. For the domain of ownership, this is accomplished by the definition of what constitutes a property relationship.

Property relationships consist of (1) a scarce good or service; and (2) the constellation of jural interests, along with their supporting sanctions, with respect to this scarce good that are held by (3) a social isolate against other social isolates within a social system.

Terminology for the Jural Realm

The next step is to develop an etic grid of the various types of social isolates that may occur in the jural realm of a society. There are terminological difficulties in doing this, as a social grouping may have a well-recognized form in the opportunity structure but still not be recognized in the social structure, in the jural realm, as a functioning entity. In other instances, a social grouping in the opportunity structure may be in the process of obtaining greater recognition in the jural realm, yet still not reach the level of a functioning jural entity. I have thus developed the following terminology to indicate levels of substantiation of social isolates in the jural realm (see also Appell 1983b, 1984).

Jural Isolate: A functioning entity in the jural system I refer to as a jural isolate. To be a functioning entity it must have the capacity to enter into jural relations. It is a right and duty bearing social entity. It is the fundamental unit of a jural system.

Jural Aggregate: A social grouping in which interests are held in severalty by the individual members. The social grouping has no jural existence above and beyond its individual members; it cannot enter into jural relations.

Jural Collectivity: A social grouping in which interests are held in severalty by the individual members but whose social existence is recognized by the jural system in which it is lodged. The jural system thus allows a member of the social grouping to sue *on behalf of* the other members while still denying the grouping a separate jural status, a distinct jural personality.

Assumptions and Limitations of the Inquiry System

In this design I have made the assumption that all societies have social isolates, all societies have scarce goods, and all societies have, as a result, a property system. All societies also have the problem of assigning rights over property created by the efforts of a group either to the persons of that group in severalty or to the group as an entity.

This form of inquiry system, however, is not restricted to the jural realm. As I have shown elsewhere (see Appell 1976b), critical aspects of the religious system can also be analyzed and described in these terms, and their interaction with the jural realm raises interesting questions. For example, in any particular social system does ritual or jural substantiation for a social isolate come first or are these domains interactive so that change in one is mirrored in the other (Appell 1976b)?

However, let us look more closely at this inquiry system for a moment. Please note that this is a very primitive system. It has no temporal sequences, and therefore it is difficult to generate causal nets. It is not interactive with its environment with scanning functions and feedback loops. In other words, it is not an adaptive system, but it is embedded in such an adaptive system. That is the theory of a social system that I have propounded here, and of which it is a part, consisting of a social structure, a contrastructure, and an opportunity structure, does have scanning mechanisms and primitive feedback loops.

But this particular inquiry system for property relations, which is a universal system to generate uncontaminated ethnographic description, is not totally inert. Predictions can be made in situations of social change as to the impact that change will have on a particular property system. For example, the new social entities that are being created under conditions of social change along with their potential rights and duties, and the new scarce good and services that are coming into being, can be inserted into the model of the property system; and those entities, relationships, and scarce goods that are being replaced or truncated can be removed. This then provides a model of what the new property system will eventually look like.

Observational Procedures for Social Isolates in the Jural Realm: The Rungus Tree-focused Isolate as an Example

The key diagnostic trait as to whether a social isolate is a jural isolate is whether or not it can enter into jural relations. In societies in which legal personhood is not legislated, this becomes difficult to ascertain and other tests are required, particularly to distinguish a jural isolate from its near relative, a jural collectivity. These observational procedures center around the creation, management, and disposition of rights over property. I will try to illustrate these procedures by analyzing the Rungus tree-focused isolate. The term "tree-focused isolate" is chosen to avoid prejudging the nature of ownership by an inappropriate linguistic category.

The Rungus plant a variety of fruit trees. The planter of these may divide his trees before his death among his offspring to avoid disputes over rights. However, trees may be devolved on all heirs, both male and female, without division. The problem for the analyst then is to determine whether rights over these trees lie with the heirs in severalty or with the cognatic descent isolate that consists of all the descendants of the original planter.

Certain types of fruit trees require care to see that they grow well and to ensure that the fruit is reserved for the owners. Care includes clearing the undergrowth around the tree and sometimes building a rough fence around the trunks to indicate that such trees are not wild but have had a claim established over them.

There are two kinds of rights associated with these trees. First there is the right to cultivate, and this entails the right to the prior enjoyment of the fruit. Then there is the secondary right to enjoy any surplus fruit, and this is held by the noncultivating heirs.

The person who holds the rights to cultivate is usually the person who resides closest to the trees. When he has enjoyed the early ripening fruit to his family's satisfaction, he then calls his coright-holders to come and also pick fruit. The more fruit available, the more distant the kin are that will be notified, both in terms of genealogical and geographical space.

In the analysis of other societies this type of social isolate has been frequently referred to as a corporate descent group (also see Appell 1983b, 1984). I argue that it is not. I will now apply certain tests to determine what type of social form this tree-focused social isolate is; that is, whether this social isolate is a jural aggregate, a jural collectivity, or a jural isolate.

1. *Creation and Activation of the Right.* The right to cultivate a tree planted by an ancestor must be activated by the interested party. This is done informally without necessarily notifying other right-holders by the method of the person living closest to the trees caring for them. Thus, the activation of the right is not done by or through a representative for the social isolate.

2. *Approval for Exercise of Right.* This test is to determine whether the right resides with the individual member, with a local social grouping, or with a larger descent grouping. With regard to fruit trees, no approval for the exercise of the cultivation right need be secured from anyone. However, if a coright-holder is resident nearby and believes he has not had a fair share of the cultivation right, he will ask for a turn at caring for the trees from the person currently caring for them.

3. *Group Representation in the Adjudication of Disputes.* The cultivator is the person who takes jural action on behalf of the other members of the tree-focused isolate in disputes between members and nonmembers. We shall explain shortly how this occurs. There is no one, however, that

represents the group in internal disputes or arbitrates these. Instead, internal disputes must be resolved through the usual village processes of dispute resolution.

4. *Disposition of Rights on Leaving Group.* If rights over property are held by a social grouping as a jural isolate, one might expect that an individual on withdrawing from membership will receive a share of the property or will be compensated for the loss of his right to use the group's property. First, it is impossible to withdraw *de jure* from the tree-focused isolate, as these are rights defined by inheritance. Right-holders are lost *de facto* to the social entity when they move away to other villages and are unable to activate their rights, but no compensation is paid. In time their children may forget their rights as do the resident coright-holders.

5. *Sale of Rights.* If a right can be sold, there is no question as to the social locus of the right, since the owner will receive the proceeds. However, sale of tree rights occurs very infrequently, and when it does occur, it must be of all the rights and all the trees as a physical unit. An individual right-holder effectively cannot sell his rights as no one would want to purchase rights the exercise of which is based ultimately on a kinship morality, and therefore can involve potential exclusion. However, when a grove of fruit trees is sold, the method of sale and distribution of the proceeds follows the same procedure as in involuntary conversion.

6. *Involuntary Conversion and Destruction.* When a piece of property is involuntarily converted or destroyed through an action by a third party, the locus of the rights can be established by ascertaining whether a representative sues for the group or whether each individual must take his own action. The distribution of compensation can also be an important diagnostic feature. When fruit trees are destroyed, the cultivator has the responsibility of taking jural action for restitution. He contacts the person who perpetrated the delict and arranges for a date to argue the case. The cultivator then has the duty to notify all other right-holders of this date. His coright-holders then decide whether to come and join in the jural action or not. If they do not appear, they receive no part of the settlement. The cultivator receives half of the settlement and the remainder is divided among those parallel right-holders who are present.

7. *Delicts Committed Against the Property.* Again this test helps us identify the locus of ownership. As in Test 6, it is the cultivator who must take action but those who have an interest must also be present if there is a restitution involved to receive a share of the award.

8. *Does the Social Isolate Have Explicit Social Boundaries?* The nature

of recruitment and therefore entitlement to rights and the temporal duration of the social isolate give some clue as to the degree of entification of the isolate. For the Rungus tree-focused isolate, theoretically there are no temporal boundaries; it exists as long as the trees bear fruit which with some varieties can last for a number of generations. Membership in the isolate is clear and precise. It includes all the descendants of the original planter. Yet in actuality, right-holders forget their rights if they move away, or if there are a large number of coholders to a small stand of trees while the holder in question has access to more productive rights. Tree-focused isolates are also not discreet. An individual may belong to as many isolates as he has had ancestors who planted trees. This in fact indicates the general attitude towards these rights in Rungus society. They are not considered to be a very important scarce good, and frequently right-holders will not bother to join in jural action.

9. *Does the Social Isolate Have a Jurally Recognized Representative and Can He Enforce Sanctions Within the Group?* The answer is no. While the cultivator is recognized in the jural system as the person who may initiate action *on behalf of* other right-holders, he has no power to enforce any types of behavior on the members of the social isolate that is different from those of nonmembers. If a coright-holder violates the cultivator's right to the first fruit, the cultivator has no formal sanctions available to employ other than bringing the case to the village moot. This he would refrain from doing because of the kin relationship. However, there are informal sanctions such as not meeting his obligations in other domains to the offender.

10. *What is the Nature of Interaction and Coactivity in the Social Isolate?* The position of cultivator has no formal title, as does the headman of the village, and there is a certain amount of turnover in the occupancy of this position, as when a right-holder moves to another hamlet or village or when his right to cultivate is challenged by another. Most importantly, the nature of interaction within the isolate is very irregular and seldom, if ever, includes all right-holders at any particular point. Only if there is an unusually large harvest are all right-holders in other villages informed; and even then there may well be right-holders in villages too far distant to get the information on the harvest to them in time.

Where then do the rights over fruit trees lie? I think we can conclude that they reside with the individual members of the descent isolate and not with the isolate as a jural entity. The evidence for this lies in the fact that the personnel of the isolate involved in cultivating and enjoying a specific grove of trees fluctuates; secondary right-holders do not all enjoy the harvest equally; the activation of rights to enjoy fruit is primarily a decision of the individual involved, for even if he has been informed of the fruit harvest he may decide not to go and participate; and because not each right-holder shares in any settlement on the destruction of trees unless he appears on his own to receive a share of the claim. There is no one who represents his interests at the jural action and ensures that he gets his proportionate share, if he does not himself appear.

However, neither is the descent isolate a jural aggregate, for the Rungus jural system does permit one person to take action *on behalf of* the other members that are present. Each person does not have to initiate separate proceedings for himself. In addition, in the jural system of the Rungus, the cultivator is given the power to fence off the trees to prevent others using the fruit, and this is done partially on behalf of the other parallel right-holders. Therefore, I believe one must conclude that the descent isolate is in fact a jural collectivity.

Finally, what type of social entity is the tree-focused descent isolate? The problem of classification is a difficult one, for, at first glance, there does appear to be a hierarchical ordering of interaction within the isolate. The cultivator calls his coright-holders to participate in the harvest of the fruit or notifies them of the time and place he plans to take jural action for restitution after a tree or stand of trees has been destroyed. Since this descent isolate never meets in face-to-face interaction, are we thus dealing with a secondary social grouping? I judge not for the following reasons. First of all the social boundaries of the isolate are very ill-defined in terms of actual coactivity. Secondly, the cultivator has no sanctions lodged in his position as cultivator to control deviant behavior within the social isolate separate from those available to all in the larger jural system. Therefore, I would prefer to class this type of tree-focused social isolate as a social collectivity (see Appell 1967). It is also a jural collectivity since it has a jurally recognized representative to sue on behalf of the other members.

In conclusion, I would like to emphasize the amorphic quality of this tree-focused descent isolate. There is no special term in the Rungus language to identify this type of social isolate. Nor are these social isolates named. Consequently, I would conclude, as I have previously (Appell 1968; Appell and Harrison 1969), that there exists no descent grouping in Rungus society. For those who disagree with my analysis of the social nature of the tree-focused descent isolate and believe it to form a secondary grouping, they could then argue that the Rungus do have cognatic descent groups at some level of substantiation.

This raises questions as to the relation of observational procedures to the evidential chain and the social locus of social forms; that is, whether social forms exist or are only the product of our analysis.

Observational Procedures and the Evidential Chain[8]

Quine argues that science is a linguistic structure that is keyed to observation at some point (1975:72). It consists of an evidential chain that links theoretical constructs with observation. But in my argument here I have not provided the observational procedures for each link in that evidential chain. I have not dealt with procedures for identifying primitive observational sentences such as "this is a fruit tree" or "A is the brother of B."

I have also not discussed the construction and conversion of such sentences into elementary standing reports of observation. These form the basic data of science (see Quine 1975:75). I refer to sentences such as "The descendants of Wind, A, B, C, but not descendants X and Y, collected fruit from the fruit trees a, b, c, located in Bee Tree Valley on Monday, October 10, between sun up and noon." Standing reports involve temporal, spatial, and social coordinates.

In my analysis, standing reports of observation also include those reports by informants as to the ownership of trees, the use of trees, and jural cases that formed precedents in disputes over fruit trees (see Appell 1969 for a discussion of methods for verifying the community truth value of such statements).

I have also not dealt with the conversion of these standing reports into the next level of generality in the evidential chain. I refer to this level as generalized standing sentences, or descriptive generalizations. This requires testing the data to reach statements such as "disputes over fruit trees of x variety never have arisen while there are many cases involving disputes over variety z." Or, "in every dispute case collected involving the payment for the destruction of a grove of fruit trees, the cultivator received one half of the payment."

Instead I have concentrated on the procedures by which generalized standing sentences can be linked to the theoretical constructs of jural isolate, jural aggregate, and jural collectivity. However, the building of the evidential chain from primitive observational sentences to generalized standing sentences, which are then amenable to analysis, is not done in a theoretical vacuum. The observational procedures which inform the theoretical constructs provide the very conjecture and queries that are put to the evidential chain at each level.

Conclusion

Choice behavior is the fundamental element of the opportunity structure. It has consequence only for the social structure when choices result in actions that violate the rules of the social structure or when choices result in the emergence of new social forms that are then transformed into the social structure. For example, if certain cultivators of Rungus fruit trees began to conclude that it is only fair to divide among all coright-holders any compensation received for the destruction of a fruit tree irrespective of whether the coright-holder was present at the hearing or not; and, if other members of the society in scanning the activation of the opportunity structure decided that this behavior was more appropriate and followed it themselves, then this new form of social action in the opportunity structure would be on the edge of creating a new social form in the social structure. The next step in this process would be for a coright-holder who had not received payment to sue the cultivator and win the suit on the basis of the precedents established in the opportunity structure. Then this action would have become legitimized and transformed into the social structure, changing the jural nature of the tree-focused social isolate. For by adding this new type of interest to this social form, it transforms it and moves it further along the continuum toward a newly-emerging social form: a corporate descent group that holds rights as a whole over fruit trees.

Notes

1. My approach to epistemology has its roots in Popper's "Epistemology Without a Knowing Subject." He argues that from the point of view of objective knowledge, epistemology becomes the "theory of the growth of knowledge . . . the theory of problem-solving, or, in other words, of the construction, critical discussion, evaluation, and critical testing, of competing conjectural theories" (1972:142). This is what I hope to do here with certain anthropological theories.

2. An earlier version of this paper was delivered at the Department of Anthropology, McGill University. I would like to thank the Department for the opportunity to test the ideas expressed in this paper and the audience for useful comments which have been incorporated into the paper. I would also like to thank Dr. Anton Ploeg for a critical reading of an earlier version of this paper. It is important to note that the terminology presented in the first part of the paper and the argument differs from that presented in Appell (1974) with, I hope, an improvement. Fieldwork among the Rungus of northern Borneo was carried out under the auspices of the Department of Anthropology and Sociology, Institute of Advanced Studies, the Australian National University, under the direction of Derek Freeman. I would like to thank the university for the support of this project and Dr. Freeman for his energetic direction and help. The analysis of our Rungus data and the preparation of this paper for publication was facilitated by National Science Foundation Grant BNS–79–15343, an ACLS–SSRC grant, and by National Science Foundation Grant GS–923.

3. Unfortunately Turner (1969) has already appropriated the term "antistructure," which would probably be more appropriate here. I would tend to view antistructure

as only another mode of structural action with communitas as the dominant theme. It is not really anti since it does not involve the constant testing of the social structure and its sanctions by actors trying to expand the limits of the opportunity system. A more appropriate term for the sphere of social action involving communitas should be "eustructure."

4. I have not discussed here in any detail the processes by which past jural actions are brought into the inventory of case materials and used as precedents for the resolution of disputes. This in itself is an interesting process in a society that lacks written records of decisions of the village moot, which thus permits change to occur through memory failure or through the manipulation of faulty memories. Roberts describes this process nicely among the Zuni: "It is interesting to note that the normal gossip of any group is actually a slow scanning of the total informational resource of the group. In Zuni, for example, it is striking how this process of informal gossip has contributed to the storage of the salient judicial cases of the last thirty or forty years in the heads of fully participating adults in the culture and how the same process contributes to the mobilization or retrieval of these salient cases when they become pertinent as precedents to on-going court trials or to discussion of these trials ..." (1964:441).

5. See Appell (1973) for a discussion of this issue.

6. See Appell (1983b) for a further discussion of this.

7. I am of course heavily dependent on the pioneering work of Hallowell (1943) for the design of an inquiry system for the property domain.

8. I am indebted to Quine (1975) for the distinction between observation sentences and standing sentences, and his argument forms the basis of much of the discussion in this section.

References

Appell, G. N.

1967   Observational Procedures for Identifying Kindreds: Social Isolates Among the Rungus of Borneo. *Southwestern Journal of Anthropology* 23:192–207.

1968   Ethnographic Profiles of the Dusun-speaking Peoples of Sabah, Malaysia. *Journal of the Malaysian Branch Royal Asiatic Society* 41:131–147.

1969   Social Anthropological Census for Cognatic Societies and Its Application Among the Rungus of Northern Borneo. *Bijdragen tot de Taal–, Land– en Volkenkunde* 125:80–93.

1973   The Distinction Between Ethnography and Ethnology and Other Issues in Cognatic Structuralism. *Bijdragen tot de Taal–, Land– en Volkenkunde* 129:1–56.

1974   The Analysis of Property Systems: The Creation and Devolution of Property Interests Among the Rungus of Borneo. Paper delivered at the Conference of the Association of Social Anthropologists, University of Keele, Keele, England, 1974.

1976a Introduction. The Direction of Research in Borneo: Its Past Contributions to Anthropological Theory and Its Relevance for the Future. In *The Societies of Borneo: Explorations in the Theory of Cognatic Social Structure*, edited by G. N. Appell. Special Publication 6. Washington, D. C.: American Anthropological Association.

1976b The Rungus: Social Structure in a Cognatic Society and Its Symbolization. In *The Societies of Borneo: Explorations in the Theory of Cognatic Social Structure*, edited by G. N. Appell. Special Publication 6. Washington, D. C.: American Anthropological Association.

1978   The Rungus of Sabah, Malaysia. In *Essays on Borneo Societies*, edited by Victor T. King. Hull Monographs on South-East Asia 7. Oxford: Oxford University Press.

1980   Epistemological Issues in Anthropological Inquiry: Social Structuralism, Cognitive Structuralism, Synthetic Structuralism and Opportunism. Part 1. *Canberra Anthropology* 3, 2:1–27.

1981   Epistemological Issues in Anthropological Inquiry: Social Structuralism, Cognitive Structuralism, Synthetic Structuralism and Opportunism. Part 2. *Canberra Anthropology* 4, 1:1–22.

1983a Ethnic Groups in the Northeast Region of Indonesian Borneo and Their Social Organizations. *Borneo Research Bulletin* 15:38–45.

1983b Methodological Problems with the Concepts of Corporation, Corporate Social Grouping, and Cognatic Descent Group. *American Ethnologist* 10:302–311.

1984   Methodologial Issues in the Corporation Redux. *American Ethnologist* 11:815–817.

Appell, G. N. and Harrison, Robert
1969   The Ethnographic Classification of the Dusun-speaking Peoples of Northern Borneo. *Ethnology* 8:212–227.

Barnes, J. A.
1962   African Models in the New Guinea Highlands. *Man* 62:5–9.

Firth, Raymond
1954   Social Organization and Social Change. *Journal of the Royal Anthropological Institute* 84:1–20. (Reprinted in *Essays on Social Organization and Value* by Raymond Firth. L. S. E. Monograph 28. London: Athlone Press, 1964.)

Garbett, G. Kingsley
1970   The Analysis of Social Situations. *Man* 5:214–227.

Hallowell, A. Irving
1943   The Nature and Function of Property as a Social Institution. *Journal of Legal and Political Sociology* 1:115–138. (Reprinted in *Culture and Experience* by A. Irving Hallowell. Philadelphia: University of Pennsylvania Press, 1955.)

Leach, E. R.
1957   The Epistemological Background to Malinowski's Empiricism. In *Man and Culture*, edited by R. Firth. London: Routledge & Kegan Paul.

1960   The Sinhalese of the Dry Zone of Northern Ceylon. In *Social Structure in Southeast Asia*, edited by G. P. Murdock. Viking Fund Publications in Anthropology 29. New York: Wenner-Gren.

1961   *Pul Elyia: A Village in Ceylon.* Cambridge: Cambridge University Press.

Lee, Dorothy
1963   Freedom and Social Constraint. In *The Concept of Freedom in Anthropology*, edited by David Bidney. The Hague: Mouton.

Mitchell, J. Clyde
1971   The Concept and Use of Social Networks. In *Social Networks in Urban Situations: Analyses of Personal Relationships in Central African Towns*, edited by J. Clyde Mitchell. Manchester: Manchester University Press for the Institute of African Studies, University of Zambia.

Popper, Karl R.
1972   *Objective Knowledge: An Evolutionary Approach.* Oxford: Clarendon Press.

Quine, W. V.
1975   The Nature of Natural Knowledge. In *Mind and Language*, edited by Samuel Guttenplan. Oxford: Clarendon Press.

Roberts, John M.
1964   The Self-Management of Cultures. In *Explorations in Cultural Anthropology: Essays in Honor of George Peter Murdock*, edited by Ward H. Goodenough. New York: McGraw-Hill.

Turner, Victor W.
1969   *The Ritual Process: Structure and Anti-structure.* Chicago: Aldine.

Velson, J. van
1967   The Extended-Case Method and Situational Analysis. In *The Craft of Social Anthropology*, edited by A. L. Epstein. London: Tavistock.

2

From Choice to Meaning

GEORGE DEVEREUX

It is almost presumptuous for the nonspecialist to contribute an article on the problem of choice to a festschrift in honor of so important an innovator in this field as Derek Freeman.[1] Yet, despite many misgivings as to my competence to discuss choice, I have accepted the assignment—which represents a choice, for my hesitancy was overcome by my regard for Derek Freeman's achievements which is matched only by my personal indebtedness to him. Such as it is, this modest contribution to the study of the problem of choice seeks to reaffirm the importance of the problem Derek Freeman has tackled and the value of his contributions to the elucidation of this complex problem.

CHOICE, MEANING, AND MAXWELL'S DEMON

It is my purpose to clarify certain aspects of the problem of "choice" which have not yet been adequately clarified.

All analyses of choice presuppose, in addition to the existence of the chooser, at least two entities, which, contrary to what seems to be tacitly taken for granted, need not belong to even remotely similar classes.

It is assuredly a choice effected by a very hungry man to choose a stew rather than a steak for his repast. But if he must choose between a half-rotten apple and few Burgundy snails, it is not absolutely certain that his choice of the smelly half-rotten apple as against the appetizingly smelling dish of snails is genuinely a choice, if the subject's culture defines snails as totally repulsive and, hence, unimaginable as nourishment, or if a traumatic subjective experience with snails renders their swallowing phobically impossible.

The decision of an adolescent to masturbate or not to masturbate is also a choice different from most types of choices analyzed by specialists. Here no "external" objects between which one must choose exist—even though more than one neurotic adolescent finds it difficult to incorporate his penis into his body image, sufficiently to deny it any trace of "total autonomy" (Devereux 1981). The choice he makes is therefore in one sense simply between "doing" and "not doing." The tug of war between the two alternatives is fully interpretable either in cultural or in psychological terms, according to the complementaristic method (Devereux 1978).

My last example concerns a well-known psychological experiment. A few yards of wire fencing separate a hungry dog from a bowl of food. If the bowl is very close to the fence, the dog cannot tear itself away from the food long enough to reach it by going around the fence. However, if the bowl is not directly by the fence, the dog can discover the alternative of briefly increasing the distance between himself and the bowl so as to reach it by walking around the fence.

Can one speak of a choice confronting the dog when the bowl is placed very near the fence? I think not. The "alternative" of walking around the fence may "exist" for the experimenter; it does *not* "exist" for the dog. Incidentally, the example chosen is of more than academic interest. It has a direct bearing on the theory of the "irresistible impulse" in criminal law. But that is by the way.

After these preliminary caveats, I propose to define choice as an entropy reducing, sorting technique. Maxwell's demon makes a choice whenever he closes the passage to every oxygen molecule but lets nitrogen molecules pass through. He sorts out the two, thereby reducing the entropy of the gas model.

A great many psychological tests are, essentially, sorting tests, though they are not always recognized as such.

I. One test of this sort can consist in presenting the test subject with a pile of chips, all of which are either triangular or else round *and* also either red or green. The subject is told to divide the pile in two. If no additional instructions are given, the end product will consist of two piles. But, depending on the subject, there will be either (1) one pile of triangular and one pile of round chips; *or* (2) one pile of red and one pile of green chips.

An inspection of the end product will automatically indicate that the subject had been instructed to divide the pile into two. But it will not indicate whether the subject had been given instructions also as regards the criteria of separation, i.e., form vs. color. This implies that the test, which seemingly required only one type of choice, may actually have required two, the second choice being motivated by subjective criteria only. That is, by a preference for orientation in terms of form as against color—or vice versa.

I note in passing that this test would be univalent only in the case of a daltonian test subject, who is unable to differentiate between red and green.[2]

II. Let this test now be refined further. All triangular chips will be red;

all circular chips will be green. In such a case sortings effected by normal and by daltonian test subjects will overlap completely. However, in the case of the daltonian subject the division (triangle vs. circle) will be indisputably univalent and its criteria determinable a posteriori by inspection only, while in the case of the normal subject the choice remains bivalent even if a subsequent interrogation of the subject determines whether his choice was guided by form or by color.

III. Matters of choice become even more complex if the pile of chips still consists of triangular as against round and red as against green chips, but where there is no longer a strict one-to-one correspondence between the form and the color of the chips to be sorted. Triangular chips will be either red or green; the same would be the case also for round chips.

At that point a normal subject can, if told to do so, sort them into two piles in two ways: (1) triangular vs. round; (2) red vs. green.

An inspection of the results will show at a glance what criterion of choice had been imposed on the normal subject.[3]

Let it be supposed, however, that the subject is told only to sort the chips in whatever way you wish. This leaves the subject free to sort in terms of four criteria: (1) triangular/red; (2) triangular/green; (3) round/red; and (4) round/green.

An inspection of the results will permit one to infer the sorting criteria used by the subject, though it cannot tell one whether or not he first separated the chips into two piles (form *or* color) and then divided each of the two piles into two other piles in terms of the initially disregarded quality (color or form).

If all chips are triangular or round and red or green, but are of various sizes and made of various substances, quite unpredictable other criteria of sorting may be used: weight, size, thickness, material, and so forth, of the chips. Here the criteria of choice can, as a rule, not be determined a posteriori, without an interrogation of the subject. The sorting principle adopted may even be of value to the clinical psychologist. But it can be of value also to the anthropologist, as the well-known maxim: "all Arara are Bororo, but all Bororo are not Arara" shows. Here, as so often, the genius of Marcel Mauss (Mauss and Durkheim 1901–1902) showed the path the end of which is still far out of sight. What matters here above all is the fact that in some ways—though not all!—in such instances the crux of the problem of choice is not the description of the product of the choosing (sorting) process, but the principles in terms of which the sorting was effected and the meaning—the mentally pre–existing and aimed at meaning—the choice aims to attain.

IV. The "test" I now propose to examine is closely related to the game of scrabble and is even closer to the art of the printer (typesetter). Type blocks replace the chips of the earlier example.

Let there be a large quantity of type blocks, each marked with one of the letters of the entire alphabet. If one selects three types marked with the letters "a," "c," and "t," respectively, one can compose with them the words "cat" and "act." On inspection, an English-speaking person will feel that either of these choices was "meaningful"—that both fitted certain (implicit) criteria of selection. But even this person will not be able to tell which of these two was the "correct" choice. In order to decide this, he would either have to know the preliminary instructions given to the testee, or else see the word in context.[4]

But whether the test subject composes "cat" or "act" out of the three selected letters, his product will not be recognized as a meaningful choice by a Frenchman, whose language does not include words that read "cat" or "act." For him, the selection of these letters would have been meaningful only if they had been selected in order to compose the word "tac" which is meaningless in English.[5] By contrast, an Anglo-Saxon will not identify the combination "tac" as a meaningful selection or choice of letters.

Sometimes a selection of letters is deliberately effected so that the letters when combined in a particular order will *mean nothing at all.* Thus, according to the weekly *Der Spiegel*, the company name "Exxon" was selected only after ascertaining that it had no meaning (improper or other) in any language.

The crux of the matter is the following: the type of choice described under heading I, in which the "criteria" of selection can be inferred from the inspection of the results, is of no particular importance in the study of man. It matters only in physics (decrease of entropy) and in some of the more esoteric forms of idealism.

Type II is somewhat more useful in behavioral science, even if we cannot be quite sure whether the red/green or the triangle/circle criterion brought about a particular result. Did Alice marry John because she loved him or because she was not getting any younger and there was no other eligible man around? In Euripides' *Trojan Women*, did Helen follow Paris to Troy for his beauty's sake (p. 987 ff.) as Hekabe claims, or because Aphrodite had offered Helen to Paris as a bribe (p. 949 ff.) as Helen asserts?

A special case of type III is more complex. The test subject was instructed to pick out all triangular and red chips—and "it so happens" that all the not chosen (rejected) chips were round/green. Such "unintended" two-criteria choices are quite common in human affairs. Among the Sedang Moi of South Vietnam, the religious and the economic choices are, for all practical purposes, undistinguishable in many decisions. Moreover, the two ways of interpreting the course decided upon—the choice effected—do not stand in a complementarity relationship (Devereux 1978) to each other. They converge to such an extent that quite often the religious and the economic are indistinguishable even as motivations: ritual acts are a *sine qua non* presupposition or even a minimum harvest and only the harvest makes rituals possible, for without a harvest there can be no rice beer.[6] This rule applies only to persons living in Sedang Moi society. An exile can plant and harvest without performing rites, since he no longer rates as a man—he is socially, legally, etc., a wild boar.

Situations of type II can also arise when—even though the results of selections in terms of either angular/rounded of red/green are identical—the two "antinomies" serving as criteria of classification are none the less perfectly distinct. "Honesty is the best policy" exemplifies this choice perfectly, and this even if one is tempted to ask whether (in J. P. Morgan's parlance) it is honesty or good policy that is the "real" reason and the other only the "good" reason of the choice made.

Misconceptions in this sphere abound, even amongst experienced fieldworkers. B. Malinowski (1932) cited the castration of all young male pigs as "proof" of the reality of the Trobrianders' conviction that coitus is not a cause of pregnancy. Yet, in my estimate, Malinowski's own data prove that their nescience is simply a denial that all their domestic pigs were sired by bush boars, which are taboo as food. The Sedang Moi, who also castrate all young domestic boars, but are free to eat wild boar, have no illusions on this score, and neither had Malinowski's (later inexplicably repudiated) early Trobriand informant, who remarked about pigs: "They copulate, copulate, presently the female will give birth."

In his book, however, Malinowski arbitrarily backs away not only from what his informant had said, but even from his own 1916 comment (on this remark), that "here copulation appears to be the u'ula (cause) of pregnancy" (1916:163). I might further add that Malinowski's goat example lacks a key detail—as do all his pig examples, by the way. The allegedly continued procreation of the nanny goat, even if her male should be killed, fails to specify whether she had already had a kid or was still nulliparous (virgin).

In the latter case, she could not (if animal procreation fitted the human model) procreate at all, since only the nonvirgin woman's distended sex organ is open to the "impregnating spirit." The same remark may also be made of the domestic sow: If some male (bush) pig did not "dilate" her, she could not procreate.

Matters do not improve even if one accepts Malinowski's very shaky distinction between native theories of human and animal births. There remains, even in the case of the latter, the basic need of a "dilatation" of the sow's vagina. That, presumably, only a male pig can accomplish. Malinowski himself recognizes this (1932:163): "vaginal dilation is *as necessary in animals* as in human beings" (my italics). This, as Malinowski did not see, obviously brings us back to his early informant's remarks: "They copulate, copulate, presently the female will give birth," quoted in his 1916 article. Just what creature coitizes the sow and "dilates" her?

Malinowski does not provide the crucially needed answer. Anthropologists are simply too prone to fall for the exotic. So excellent a fieldworker as Verrier Elwin (1943) hypothesizes that by castrating all boars in the first few weeks of their lives, the Agaria have (involuntarily?) bred a race of pigs whose farrows, when still only a few weeks of age, are already able to copulate and to impregnate the mother sow. This would incidentally imply also the biological enormity of the suckling sow entering a period of rut, i.e., ovulating. Also, by impregnating his nursing mother, the farrow would also cut off his own milk supply, since the sow would stop giving milk as soon as she is again pregnant. Just how all these biological conjuring tricks can come about, and perhaps transmitted by pigs, is left unexplained.

These examples suffice to show that the choice the mind of the culturally distant informant effects between what strike the fieldworker as being simple red/green type alternatives are much less unambiguous in reality.

The most important choice for the student of behavior is, however, of type III, to which I must now return. The classical paradigm is that of the million monkeys pounding for a million years on a million typewriters so that, in so doing, one of them will type out the works of Shakespeare.

Before I go further, I must give a somewhat comparable real example. Some forty years ago a man born deaf studied intensively the rules of harmony and counterpoint and sent his "compositions" to a musician who I myself had known when I was of high school age. In the opinion of this musician, the "music" the deaf man had composed was very bad, though he had carefully obeyed all the technical rules. However, in my opinion, what this man, deaf from birth, had "composed" was not music in any real sense. It was a series of mathematical puzzles and would not have been music even if he had, by chance, written note for note the complete score of a Mozart symphony. Otherwise expressed, this "composer's" choices were not musical but (perhaps) algebraic ones. The "computer" was not programmed for music but for the rules of harmony and counterpoint.

The problem can be further clarified by examining the task of the person who fills the holes of a printer's type case with the necessary letters: All A's in one box, all B's in another, and so forth. An "order" of a particular kind is thus created; choices are made in terms of a particular kind of programming. In terms of that system, "entropy" is at a minimum; all letters of one kind are in one box only.

At that point the typesetter begins his work and arranges the letters to "read": "Sabermula maka tersebutlah perkataan, and so forth." For the arranger of the type case the "entropy" is greatly increased. His "order," the product of (his kind of) careful sorting, is destroyed. It is destroyed also for anyone who does not know classical Malay and does not recognize in the words just cited the opening sentence of the main body of the prose epic, *The Story of Mr. Tuah*. For the Malay scholar the disruption of the type case's next-to-zero entropy has led to an even closer-to-zero entropy of the letters, *through the emerging of a meaning*, precisely by the disarranging of the very narrow gauge (alphabet) sort of meaning possessed by the types as long as they were left in their "proper" cases.

Essentially the choices that Derek Freeman's pioneering studies explore are choices that create—or at least give tangible substance to— more meaning (and, if one wishes, also less entropy) than the alternative(s) that confronted one initially. Derek Freeman's sounding indicated the need to differentiate between the purely "external" order of the red/green piles and the "inner" meaning of test, test instructions, test performance and test evaluation complex. It calls for the discovery of a way of distinguishing between choice results, the mere inspection of which reveals the nature of the preliminary instructions given to the subject, and choice results which, on simple inspection, do not reveal the crucial instructions given to the testee.

Aeschylus' *Agamemnon* was assuredly written according to the rules. One of the poets' objectives was to be crowned victor of the dramatic competition of the Dionysia. What other—often unconscious— "instructions" went into Aeschylus' arranging tens of thousands of Greek letters in this particular way can only partly be conjectured.[7]

I venture to conclude with an admittedly bold hypothesis: The higher a cultural product is, the more sublimation it represents, the more inexhaustible will be the many choices whose collective print it happens to be.

Notes

1. My task was not rendered any easier by its having been assigned to me at the end of about half a year of near-fatal illness, some of whose after effects are still not fully overcome.

2. In order to avoid gratuitous complexity mongering, I relegate to a footnote the finding that a blind subject who is *also* paralyzed, i.e., one unable to determine the form of the chips, could also sort the chips into two piles if half of them were made of sandalwood, which he can identify by smell. This recalls Henri Poincaré's (1913) remark that a man whose sole functioning sense was his smell could, on the basis of odors alone, contrive an impeccable geometry.

3. The daltonian would, of course, be able to sort the chips in one way only: on the basis of form.

4. At this point, I wish to explain my choice of the example in question and the

parapraxis underlying it. I had found one misprint in my book *Mohave Ethnopsychiatry* (1961). As I (correctly) recalled, the printed word was "cat." My recall was, however, faulty when I thought I knew the word should have been "act." On verification, I found that it should have been "fact" (p. 493, 1.2 from bottom). I am unable to explain my false recall (lapsus) otherwise than by my wish to find that the misprint constituted a perfect anagram for "cat."

5. Click (of steel), clack (of mill); *riposter du tac au tac*, to make a very fast retort.

6. ō njō = religious feast, literally: "drink alcohol."

7. In my *Dreams in Greek Tragedy* (1976), I devote some sixty pages to the exegesis of only seventeen verses of this drama.

References

Devereux, George
1961 *Mohave Ethnopsychiatry and Suicide: The Psychiatric Knowledge and the Psychic Disturbances of an Indian Tribe* [Bulletin 175.] Washington, D. C.: Smithsonian Institution, Bureau of American Ethnology.

1976 *Dreams in Greek Tragedy*. Oxford: Blackwell.

1978 *Ethnopsychoanalysis: Psychoanalysis and Anthropology as Complementary Frames of Reference*. Berkeley: University of California Press.

1981 *Baubo, die mythische Vulva*. Frankfurt am Main: Syndikat.

Elwin, Verrier
1943 *The Agaria*. Bombay: Oxford University Press.

Malinowski, B.
1916 Baloma, the Spirit of the Dead. *Journal of the Royal Anthropological Institute* 46:353–460.

1932 *The Sexual Life of Savages in North-Western Melanesia*. London: Routledge & Kegan Paul.

Mauss, M. and E. Durkheim
1901–1902 De quelques formes primitives de classification primitives. *Annee Sociologique* 6:1–72.

Poincaré, Henri
1913 *The Foundations of Science*. Garrison, NY: The Science Press.

3

Corpus Morale Collectivum: Social Anthropology Without Tears?

PETER LAWRENCE

Social anthropology in Australia, although by no means in disarray, has lost its self-confidence since the 1960s. For some fifteen years after the Second World War, very many of our scholars were satisfied to be included in the then British School, which specialized in the analysis of the structures of stateless societies in group, or collectivist terms. They thought that this approach would be able to provide complete answers to all the problems they should study in Oceania, especially Papua New Guinea and aboriginal Australia. In so far as they were interested in him, they treated the individual as virtually an automaton: a microcosmic stereotype of his society. Then suddenly, with the publication of Barnes' (1962) paper, which dismissed the relevance of the African unilineal model to the Papua New Guinea Highlands, it was almost as if a house of cards had collapsed. Disciples lost faith in received dogma and began to experiment with new lines of inquiry, none of which so far has had a lasting impact.

My own experience in Papua New Guinea (cf. Lawrence 1984) had made me suspicious of the uncritical use of the collectivist approach (which I satirized in verse [Lawrence 1964]), but I was no revolutionary. I still believed that British or, as I now prefer, Anglo-Australian social anthropology could be modified to suit Oceanic conditions. About the same time, Derek Freeman also became dissatisfied with the holistic tradition, although he was far more radical than I could ever be. He was prepared to move into several fields of inquiry—psychology, ethology, and biology—in which I had neither interest nor skill. In the mid-1970s, he opted for the study of the individual's ability to make his own choices both within and, if need be, beyond his own sociocultural milieu. This was closer to my own position. Thus, when he invited me to read a paper on this topic at the Australian National University in December 1977, I was happy to accept. I now offer a revised version in his honor.

My argument rests on the moderate Greek ideal: that in any structural[1] analysis the individual and his society must be seen as complementary. Yet my aim is to write about this relationship not as I think we should examine it but as Western thinkers have conceived it for the last two and a half millennia. I suggest that Anglo-Australian social anthropologists embraced the collectivist approach for two reasons. First, it seemed to make analysis simpler. With defined social units, it was easier to work out regular behavior patterns—even, perhaps, sociological laws—which individuals, always idiosyncratic and unpredictable, were bound to distort. Second, by the late nineteenth century, it had crystallized as orthodoxy in much of European, especially French, sociology. With total disregard of its internal contradictions, which were already obvious, the savants used it as an elixir or philosopher's stone for a kind of social alchemical inquiry. Their axiom was that there could be no sociology without a corporate group.

I began my argument by sketching the situation in Oceania to which I have referred, in which Anglo-Australian anthropologists[2] unsuccessfully used the collectivist approach in Papua New Guinea and aboriginal Australia. I then trace the history of the concept of collectivism in Europe since the fifth century B.C. I try to show that it emerged in its modern form—society as the *corpus morale collectivum*, or collective moral body of Natural Law—in the eighteenth century but with a new and special meaning—after a long and ambivalent relationship between two ideal forms: the small integrated society, typified by the Greek city-state, and the world community, represented by the empires of Alexander the Great and of Rome. In the city-state, the individual citizen was tied to his fellows in a mesh of mutually beneficial relationships, while in the world community he could be comparatively free-ranging. I illustrate this theme by reviewing the following periods: the Greco-Roman world; Europe in the Middle Ages; Europe from the Reformation until the Enlightenment; and France during and after the revolution and First Empire. I conclude by examining Anglo-Australian social anthropology's adoption of collectivism as a heuristic device.

THE SOCIAL COLLECTIVIST APPROACH IN OCEANIA

Anglo-Australian structuralism founded on a collectivist vision came of age at the beginning of the Second World War with the publication of three now classic works: Evans-Pritchard (1940), Fortes and Evans-Pritchard (1940), and Fortes (1945). In Australia, where Radcliffe-Brown gave it its initial impetus, anthropologists exploited it for what they thought were sound academic and practical reasons. As I have already foreshadowed and shall argue later, it made sense of a mass of hitherto amorphous data. Also, it seemed to solve the two most pressing problems federal and state governments had to face: the preparation of the then Territory of Papua and New Guinea for eventual self-determination and the growing need to come to terms with an aboriginal minority. In brief, it seemed to package, even streamline, all the necessary information that would enable us to advance the former and reach a compromise with the latter.

The weakness of the collectivist approach in Oceania was first demonstrated, as I have indicated, for the Papua New Guinea Highlands. In his seminal paper, Barnes (1962) commented that the first social anthropologists in the area in the 1950s had found large populations which, *prima facie*, they could divide into patrilineal segmentary groups. But they did not look closely enough. Although these groups were formed around agnatic kernels, they could incorporate also enates and affines, and were by no means genealogically regular. There followed a spate of articles endorsing this view (Barnes 1967; de Lepervanche 1967–68; McArthur 1967; and Langness 1972–73). More recently Brown (1978:183), already well known for her publications on the Chimbu, has written what is perhaps her apologia for the pioneer workers in the Highlands: "The earlier observers of highland life were concerned with the stability and continuity of corporate groups, following what was the usual emphasis in the study of groups in social anthropology." If she means to imply by this that these "early observers" intended to do no more than produce tentative sketches that would lead to more precise studies later, as is possibly insinuated by her own valiant attempt in the same context to offer an interpersonal network analysis of Highlands societies, nothing could be farther from the truth. In fact, these workers set out for the field convinced that they would soon find examples of classical segmentary societies and returned to present their analyses firmly on that basis. They did not conceive any alternative. Langness (1972:930; 1973:160–61) documents three examples of this and concludes: "this unilineal bias . . . has prevented workers in Papua New Guinea from coming to grips with the distinctive features of social and political organization." It is quite clear that he has in mind the person to person network analysis that Brown posits but has insufficient material to substantiate.[3]

Moreover, there is now strong evidence of the inadequacy of the collectivist approach also in aboriginal Australia. In his influential publications on traditional aboriginal societies, Radcliffe-Brown (1930–31 and 1934–35), the father of Anglo-Australian structuralism, stated that rights to land were held by a corporation which he called the patrilineal horde and which had joint "dominion" over its own exclusive tract, thereby

partaking "of the nature of the relation of a modern state to its territory..."
(Radcliffe-Brown 1934–35:288 passim). Gumbert (1981:103ff.), capital-
izing on previous criticism by Hiatt (1962) and Meggitt (1962), makes a
powerful case that this misrepresents aboriginal land tenure and local
organization. Rights to any one area are not restricted to a single unilineal
descent group but are diffused throughout the society by the whole complex web of cognatic kinship and marriage ties as well as by descent. The
individual, *qua* individual, exercises rights in many areas, inheriting them
from his father and mother, and acquiring them through his wife. This is
not in keeping with Radcliffe-Brown's equation between horde and embryonic modern state. The issue came to a head in the Gove Land Rights
Case in 1970. In court, two expert anthropological witnesses stoutly testified that the patrilineal horde was the aboriginal land-owning body. Their
evidence did not accord with that of the aboriginal plaintiffs, who were in
no sense representatives of a single defined agnatic group, so that the
claim was dismissed. The anthropologists had clearly gotten it wrong.

These two examples make it clear that, certainly in Oceania, anthropologists must reappraise their approach to the study of the individual
and his society. The collectivist tradition, which, as I have indicated, once
promised to simplify and add precision to social analysis, has been found
sadly wanting. They will do no good with "band-aid" treatment. They must
go to the heart of the matter, first looking behind the facade of collectivism,
which they must recognize as a fairly recent phenomenon accepted by
European thinkers because of particular problems in their own society at
a particular time and which, therefore, has no necessary immemorial and
ubiquitous relevance. For this reason, as I have said, I attempt to trace
the development of the concept since the era of the classical Greco-
Roman world.[4]

THE GRECO-ROMAN WORLD

For our present purposes, we must consider the Greco-Roman world
from two points of view: the continuity of its broad class structure until
the Middle Ages; and, from the end of the fourth century B.C., the vast
change in the accepted scale of society. In the first place, both Greek and
Roman society consisted of a hierarchy of social classes—aristocrats,
wealthy commoners, free plebeians or artisans, and slaves—that was taken
for granted in times of both political tranquility and political turmoil. There
was never a threat of genuine revolution. True, there was faction-fighting
(*stasis*) in the Greek cities on the eve of the Peloponnesian War in the
fifth century B.C. There was civil strife in the Roman Republic in the second
and first centuries B.C.: the insurrections of the Gracchi and Catiline, the

struggle between Marius and Sulla, and the Civil War that lasted until 31 B.C. Yet it is doubtful whether any of these events could have led—or was intended to lead—to the complete overthrow and transformation of the social order. Although towards the end of the Roman Republic there were signs of improvement in the condition of slaves, there was never any suggestion that they could use their own initiative to hasten the process, as the brutal reprisals against the revolts in Sicily and that led to Spartacus made clear. If a slave killed his master, not only he but all his fellows in the household were put to death.

In the second place, the rise of Macedon as an imperial power about 350 B.C. initiated a vast change in the sociopolitical horizon of Mediterranean man. For Greeks until about fifty years after the end of the Peloponnesian War—as, indeed, for Romans before the expansion of their military and administrative power—the ultimate sociopolitical reality was the *polis* or city-state, whose members—at most some 250,000—had defined and regular obligations towards each other: a network of interdependent relationships, which in their aggregate represented, and guaranteed the stability of, the community. Society and the individual were compounded. Neither was conceivable apart from the other. Three different authors—one liberal, one authoritarian, and one scientifically objective—expressed this view. In the famous and moving Funeral Oration attributed to him by Thucydides, Pericles lauded the personal democratic freedoms of Athenian citizens. They were the original open society. Yet they had to preserve their city, which alone gave their lives meaning and value. Plato in his *Republic* and *Laws* allowed the citizens of his model society little personal freedom. Their correct indoctrination—especially under the aegis of the philosopher-king—would perfect it, an idea that Rousseau was to revive many centuries later. The polis was good only in so far as its citizens were moral, upheld justice, and so promoted harmony between its component classes. Finally, Aristotle saw the good man and the good citizen as identical. The duty of the city-state was to produce moral human beings. Only the city-state could do this, for man was "by nature an animal intended to live in a polis" (Barker 1948:6).

Then suddenly, in the middle of the fourth century B.C., the Greek city-state ceased to exist in its own right. It was absorbed into an entirely new political phenomenon, the multiethnic empire: first, that of Philip and Alexander the Great and, later, that of Rome. As an ideal, it remained dormant until the Middle Ages, when it reappeared as a vital ingredient in European thought.

The new empires were more than political reality. They established a new social concept: the worldwide or universal society, in which countries became provinces and city-states administrative units or centers within them. There was a corresponding emphasis on individualism. Ego, once a fixed integer within the self-governing polis, the only structure that Pericles, Plato, and Aristotle ever envisaged, now became a person with wider responsibilities. He had himself to regulate his own conduct and his relationships with other members of the cosmopolitan order. That this subjected him to considerable social pressure and anxiety is apparent in the general rise throughout the Mediterranean world at this time of religions that offered the hope of personal immortality, and the new social philosophies, to which I now turn.

Two of the new philosophies, Epicureanism and Stoicism, grew up at Athens seemingly automatically in response to the new social order after the death of Alexander in 323 B.C. Epicureanism stressed the secular world. God was not to be feared; there was nothing to feel in death; the good was obtainable; and evil was endurable (Harvey 1937:162). It endorsed nature's cause and effect, as hymned by Lucretius in his De Rerum Natura in the first century B.C.: man had created his own society and it was up to him to make it work. Hence the philosophy's social theme was the need to promote individual self-sufficiency and happiness by the avoidance of all pain, worry, and anxiety. A man should have congenial friends and, in contrast to the ideal of the polis, avoid the cares of public office.

Stoicism was perhaps even more relevant to the present argument. Although it made heavy use of religion—for example, divination and astrology—its sociopolitical teachings were more explicit than those of Epicureanism. It preached the universal brotherhood of man, without distinction between Greek and barbarian, freeman and slave: there had to be universal benevolence and justice. It had a strong impact on Rome by the second century B.C. and was the medium through which Greek philosophy influenced the initial stage of Roman jurisprudence, which provided a third, and in the long run more important, universal doctrine.

This third doctrine, established in the first century B.C., was Ius Naturale, Natural Law, a coalescence between Stoicism and Roman jurisprudence. Its first great exponent was Cicero, for whom it represented ". . . a true law—namely, right reason—which is in accordance with nature, applies to all men, and is unchangeable and eternal" (Cicero, Republic III:22, quoted in Sabine 1964:164). It arose from the providential government of the world by God, to whom human beings were akin because of their rational and social nature. Hence, as in Stoicism, all men were equal. In contrast to Aristotle's view, the slave was no longer a mere "living tool" but became a persona, protected by the law and eventually a greater chance of manumission.[5] Natural Law was, of course, embraced by the early Fathers of the Church. Because it could be regarded as God's Law, it became a pillar of European Christianity until its decay in the eighteenth century. Nevertheless, again like Stoicism, it remained essentially an ideal.

It was never allowed seriously to challenge the class structure I outlined above.

MEDIEVAL EUROPE

The classical world ended in the West in 410 A.D. with the capture of Rome by the Visigoth Alaric the Bold. Although he probably did not intend it, he destroyed the Empire in Europe for the next four centuries until Charlemagne restored it for a brief period. The new imperial structure was eventually replaced by the feudal system of fragmentary states loosely coordinated by the Catholic Church under the Pope and the Holy Roman Emperor, to whom kings and nobles owed allegiance.

The fall of Rome was a traumatic event. Even in the 1770s, Gibbon (1960:1, orig. 1896) wrote of it as "a revolution . . . still felt by the nations of the earth." Nevertheless, despite the demise of imperial power, there was no immediate return to the ideology of the city-state. Almost at once St. Augustine wrote his *De Civitate Dei*: men had to choose between a "celestial city"—a ubiquitous community of the righteous on earth and saints in Heaven, living according to God's will—and its antithesis, a "worldly city" guided by selfishness and concupiscence. Eventually, by the twelfth century, his doctrine was equated with the old imperial concept of a universal society: a worldwide Christian community, the Heavenly City of God, directed by divinely ordained Natural Law (Sabine 1964:225). In 1159, John of Salisbury wrote his *Policraticus*, in which he ignored the reality of feudal fragmentation and discussed the *republica*, the multiethnic commonwealth formulated by Cicero and his successors. Even one and a half centuries later, about 1310, Dante (1957, orig. 1310–13) in his *De Monarchia* described the Old Empire as if it still existed in all its grandeur (Sabine 1964:246–47, and 257ff.).

These scholars envisaged this universal society as corpus morale collectivum, as it was called in Natural Law (Barker 1960:xxxvii). Yet this could not be a precise concept. There were at least two issues that called into question its twin assertions of morality and collectivity: the class structure and effective administrative boundaries. In the first context, according to Natural Law, all men were theoretically equal. In the twelfth century, Gratian (quoted in Tawney 1948:45) had written that ideally "the communal use of everything in this world should be made possible for all men."[6] Yet clearly this was not viable. Adam's sin brought greed and envy into the world, and made personal property a necessity. People worked harder and disputed less when goods were private rather than held in common. Thus the class structure, which was based partly on differences of wealth and had survived the switch from city-state to world empire, passed into Medieval Europe with little change: nobles, knights, wealthy commoners, artisans, and serfs. It now took its place in a cosmic pyramid that reached down from God at its apex through the Company of Heaven to the Pope, the higher church dignitaries, and the lesser priests, under whom, officially, were the secular authorities: the Emperor, kings, and their vassals. The structure had to be preserved at all costs from the political chaos from which it had extricated itself. It was justified by reference to St. Paul's returning the runaway slave to his master, the early Fathers' defense of slavery, despite their acclaim of Natural Law, because of the need for order, and Dante's (1957:48–49, orig. 1310–13) argument that Christ having been born in Bethlehem in the reign of Augustus Caesar obviously approved of the social system of his day. Above all, both ecclesiastical and lay rulers opposed anything that might cause unpredictable fluctuations of wealth and hence changes in the class structure. There was, in theory, no place for private initiative that could alter personal status. Usury, which by creating sudden wealth and poverty had precisely this effect, was condemned as mortal sin. Yet this was a clear denial of the individual freedom implicit in the concept of universal society.

This limitation of personal liberty was relevant to the second context: the effective administrative boundaries of the moral collective social body. The universal society was a pipe dream. It could not function without the imperial power that Rome once exercised but the Popes and Holy Roman Emperors obviously lacked. In a word, it could be neither moral nor collective. Individuals ignored the restriction of their freedom. Usury was widely practiced because commerce would have collapsed without it. Even the Popes employed Jewish bankers, whose religion did not find it evil. Merchants were guilty of the grossest antisocial conduct. For example, the two Marseilles entrepreneurs who sold the children assembled for the Crusade of 1212 into slavery on the Barbary Coast (Runciman 1954:141–44).

The actual communities in which dependable moral bonds and efficient administration had been reestablished were very small. Of the kingdoms, only England with her strong central government could be said to qualify, but she had a distinct advantage because of her limited size and population. France was no more than a congeries of fiefs or provinces under the crown, each of which was in most of its concerns a virtually independent unit. Hence, when Aristotle's works became known in Western Europe during the thirteenth century, especially his writings on politics, they aroused great interest among Catholic thinkers, especially in Paris and Italy.

The most famous of the neo-Aristotelian savants was, of course, St. Thomas Aquinas (1225/6–74 A.D.), Dominican Professor of Theology at the University of Paris. From the present point of view, his contribution was to put the Christian ideal and the politically real in proper perspective. At the ideal level, he endorsed the concept of the universal society under the aegis of the Church, which he regarded as "the fullest embodiment of the unity of human kind" (Sabine 1964:256). But at the level of the real, he followed Aristotle. The politically effective society, the *de facto corpus morale collectivum*, was the equivalent of the city-state based on "a mutual exchange of services for the sake of a good life to which many callings contribute, the farmer and the artisan by supplying material goods, the priest by prayer and religious observance, and each class doing its own proper work" (Sabine 1964:249).

In short, about nine hundred years after its disappearance in ancient Greece, St. Thomas restated the concept of the polis, in which the individual ceased to be free-ranging and was fused with society. His argument, which endorsed the principles of feudalism already widely accepted, was important in that it was applied to the small and compact rather than the universal society, which was too amorphous to be an expression of it. He was followed in the fourteenth century by two other thinkers who wrote in similar terms: John of Paris about the fragmented French kingdom and Marsilius of Padua about the Italian city-states.

The Thomist synthesis of the social theories of Aristotle and Christian Natural Law were incorporated in Catholic teaching but was undermined two centuries later by the very economic forces that had originally promoted it. Since the Age of Discovery at the end of the fifteenth century, European trade, especially with the Orient and Americas, became so great and geographically extensive that the small close-knit community could not hope to handle it. Especially in Northern Europe, where commerce burgeoned, the situation called for a new kind of economic man: bold, enterprising, fearless of risk and, above all, ready to override the ban on usury. Although such persons flourished during, and were sanctified by, the Reformation, they anticipated it. In 1516, three years before Martin Luther promulgated his theses, Sir Thomas More published his *Utopia*, in which he looked back nostalgically to Plato's *Republic* and ridiculed the rising "acquisitive society in which it was becoming good morals to 'buy abroad very cheap and sell again exceeding dear'" (Sabine 1964:436; Sampson 1910:41). This was the last *cri de coeur* for the Middle Ages. The ideal of the small integrated society, that More like St. Thomas upheld, was to be challenged and in many places supplanted by a new version of the universal individualistic order until the mid-eighteenth century.

EUROPE FROM THE REFORMATION TO THE ENLIGHTENMENT

In contrast to the Iberian experiment in Latin America, where Spaniards and Portuguese recreated their own form of society with its ranks and feudal privileges (Spate 1979), the commercial domains of the Northern Europeans, especially in their early days, were purely economic enterprises (Spate 1983). The initial aim of the British and Dutch was not so much to take over territory as to establish stations from which to trade with the indigenes—a policy which was short-lived in North America but persisted into the eighteenth century in India and the East Indies. This was the world through which the new economic man was free to roam, amassing profit by lending out his money at reasonable rates of interest without fear of spiritual damnation. Yet he did not have a completely free hand. He was still under God's rule and had to be moral in God's sight, even though the new morality of the Reformation was often at variance with that of the Middle Ages.

Weber (1958), the sociological authority on this period, argues that the achievement of Luther, who initiated the Reformation, was to break the institutional control of the Catholic Church and make the person, through his calling, an individual directly responsible to God. Yet Luther was overshadowed by the real giant of the Reformation, John Calvin of Geneva (1509–64).

Unlike Luther, who ultimately accepted the old class structure, Calvin boldly geared his teachings to the economic reality of the day: the need to validate and stabilize a society, which rejected the static feudal order, one in which men grew rich or poor by trade, and in which, above all, they found it essential to lend or borrow money at interest to carry on their business. He resolved these problems with the aid of the two doctrines of the Dignity of Labor and Predestination. God approved of those who worked hard, and by His inexorable will He determined the fate of every person in the world, as a member of either the Elect or the Damned, at the instant of birth. Not even He could change that decision thereafter. This imposed considerable strain on the individual, who naturally wanted *certitudo salutis*, the assure of personal salvation. Thus, although neither faith nor good works could affect his fate, a man could still demonstrate his inclusion in the ranks of the Elect through success in worldly affairs, especially commercial enterprises, which ceased to be disdained as in the Middle Ages. What was most important, usury within reasonable limits was no longer a sin.

As Dumont (1983:24) implies, Calvin was perhaps a sociopolitical paradox. Although he was the religious leader of tiny Geneva, he did not think in terms of the integrated city-state. As his doctrine was essentially individualist, his influence spread throughout Europe and into the New World. I consider its effects in two contexts: general European society and international commerce; and English revolutionary politics in the seventeenth century.

In the first context, wherever it took root, Calvinism transformed European society. Superficially, of course, there was little change. There were still marked differences between the haves and have-nots. The old social categories remained: nobles, knights, merchants, and artisans. Yet now they were blurred. Nobody's status was irrevocably fixed by genealogy, for a man could rise legitimately by his own endeavor from rags to respectability, and even honor. In England, where the Wars of the Roses had forced the Tudor kings literally to create a new nobility, the process was particularly marked. The dynamic individual came into his own. Provided that he was not profligate and did not use his wealth for vulgar ostentation, he could ignore old social prejudices because his personal achievement demonstrated that he was of the Elect. The new volatile structure was reflected in the literature of the day. The London playwrights of the late sixteenth century—for example, Dekker, Beaumont, and Fletcher—used or satirized it in their plots. In 1583, Stubbes in his *Anatomy of Abuses* bemoaned the passing of the old order in which clothes denoted differences of rank. He found the current sartorial egalitarianism intolerable (quoted in Hogbin 1958:12). By the same token, when a man was successful in promoting commerce overseas, the Hand of God was said to be upon him. He was a true representative of the universal community under God. He could engage in any gainful activity.

In the second context, Calvinism lay at the very heart of revolutionary politics in seventeenth century England. It was there that its rampant individualism seemed at one stage to get out of hand and had to be curbed. The new capitalistic system was out of step with the sociopolitical order, so that it was inevitable that the outcry was against the Stuart monarchy, two of whose representatives misunderstood the weave of the English political fabric and were deposed. Yet, despite their common origin, the two revolutions were different in one respect. On the one hand, Charles I faced a commoners' revolt. The English were used to dethronement, even the assassination, of their monarchs, but hitherto these matters had been arranged by peers of the realm. This time it was different. Charles had to answer the charge that he was a "tyrant, traitor, murderer, and a public and implacable enemy of the Commonwealth of England," "in the behalf of the Commons assembled in Parliament and the good people of England" (quoted from Fraser 1973:283). Divinity no longer hedged a king. The mood of much of England in the next decade was republican. On the other hand, James II lost his crown because of his personal loyalty to the Church of Rome and refusal to pay even lip-service to Protestantism, as his more realistic brother Charles II had done. The leading Whig families replaced him with monarchs more amenable to their own religious and political outlook. This difference was reflected in the political philosophies published after each revolution: Thomas Hobbes (1588–1679) rejected free-ranging individualism in favor of authoritarian collectivism, while John Locke (1632–1704) argued for it as long as it was tempered with broad social consensus. Jointly, they prepared the way for Rousseau in the next century.

Hobbes's philosophy was bred of the Civil War, which he witnessed as a mature man. He was shocked by the destruction of legitimate authority and its chaotic aftermath: the death of Charles I on the scaffold and the subsequent cacophony of populist voices (Puritans, Center Protestants, Low Church Anglicans, Quakers, Levellers, Diggers, and Fifth Monarchy Men), each proclaiming its own version of political truth. Hence, in his *Leviathan*, published in 1651, he stressed the chaotic state of nature, in which "every man is Enemy to every man" and "men live without other security, than what their own strength, and their own invention shall furnish them withall." There can be no industry, agriculture, navigation, architecture or arts but only "continuall feare, and danger of violent death; And the life of man, solitary, poore, nasty, brutish and short" (Hobbes 1909:96–97, orig. 1651).

The only means of resolving this chaos was the compulsory surrender of personal freedom by vesting all authority in one person or assembly, the "soveraigne," who can reduce the "Wills" of the many to "one Will." There must be a

> ... Covenant of every man with every man, in such manner, as if every man should say to every man, *I Authorise and give up my Right of Governing my selfe, to this Man, or this Assembly of men, on this condition, that thou give up thy Right to him, and Authorise all his Actions in like manner*. This done, the Multitude so united in one Person, is called a COMMON-WEALTH, in latine CIVITAS. This is the Generation of that great LEVIATHAN, or rather (to speak more reverently) of the *Mortall God*, to which we owe under the Immortall God, our peace and defence [Hobbes 1909:131–32, orig. 1651].

Hobbes was important in my argument for three reasons. First, as I have said, he dismissed Calvinist individualism and reintroduced the idea of a collective society, although it had one special feature. Implicitly, it was greater than the sum of its parts. He based his ideas on England, which with a population still small even by current European standards, could be equated with a classical city-state. Yet he ignored the fundamental Greek principle of person to person interdependence. Integration would be imposed by his version of Plato's philosopher-king. Second, he believed that an indispensable condition of a fully collective society was the preponderance of "one Will" over many. Third, he restated the view of antiquity that societies were not necessarily ordained by God but could be made by man himself by grouping individuals in desired formations.

> For by Art is created that great LEVIATHAN called a COMMON-WEALTH or STATE ... which is but an Artificiall Man; though of

greater stature and strength than the natural . . . and in which, the Soveraignty is an Artificiall Soul, as giving life and motion to the whole body [Hobbes 1909:8, orig. 1651].

And,

The skill of making, and maintaining Common-wealths, consisteth in certain Rules, as doth Arithmetique and Geometry . . . which Rules, neither poor men have the leisure, nor men that have had the leisure, have hitherto had the curiosity, or the method to find out [Hobbes 1909:160, orig. 1651].

A hundred years later, this idea of the man-made collective with a single will indoctrinated by an "Artificiall Soul," the all-wise dictator, helped to shape the pattern of European—even world—history.

John Locke, like Hobbes, witnessed the Civil War, but as a teenager. He wrote his two most important works, his *Second Treatise on Civil Government* and *An Essay Concerning Human Understanding*, over thirty years later during the period of relative calm and reconstruction following the Bloodless Revolution of 1688. His purpose was to explain and justify the new concordat between parliamentary democracy and constitutional monarchy. This was the basis of his support of individualism within an integrated society: once again an attempt at balance between Natural Law (the sanctity of the person) and Aristotelianism (a community of persons in a network of mutually advantageous relationships). He saw this as the social contract.

The initial theme in Locke's *Second Treatise on Civil Government* was the rational and social nature of the human person. He too assumed that men once lived in a state of nature as equal and separate units with an inalienable right to private property, although they recognized that to survive each man had to accept a limitation on his power to act. In contrast to Hobbes's view, society resulted from individual acts not of surrender to an authority imposed from above but of voluntary consensus. Men themselves agreed to form an interdependent community and a government. Yet, although he acknowledged the corporate nature of society, he was far less comfortable with the idea than was Hobbes. Whereas Hobbes spelt out clearly various possible forms of his commonwealth, Locke wrote about his in general terms. His main interest was in the field of interpersonal relationships, which he saw as the essence of social life. Whereas Hobbes had no doubt about the need to re-establish a discipline corporate state, Locke was wary about such a prospect. After all, his revolution had put down the "tyranny" of James II. Yet he could not ignore the issue. At different times he stressed the supreme power of the people, of the legislature, and finally of a monarch, almost even if somewhat hesitatingly, anticipating the tripartite division of powers that Burke made famous at the end of the next century. Because of the original person to person and consensual social contract, all authority must be curbed: that of the people by the legislature and the monarch; and that of the legislature and monarch by the law, on which the people must never encroach. Yet, in the final analysis, good Calvinist and Whig as he was, Locke saw the people as having the final choice. Under extreme provocation, they were free to overturn the legislature and monarch, dissolve the constitution, and reject the old and seek a new social contract on the basis, of course, of concordance between individual human beings (Sabine 1964:523–40).

Locke's other work, *An Essay Concerning Human Understanding*, was probably equally important to the argument of this paper as his work on civil government. He published it in 1689, two years after Newton's *Principia Mathematica*, which apparently it rivalled in popular esteem. He wrote it at the height of the Scientific Revolution, setting forth the great principle on which that movement was based—human secular intellectual discovery—and dismissing the old view, attributed to the medieval schoolmen, that all knowledge was God-given, a product of divine revelation. Initially, said Locke, the mind was an "empty cabinet" or "white paper, void of all characters, without any ideas." "How comes [the mind]," he asks, "to be furnished?" Whence come all its "materials of reason and knowledge? To this I answer, in one word, from *experience*. In that all our knowledge is founded; and from that it ultimately derives itself" (Locke 1964:89, orig. 1689). This statement of the theory of the malleability of the human mind opened the way to its political correlate, indoctrination.

After about 1700, with the success of the concordat between crown and parliament, English social philosophy lost momentum. The initiative passed to France, where the character of the subject was substantially changed. Certainly, there were good reasons for the French to be interested in it. Their economic and sociopolitical systems were as much out of step with each other as those of the English seventy years earlier. The expansion of world trade had created a new, wealthy, well-educated, and ambitious middle class. Yet the country's formal structure was still feudal. The traditional ranks of nobles, seigniors, merchants, peasants, and artisans were largely genealogically fixed. By the mid-eighteenth century, the middle class felt itself alienated. There was no tradition of local or national parliamentary representation by which it could realize its political ambitions, as in England. It had even lost the advantages it had won under Louis XIV, who had curbed the power of the old nobility (*Noblesse d'epée*); he governed his kingdom with the help of able bourgeois, whom he created the *noblesse de la robe*, and appointed to high administrative and military positions. As the eighteenth century wore on, the old nobility became so impoverished by the high cost of living at Versailles that its members had to take up senior posts in the civil service and army, thereby stifling middle class aspirations.

To this extent, there was a genuine problem. We can understand Voltaire finding England in the 1720s the freest country in the world, not excepting any republic, and his contrast between English "liberty" and French "slavery," and English "sensible toughness" and French "mad superstition" (Mitford 1957:36). Yet his subsequent obsession with the domestic politics of France became unreal: "[We] live in curious times and amid astonishing contrasts: reason on the one hand, the most absurd fanaticism on the other ... a civil war in every soul. *Sauve qui peut*" (quoted in Behrens 1967:10). One is reminded of Kingsley Amis's gibe at A. E. Housman: "Wounds imagined more than seen." Whereas English social inquiry had been typically *ad hoc* and pragmatic—certainly after the demise of the Fifth Monarchy Movement in the 1660s it had few millenarian attributes—French philosophy in the eighteenth century seems to have been geared to no specific issue or problem but rather to general dissatisfaction. This and French penchant for abstract theory allowed it to become arrogantly chiliast, as de Tocqueville (1959:33–34 noted in a famous passage in the 1850s:

> The general idea of the greatness of man, of the omnipotence of his reason, of the limitless powers of his intelligence, had pene-trated and pervaded the spirit of the century. Yet this lofty concep-tion of mankind in general was coupled with a particular contempt for contemporary society.

In reality, however, there had been a switch from empirical reason to idealistic romanticism: *cogito ergo sum* had given way to *je sense, donc je suis* (Willey 1962:107). The age was ready for revolution. All it needed was a slogan. It found it in Jean Jacques Rousseau's *The Social Contract*, published in 1762. What was once conceived as a longer work of political philosophy was boiled down into a short, lucid, and in the long-run inflam-matory pamphlet (Sabine 1964:586–87).

"Man is born free, and everywhere he is in the chains." The dramatic opening sentence of *The Social Contract* was directed primarily at quasi-feudal France but also at current European society in general. Rousseau's aim was universal human liberation. His problem was: How can the indi-vidual retain the freedom with which he was born and yet live in society, which is the negation of that freedom? He saw it clearly as a problem of the relationship between the individual and his society. His solution was an idiosyncratic reinterpretation of the works of philosophers who had preceded him, especially Plato, Hobbes, and Locke. From Plato and Hobbes he took one concept in particular: the small collective or corporate society under a philosopher-king or lawgiver, who could create order by reducing many wills to one. Three factors were important. First, as Sabine (1964:524ff.) suggests, the old idea of Natural Law and the universal society under God was in decline. It had lost credibility, perhaps, after Louis XIV, that most Christian king, supported the Turks against their Christian subjects. Second, as has often been remarked, despite his long sojourn in France, Rousseau was always at heart and in fact a citizen of Geneva. He idealized—he most certainly thought in terms of—the city-state. Hence he repudiated the cosmopolitan individualism of his precursor Calvin, which he saw as harmful. Third, while planning his wider political thesis, he had spent much time reading Plato (Durant and Durant 1967:171, 178, and 188; cf. Sabine 1964:59 and 58–81). Finally, from Locke he took two ideas. First, there had to be person to person consensus. Membership in society should be voluntary and citizens should join together in it in a spirit of reason. Yet he rejected the idea that true consensus could be found or represented by a mere majority of views: 51 percent of any vote taken would be only just over half of the individual opinions and would not necessarily promote the good of the whole community. Once again the individual and his society had to be compounded, but to a degree probably never envisaged even by Plato or Hobbes. The individual would become a mere cipher. Second, the process would be facilitated by applying Locke's theory of the malleable human mind and total indoctrination.

This led to the well-known formula of the General Will, or collective ideology, which every citizen should uphold, and the civic religion, which would validate and reinforce it. To ensure interpersonal consensus but avoid the bedlam of uncoordinated individual views, a Legislator, who alone could envisage the General Will, had to impart it to the citizens so that they would singly and voluntarily embrace it and come together. This would establish the perfected society, *un corps moral et collectif*, Rousseau's translation of the corpus morale collectivum of Natural Law (Barker 1960:xxxvii). The new moral collective—not the universal society of Natural Law but his own limited city-state—had to be buttressed, as Plato had argued in his *Republic* and *Laws*, by a purely social and deintellectualized religion, a religion "viewed in relation to society":

> ... a purely civil profession of faith, the articles of which it behoves the Sovereign [people] to fix, not with the precision of religious dogmas, but treating them as a body of social sentiments without which no man can be either a good citizen or a faithful subject [Rousseau 1960:437, orig. 1762].

Talmon's (1961) thesis is compelling: Rousseau's *The Social Contract* marked a breach between British and Continental Europe, which had hitherto always seen themselves as part of the same sociocultural order. With a few exceptions to be mentioned later, the British upheld individualism: society was an aggregation of individuals and decisions were to be reached by a majority vote. There was no concept of the General Will and a structure greater than the sum of its parts. By way of contrast, Continental—especially French and German—savants became progressively collectivist. In his *A Sketch of a Historical Picture of the Progress of the Human Mind* (popularly subtitled "The Testament of the Eighteenth Century"), published in 1795, Condorcet prophesied a science that could foresee, accelerate, and direct the progress of humanity by establishing laws governing society. As Hayek (1962:108) points out, to establish such laws demanded, as Condorcet desired, the transformation of history from one that dealt with individuals to one that concentrated on the masses. But the idea was not new. Even twelve years beforehand, in 1783, in his address to the *Académie*, Condorcet had advocated structuralist inquiry: The "study [of] human society as we study those of beavers and bees" (quoted in Hayek 1962:108). With the fall of the *ancien régime* in the 1790s, collectivist ideology became a dominant force.

France During and After the Revolution and First Empire

It is probable that many of its supporters in 1789 interpreted the nascent French Revolution in strictly individualist terms. Man, by means of his own reason, would break free from the old society and thereby perfect it. This was implicit in the slogan: *Liberté, Egalité, Fraternité*. Such persons were soon to be disillusioned and their trust in personal freedom betrayed. As Lord Acton later expressed it, the "hope of liberty" was "made vain" by the "passion for equality." Indeed, equality was possible only in collectivist terms, as soon became apparent in the speeches of the Abbé Sieyès and other early demagogues at Versailles (Talmon 1961:69ff.). What Rousseau had put out as a neat theory for his ideal small community now became a frightening concept: the solidary nation with, as Burke prophesied, an inordinate concentration of state power and, needless to say, a corresponding loss of personal independence, the first genuinely modern totalitarian experiment.

After engineering the destruction of the aristocracy, the Catholic Church, the monarchy, and finally the moderate liberals (the Girondists), the hard left, the Jacobins under Robespierre and Saint-Just, seized power until they were themselves overthrown and executed in 1794. The Jacobin program was to establish the rule of Rousseauist collectivist philosophy with its own version of the General Will ("a republic one and indivisible"), in which Robespierre was cast as the Legislator, and those who resisted his indoctrination were sentenced to the hiss of the guillotine. France needed "a single will." Although the succeeding regime, the Directory, was more easygoing, to the point very often of public venality, the drive for centralization continued, especially in the field of national education (Hayek 1962:109–10).

Yet the Rousseauist dream really seemed to have come true when Napoleon had himself installed as First Consul and then Emperor. He was the final incarnation of the General Will, beyond custom, morality, and law: David's God-Man, the personalification of the new corporate nation-state. The English historian Sir Arthur Bryant (1945:2ff.) gives a graphic description of Paris as seen through the eyes of English tourists during the Peace of Amiens in 1802. The perceptive quickly saw that individual liberty had been a casualty of the guillotine. Even Charles James Fox, an early fellow traveller, was somewhat shaken by the absence of free discussion and criticism, the mainspring of English public life. The French had no misgivings. "Look at that sanguinary prostitute!" cried a Rouen merchant to his English guest as they stood before the statue of *Liberty* in the Law Courts. "For years we have had liberty and bloodshed: thank Heaven we are no longer free!"

With consummate skill Napoleon used two forces to bolster his position: religion and the plebiscite. In the first context he copied Augustus Caesar, although he did not seek posthumous deification. His masterstroke was his Concordat with the Papacy in 1802, whereby he reintroduced the Catholic Church into France, albeit without its former seigniorial rights. Although he retained a modicum of faith, his religious policy was pragmatic. Religion represented not the mystery of the Incarnation but the mystery of the social order: a form of social cement which he used to keep the support of a peasantry, both in France and Italy, that was essentially devote "but had been robbed of its altars by urban doctrinaires" (Bryant 1945:5). He used it to repress anarchy, enhance the prestige of France, and consolidate his hold on Europe. To this end, he had the catechism rewritten to stress the duty of loyalty to his person. In the second context he allowed the Senate to implore him to accept the Imperial Crown, which the people overwhelmingly supported by ballot: 3,572,329 votes in favor and 2,569 against. He could declare: "I ascend the throne where I have been placed by the unanimous voice of the people, the Senate, and the army." It was nothing for him to summon the Pope to Paris with the Crown of Charlemagne, the ultimate trophy. Even more than Louis XIV, he was the state. He was, *de facto*, Napoleon by the Grace of God and the Will of the People Emperor of the French Republic (Alison 1854:350–55).[7]

Yet this was not merely Napoleon's projection of his self-image. It was endorsed by the leading Continental philosophers of the day, both during and after his reign. They agreed with the view of the Rouen merchant. Individual liberty was the submerged rock on which the ship of revolution had foundered. They all wanted a stable collective society. In Germany, this attitude was foreshadowed by Kant (1724–1804) implicit in the later works of Fichte (1762–1814), and explicit in those of Hegel (1770–1831). In Hegel's judgment, Jacobinism had created the violence, fanaticism, and terrorism that had torn France apart. By himself, the individual was, as Rousseau had said, a wayward animal governed only by instinct. He had to be placed firmly in, and disciplined by, society, the highest form of which was the state, the physical representation of the World Spirit, whose terrestrial agents were great men such as Napoleon. The individual's highest duty was to be a member of the state (Parkinson 1958:273; Sabine 1964:652–53).

In France, both conservative Catholic counter-revolutionaries and the social progressives (heterodox millenarians) had comparable ideas. The most important of the Catholic group was de Bonald, Ballanche, de Maistre, and Lammenais. De Bonald spoke for them all when he said that it was time to speak of "*We*" rather than "*I*," for only the corporate entity was real. Far from man constituting society, society constituted man and formed him with the aid of social education. Society was the true—indeed, the only—nature of man. Ballanche wrote: "Man's movements are imprinted on him by the whole of which he forms a part. Individuality is not for him in this world." They all condemned the anarchic penchants of individualism and, like Rousseau, saw religion as a necessary buttress of collective society. Thus de Maistre asserted: "Individual reason reduced to its individual forces is impotent . . . because it produces nothing but disputes . . . There needs to be a religion of state." Likewise de Bonald wrote: "Others have defended the religion of man. I defend the religion of society" (Talmon 1960:301–4).

Except for their political views, these Catholic conservatives were little different in outlook from the millenarian thinkers who flourished in France after the Bourbon Restoration and whose ideas were later taken up by Durkheim, the godfather of British structuralism. Of these, the most influential were Saint-Simon and Comte, who repudiated individualism and proposed new forms of the Rousseauist collective social order and civil region.

Saint-Simon (1760–1825), a count of the *ancien régime*, had fought against the British in North America and had had a checkered career during the Revolution. After the Terror, he concerned himself with plans for restructuring European society by means of what he called a "regenerative revolution" in the face of two crucial and interdependent problems: individual liberty and the new industrialism that had taken root in Britain after 1750 and was now spreading to Europe. As events in the 1790s had demonstrated, multiple factional wills had to be replaced by a new incarnation of the General Will. Like the majority of Frenchmen, he hailed

Napoleon as the Rousseauist Legislator who would "give laws to all man-kind," of which he was the "scientific chief" and "political head."

Napoleon ignored this flattery. He too remembered the Terror. Having studied Rousseau, he knew the influence *The Social Contract* had had, and he did not encourage further philosophical experiments. Undeterred, Saint-Simon addressed himself to his second problem. He was probably the first Continental thinker to recognize that henceforth industrial technology and factory organization were to dominate European society. He anticipated Marx in arguing that, unless irresponsible individualism in this field were curbed, there would be continual turmoil. In the early years of the nineteenth century, he suggested the formation of a Council of Newton, consisting of twenty-one of the greatest European minds: three mathematicians, three physicists, three chemists, three physiologists, three authors, three painters, and three musicians, the chairman to be a mathematician. The Council would be the collective representative of God on earth and would legislate for society (Hayek 1962:120; Talmon 1960:42). In 1819, as the factory system became more widespread, he proposed a larger Council of Industrialists, consisting of all those engaged in productive work and organized in three tiers. A Chamber of Invention would draw up plans for public undertakings. A Chamber of Review would scrutinize these plans. A Chamber of Execution (incorporating the richest and most successful entrepreneurs) would supervise the implementation of those projects approved. Over six hundred people were to be involved (Hayek 1962:131–32). Ultimately, as with Rousseau, Robespierre (Lawrence 1968), and Napoleon, the new structure was to be validated and reinforced by yet another social religion, the New Christianity, in which God was to be Newton's Law of Gravity and which would regulate the laws made by the Council (Durkheim 1962a:229, orig. 1895). As Talmon (1960:53–54) comments, the Council was an expression of "collective sovereignty," imposing the General Will on corporate society as "an act of scientific comprehension": it had total knowledge. This implicit faith in science was the link between Saint-Simon and Comte.

Although regarded as Saint-Simon's intellectual successor, Auguste Comte (1798–1857) had an entirely different background. He was middle class, never knew the *ancien régime*, and started life as a mathematician. For a time he was Saint-Simon's secretary until he set up as a savant on his own account. Like Saint-Simon, he was a visionary, but he earnestly presented a front of scientific rigor. He coined the word *sociology* as the science of a collective society greater than the sum of its parts, the individuals who composed it. He began his analysis with a restatement of the evolutionary stages of the human mind first expounded by Turgot at the Sorbonne in 1750: religion, metaphysics, and science. Now that European society had progressed to the third stage, it too could be studied and thereby reformed scientifically provided two conditions were met. First, like the natural sciences, sociology had to be based on positivism. Every proposition had to be reduced to a simple enunciation of fact. Second, as with his predecessors—although he elaborated the idea only in the last years of his life—collective society had to be legitimized and strengthened by a new religion: the Religion of Humanity, which of course was God. In the spirit of Saint-Simon's New Christianity, creed and dogma were the discovered laws of the positive sciences.

Yet, for all his scientific front, Comte had his Achilles' heel. Try as he might, he could never completely fuse the individual with collective society and its General Will. The individual was always the joker in the pack. Comte's problem was that instead of merely hypothesizing social issues, as his predecessors had done, he had begun to analyze them. "Abnormalities" were inevitable. Thus he wrote of his positive philosophy: "It cannot be necessary to prove to anybody . . . that ideas govern the world" (Comte 1954:238). Yet by *ideas* he meant the collective mind of society. Initially, he dismissed the individual intellect: "True observation must necessarily be external to the observer . . . internal observation is no more than a vain parody of it." In other words, we cannot study the individual mind and its decisions. But a few pages later he was guilty of a vole-face: We must observe "the series of intellectual and moral acts, which belong more to history proper." These have to be the acts of individual men and women (Hayek 1962:171–73). This is the first clear example of the internal inconsistencies in the collectivist argument which I foreshadowed at the outset. As we shall see, Durkheim, to whom I now turn, was confronted with this difficulty, which he never solved but merely tried to evade.

Émile Durkheim (1858–1917) continued the tradition of the scientific study of collective society. His theories are too well-known to need summary restatement here. Yet certain aspects of them must be stressed. Although, certainly in the past, he has been regarded as the direct successor of Comte, there are grounds for believing that he was at least equally indebted to Rousseau and Saint-Simon, about whom he wrote two more sympathetic books (Durkheim 1960, orig. 1892, and 1962a, orig. 1895). He regarded Rousseau as one of the forerunners of sociology and took to extremes the idea that he had synthesized from the work of earlier thinkers: the fusion between corporate society and the individual. Society was an autonomous moral entity with its own qualities quite separate from those of its single members. Again, Durkheim's *conscience collective* (the collective conscience-cum-consciousness) was a modified version of Rousseau's General Will without its futurist messianism: the ideology of a society yet to be established. The conscience collective already existed as an actual society's idealized conception of itself. Finally, Durkheim's stress on the role of religious beliefs and ritual in endorsing and strengthening the collective social order owes much to both Rousseau and Saint-Simon.

Indeed, so seriously did Durkheim take Rousseau that he felt constrained to criticize him for a lapse into individualism in *The Social Contract*: his admission of the need for an *individual* Legislator to instruct the *collective* citizenry in the General Will.

> Neither Hobbes nor Rousseau seems to have realized how contradictory it is to admit that the individual is himself the author of a machine which has for its essential role his domination and restraint. At least, it seemed to them sufficient for the elimination of this contradiction that it be disguised in the eyes of those who are its victims, by the clever artifice of the social contract [Durkheim 1962a:122, orig. 1895].

> Again:

> [Individualism is] itself a social product ... The individual receives from society even the moral beliefs which deify him. This is what Kant and Rousseau did not understand. They wished to deduce their individualist ethics not from society, but from the notion of the isolated individual ... [It is] possible, without contradiction, to be an individualist while asserting that the individual is a product of society, rather than its cause [Durkheim 1898:12, quoted in Lukes 1973:339–40].

I regard this as sophism: an enormous tail wagging a minuscule dog. What is equally important, it is another example of the contradictions inherent in collectivist dogma. For all his brave talk about the total derivation of the individual from the collective, there were times when Durkheim, like Comte, had to admit the primacy of individualism. Thus, after his criticism of Hobbes and Rousseau in the first quotation above, he went on to say: "In principle, we have only to leave individual forces to develop freely and they will tend to organize themselves socially." Again, in his great and seminal work on religion and magic, just as he had to admit the existence of *private* religions, which he unconvincingly tried to distinguish from magic as he had defined it, he remarked lamely that "to make [collective representations], a *multitude of minds* have associated, united, and *combined* their ideas and sentiments" (Durkheim 1954:16, orig. 1912; my italics). In other words, before there can be a General Will and collective, there must be individual minds, as Hobbes and Rousseau doubtless would have retorted. *Naturam expellas furca tamen usque recurret.*

THE CONCEPT OF THE COLLECTIVE IN ANGLO-AUSTRALIAN SOCIAL ANTHROPOLOGY

Radcliffe-Brown became an admirer of Durkheim before the First World War (Langham 1981:268), and it has often been supposed that this alone was responsible for the introduction of the concept of the collective into Anglo-Australian social anthropology after 1920. Although by no means incorrect, such an explanation on its own is far too simple. It ignores over two thousand years of intellectual history. As I have argued, the idea of the collective had its roots in the ancient world and finally became established in European thought in the eighteenth century after much debate and as the result of local historical accidents. It was taken up mainly by Continental theorists but even in Britain, the fortress of individualism, especially after 1688, it had its adherents. Apart from the fellow travellers during the French Revolution—members of the Lunar Club in Birmingham, Tom Paine, and poets Wordsworth, Coleridge, Southey, and Byron—there were other Britons who had studied collectivist theory closely and been influenced by it at least to some extent: such people as Harriet Martineau (friend of Florence Nightingale and translator of Comte), J. S. Mill, Herbert Spencer, and T. H. Green.

Yet by and large, before Durkheim, collectivist doctrine never struck root in Britain for two reasons. First, as Mill came to realize, it represented a form of tyranny which denied the kinds of freedom for which he and his fellows stood. Second, especially after Napoleon had ultimately failed to hold the French together despite his initial advantages, the new national societies, with populations now numbering many millions, were too huge to be conceived as single integrated wholes. The world had yet to witness the brutal Left and Right totalitarianism of our own century. Hence collectivism at the national level was only a pipe dream, not to be taken seriously. Indeed, the only French social concept that might have made a deep impression was the phalange of the visionary Fourier, a successor of Saint-Simon: a human productive group of some 1600 people on five hundred acres of land (Talmon 1960:148–56). This was certainly small enough to have been considered as a viable collective but, as Fourier envisaged a world population consisting of six million such units, the idea was ignored.[8]

This, I believe, explains Durkheim's rapid success in Britain, especially after the publication of *The Elementary Forms of the Religious Life* (Durkheim 1954), in French in 1912 and in English only three years later. In this work, he presented the argument, already implicit in his earlier writings, that religion must be studied in collectivist terms, as an affair of the group. Yet, although his ultimate aim was to project his conclusions onto French society, sadly anarchic and lacking a solidary morality since

the failure of the Revolution, the actual collective he purported to describe
and analyze was conveniently small: the patriclan of the Aranda in Central
Australia. Like Fourier's phalange, this was something that could be
accepted as a fully integrated totality without individualist deviations, the
prerequisite of the sociological law. Furthermore, it could be regarded not
as a pipe dream but as an existing reality. It is significant that two sets of
scholars at once took notice of the work: those interested in classical
antiquity and the early social anthropologists.

Of the classical scholars, the two most important were Gilbert Murray,
Regius Professor of Greek at Oxford, and Jane Harrison, a Newnham
(Cambridge) don. Both were eminent for their studies of ancient and
classical Greek religion. Although they did not accept it without criticism,
they were sympathetic to Durkheim's approach on two grounds. Its anti-
intellectualist bias (Lawrence 1968) was in keeping with the secular scientific outlook and urbane religious skepticism of fifth and fourth century
Athenians (Murray 1912:95–99). Again, Durkheim's collective, the Aranda
patriclan, was relevant to ancient Greek society: it was a mini*polis*. Inter-
estingly, in the same year that the French edition of *The Elementary
Forms of the Religious Life* appeared, Murray (1912:19 fn.1) referred to
it as a "famous analysis."

The social anthropologists—Radcliffe-Brown, Marett, and their
students—were quick to follow, although their impact on the study of
stateless societies was not apparent until the end of the 1920s because
of the internal politics of their subject. As Langham (1981) has demonstrated, for at least a decade after the First World War, there was the bitter
struggle between social anthropology (structural-functionalism) and diffusionism. Moreover, even within the structural-functionalist camp itself
there were at that time influential scholars other than Durkheim. W. H. R.
Rivers—before he turned to diffusionism—and Lewis Morgan (cf. Fortes
1970) did much to stimulate Radcliffe-Brown's interest in the structural
analysis of stateless societies. Yet much of this work (cf. Rivers 1968) was
based on the examination of individualistic or interpersonal kinship relationships, which by themselves seemed fragmented and formless. With
Durkheim's corporate patriclan, shorn of Lewis Morgan's tortuous, and
by then unfashionable, evolutionism, and fortified by Maine's (1965:110,
orig. 1861) concept of the "corporation aggregate"—eventually an axiom
of anthropological faith that can be defined as a *united* body of persons
authorized to act as an individual—it became possible to comprehend
the parts of stateless societies, and combine them as recognizable and
seemingly operative wholes. To cut a long story short, Radcliffe-Brown
(1930–31) then at the University of Sydney, applied this holistic concept
to Australian aboriginal societies by positing the patrilineal horde as the land-
owning group. The Africanists,[9] very much under Radcliffe-Brown's aegis,
used the same approach in an expanded form in their large segmentary

societies in the 1930s and 1940s. The anthropologists working in the Papua New Guinea Highlands in the 1950s repatriated it to the Antipodes.

In conclusion, it would be invidious to dismiss Anglo-Australian collectivist anthropology without recognizing its achievements. Broadly, especially in the field of indigenous politics, it helped make us aware that we were dealing not with mere ragbags of custom but with organized sociocultural systems which we should treat with respect. But the approach proved inadequate, as it did in the case of Comte and Durkheim, because it made no provision for the free-ranging individual, who was always bound to intrude. Had the early holist analyses been intended only as stop-gaps, as preludes to more detailed and subtle interpersonal studies, there might have been no problem. But, as Langness (1972) forthrightly observed, this was not so. Collectivist research was seen as an end in itself, only to prove in the long-run a cul-de-sac.

Essentially, it is a matter of returning to something resembling the tolerant Periclean ideal: that the individual and his society should be kept in reasonable perspective. This has always been a difficulty in our understanding of the so-called Third World, particularly Africa and Oceania, during the last 150 years, in which we have had close dealings with its peoples. The problem is neatly illustrated by a passage in Lucretius' *De Rerum Natura* (Book II, 308–32). The poet compares a human body, at rest but composed of innumerable atoms in motion and hence difficult immediately to comprehend, to a flock of sheep grazing on a hillside or legions practicing military exercises, when seen from afar. All we can discern is a deceptive, large white blaze or single sheen of metal. The implication is that to see the single sheep or soldiers we must get nearer. By the same token, we first saw Africans and Oceanians as a non-Caucasoid blur, about which we had so little knowledge that we could use it only for dubious armchair evolutionary surveys. Yet when we turned to structural-functionalism and the field research it entailed, we tried to simplify—and thereby short-circuited—our inquiries by going no farther than delineating groups. To grant these peoples full humanity and dignity we must move yet closer to them and observe individuals operating in depth within the frameworks of their societies. In short, future researchers will have to be better linguists and spend longer in the field than has hitherto been possible. To this end, Derek Freeman's projected studies of individual choice and action will be both timely and welcome.

Notes

1. Throughout this paper, the terms "structural" and "structuralism" refer to British or Anglo-Australian social structural studies and not to French, or Lévi-Straussian, structuralism.

2. In this paper, I treat as an Anglo-Australian anthropologist any scholar who has carried out research in Oceania under the auspices of a British or Australian university, regardless of nationality.

3. From personal knowledge, I could add to Langness's list, but this is not to be "holier than thou." As I have recorded in Lawrence (1984:1–2), when I went to the southern Madang Providence of Papua New Guinea in 1949, I had exactly the same expectations as the workers in the Highlands in the 1950s. Fortunately, I found a society that I could in no way squeeze into a unilineal mold.

4. I stress immediately that this brief survey cannot be definitive. At most, I hope that it will encourage others to pursue (in greater detail) the issues I have raised. Nor is it based exclusively on primary sources: the relevant literature is too vast. I acknowledge my debt to Parkinson (1958), Talmon (1960 and 1961), and Sabine (1964). I learned also from Anthony Darcy's B.A. Honors thesis (Department of Anthropology, University of Sydney, 1982): "The Rise of Individualism and the Development of Social Theory." I cite other works in context.

5. This explains a comment by Maine (1965:97–98, orig. 1861) that slaves in those American states that derive their law from "the highly Romanized code of Louisiana" had better prospects than those in states that had only English Common Law, "which, as recently interpreted, has no true place for the Slave, and can only therefore regard him as a chattel."

6. My translation. The original Latin reads: "Communis enim usus omnium, quae sunt in hoc mundo, omnibus hominibus esse debuit." Gratian, Decretum, pt. ii, Causa xii, Q.1, c.ii 1.

7. For a recent sympathetic biography of Napoleon, see Cronin (1971).

8. Fourier's idea of the phalange had, of course, its empirical counterpart in Britain: Robert Owen's socialist experiments in reforming factory organization at the New Lanark Mills in Scotland and elsewhere.

9. At least one Africanist did not conform to the stereotype: the late Emeritus Professor Meyer Fortes of Cambridge, one of the first two exponents of the African Segmentary Model. As his general work on kinship (Fortes 1970) makes clear, his thinking went well beyond segmentary collectivist analysis. I record this with deep appreciation and gratitude. As he has stated in his Foreword to Lawrence (1984:ix), he was initially cautious about my analysis of Garia social structure in terms of networks of interpersonal relationships. Yet, as is manifest in his Foreword, having examined my work in toto, he gave it his full, consistent, and most generous support. He was the kind of man whom convention and dogma could never constrain. I should mention also in this context that my summary in this paragraph owes much to Gumbert (1981).

References

Alison, Sir A.
1854 History of Europe. Volume 5. Edinburgh and London: Blackwood.

Barker, Sir E.
1948 The Politics of Aristotle. Oxford: Oxford University Press.

1960 *Social Contract*. Oxford: Oxford University Press.

Barnes, J. A.
1962 African Models in the New Guinea Highlands. *Man* 62:5–9.

1967 Agnation Among the Enga. *Oceania* 38:33–43.

Behrens, C. B. A.
1967 *The Ancien Régime*. London: Thames and Hudson.

Brown, P.
1978 *Highland Peoples of New Guinea*. Cambridge: Cambridge University Press.

Bryant, Sir A.
1945 *Years of Victory*. London: Collins.

Comte, A.
1954 (orig. 1830–42) The Positive Philosophy. In *The Philosophers of Science,* edited by S. Commins and R. N. Linscott. New York: Modern Pocket Library.

Cronin, V.
1971 *Napoleon*. Harmondsworth: Penguin.

Dante, Alighieri
1957 (orig. 1310–13) *On World-Government (de Monarchia)*. New York: Bobbs-Merrill.

Dumont, L.
1983 A Modified View of Our Origins: The Christian Beginnings of Modern Individualism. *Contributions to Indian Sociology* 17(1).

Durant, W. and A. Durant.
1967 *Rousseau and Revolution*. New York: Simon and Shuster.

Durkheim, É.
1898 L'Individualisme et les intellectuels. *Revue Bleue* 4, x:7–13.

1954 orig. 1912) *The Elementary Forms of the Religious Life*. London: Allen and Unwin.

1960 (orig. 1892) *Montesquieu and Rousseau*. Ann Arbor: University of Michigan Press.

1962a (orig. 1895) *Socialism*. New York: Collier.

1962b (orig. 1895) *The Rules of Sociological Method*. New York: Free Press.

Evans-Pritchard, E. E.
1940 *The Nuer*. Oxford: Oxford University Press.

Fortes, M.
1945 *The Dynamics of Clanship Among the Tallensi*. Oxford: Oxford University Press.

1970 *Kinship and the Social Order.* London: Routlege and Kegan Paul.

Fortes, M. and E. E. Evans-Pritchard
1940 *African Political Systems.* Oxford: Oxford University Press.

Fraser, Lady A.
1973 *Cromwell.* London: Weidenfeld and Nicolson.

Gibbon, E.
1960 (orig. 1891) *The Decline and Fall of the Roman Empire.* Volume I. London: Dent.

Gumbert, M.
1981 Paradigm Lost. *Oceania* 52:103–23.

Harvey, Sir P.
1937 *The Oxford Companion to Classical Literature.* Oxford: Oxford University Press.

Hayek, F. A.
1962 *The Counter-Revolution of Science.* New York: Free Press.

Hiatt, L. R.
1962 Local Organization Among the Australian Aborigines. *Oceania* 30:267–86.

Hobbes, T.
1909 (orig. 1651) *The Leviathan,* edited by W. G. Pogson Smith. Oxford: Oxford University Press.

Hogbin, I.
1958 *Social Change.* London: Watts and Co.

Langham, I.
1981 *The Building of British Social Anthropology.* Dordrecht: Reidel.

Langness, L. L.
1972 Political Organization. In *Encyclopedia of Papua and New Guinea.* Melbourne: Melbourne University Press. (Republished as Traditional Political Organization in *Anthropology in Papua New Guinea,* edited by I. Hogbin. Melbourne: Melbourne University Press, 1973.)

Lawrence, P.
1964 *Don Juan in Melanesia.* Quadrant No. 29, April–May. (Republished by the University of Queensland Press, 1967.)

1968 *Daughter of Time.* Queensland: University of Queensland Press. (Reprinted in *Cultures of the Pacific,* edited by T. G. Harding and B. J. Wallace. New York: Free Press, 1970.)

1984 *The Garia.* Melbourne and Manchester: Melbourne and Manchester University Presses.

Lepervanche, M. de
1967–68 Descent, Residence and Leadership in the New Guinea Highlands. *Oceania* 38:135–58, 163–89.

Locke, J.
1960 (orig. 1690) Second Treatise on Civil Government. In *Social Contract* by Sir E. Barker. Oxford: Oxford University Press.

1964 (orig. 1689) *An Essay Concerning Human Understanding.* London: Collins (Fontana) Paperback.

Lukes, S.
1973 *Émile Durkheim: His Life and Work.* Harmondsworth: Penguin.

Maine, Sir H.
1965 (orig. 1861) *Ancient Law.* London: Dent.

McArthur, M.
1967 Analysis of the Genealogy of a Mae-Enga Clan. *Oceania* 37:281–85.

Meggitt, M. J.
1962 *Desert People.* Sydney: Angus and Robertson.

Mitford, N.
1957 *Voltaire in Love.* Harmondsworth: Penguin.

Murray, G.
1912 *Four Stages of Greek Religion.* New York: Columbia University Press.

Parkinson, C. N.
1958 *The Evolution of Political Thought.* London: University of London Press.

Radcliffe-Brown, A. R.
1930–31 The Social Organization of Australian Tribes. *Oceania* 34–63, 322–41, 426–56.

1934–35 Patrilineal and Matrilineal Succession. *Iowa Law Review* 20.

Rivers, W. H. R.
1968 *Kinship and Social Organization.* New York: Athlone Press.

Rousseau, J. J.
1960 (orig. 1762) The Social Contract. In *Social Contract* by Sir. E. Barker. Oxford: Oxford University Press.

Runciman, S.
1954 *A History of the Crusades.* Volume III. Harmondsworth: Penguin.

Sabine, G. H.
1964 *A History of Political Theory.* London: George C. Harrap and Co.

Sampson, G. (ed.)
1910 *The Utopia of Sir Thomas More.* London: Bell.

Spate, O. H. K.
1979 *The Pacific Since Magellan: 1. The Spanish Lake.* Canberra: The Australian National University Press.

1983 *The Pacific since Magellan: 2. Monopolists and Freeboaters.* Canberra: The Australian National University Press.

Talmon, J. L.
1960 *Political Messianism.* New York: Praeger.

1961 *The Origins of Totalitarian Democracy.* London: Mercury.

Tawney, R. H.
1948 *Religion and the Rise of Capitalism.* London: Pelican.

Tocqueville, A. de
1959 *The European Revolution and Correspondence with de Gobineau.* New York: Doubleday, Anchor.

Weber, M.
1958 *The Protestant Ethic and the Spirit of Capitalism.* New York: Scribner.

Willey, B.
1962 *The Eighteenth Century Background.* Peregrine Paperback.

4

The Morality of Exchange

D. K. Feil

At least since *The Gift*, anthropologists have been fascinated by forms of exchange and modes of reciprocity in primitive societies. The power of the gift to express the full range of cultural values, to sanctify or subvert social relations, has made it a conceptual key for understanding the "archaic" societies with which Mauss was primarily concerned. Less often remarked upon, however, were his views on society in which gift exchange no longer played the pre-eminent role it once did; that is in predominantly Western societies with market economies. For Mauss these societies were patently morally inferior. The overlay of social and community constraints on the economy had been eroded and new men thereby created. "*Homo oeconomicus* is not behind us, but before ... For a long time man was something quite different—and it is not so long now since he became a machine—a calculating machine" (Mauss 1954:74).

In his sorrow for the passing of societies in which man was no mere "economic animal," Mauss may, in fact, have underestimated the "dual nature" of gifts and the exchange process itself in just those societies in which the ramifications of a gift exchange economy were most apparent. Some modern commentators of Mauss have stressed this very point. Godelier describes precious objects, gifts, as being "both goods and non-goods," "money" and "gifts" depending on the contexts in which they are exchanged (Godelier 1979:128). Objects change their function with the status and identity of those who exchange them. Van Baal (1975) similarly writes of gifts as embodying two distinct forms of communication: one, in which the object itself and its exchange value are primary, the other in which the object is secondary to the expression of common bonds and the sociable intentions of the partners to the exchange.[1] In the latter kind of communication, the fundamental message conveyed by exchange is "addressed to the recipient's person," its aim is to affirm a person's "full participation in the[ir] universe" (Van Baal 1975:55, 54). Van Baal, as did

Mauss before him, sees one form of exchange as giving way to the other through time.

Across Melanesia, there is great variation and emphasis on these themes of communication and the dual capacity of objects in exchange. The situation is complicated by the fact that some systems of exchange have undergone profound changes in the colonial and post-colonial period, and their economies seem on the verge, if they have not already passed it, of emphasizing the production of "exchange [object] values" rather than "use [social relations] values." The introduction of cash cropping and money have obliterated some gift economies, while others, of course, have apparently incorporated these new valuables and practices into the "traditional" pattern of ceremonial exchange. Still, it would appear that one could characterize systems of exchange as emphasizing one type of communication or the other, of valuing more highly objects or social relations in the transactional sphere. Thus, the dichotomy set up by Mauss might disappear if the so-called "gift exchange" systems were differentiated in terms of emphasis on objects or social relations. The result might form some sort of "moral continuum" akin to Mauss's developmental view of gift to commodity exchange. In the Trobriands for example, it is *kula* that is emphasized and the interpersonal relations validated through it. It is incompatible with the commodity haggling of *gimwali* (trade), which involves different relationships and emphasizes the transfer of economically necessary objects. The two spheres of exchange do not overlap and despite decades of cash cropping, money has not penetrated kula dealings. One set of social relationships clearly are valued more than those of the opposite sort, and there can be no admixture of them. In the New Guinea Highlands, the *moka* system of Mount Hagen (Strathern 1971) authorizes, even demands, inherent increments in transactions, "overgifting," virtual profits in its exchanges. In the modern period, the moka has apparently proved resilient in the face of the encroaching cash economy and the advent of wage labor (A. J. Strathern 1979, 1982a). Writing more generally, Strathern (1982b) recently made the point that there appears to be a "remarkable mapping of Highland systems of prestige gift-giving ... on to an introduced capitalist system" (1982b:551). The implications of this blend of gift and market exchange will be taken up briefly later. The point here is that the moka seems to differ profoundly from both kula and the *tee* of the Enga, to be discussed more fully here. The Melpa of Mount Hagen apparently see no contradiction in moka and cash related transactions, or more precisely perhaps, the inherent contradiction has not yet manifested itself to them.

The tee system of the Tombema-Enga gives primary value to social relations which exchange makes possible. Most transactions are *quid pro quo,* and do not involve transactors in blatant, invidious evaluations of superiority and inferiority. The partnership itself is what matters most. As Van Baal might say of them, tee partners are a "dear thing to any man" and gifts are merely "an invitation to a partnership and is as wholeheartedly accepted as it is returned" (Van Baal 1975:53). Money and the cash nexus have not infiltrated tee dealings; "business" and tee are quite separate affairs.

Tee partnerships are not quite as morally unproblematic, however, as this characterization suggests. Every transaction (or failure to make an expected one) between partners reflects a choice, a choice seen in fundamentally moral terms in Tombema-Enga eyes. A person can often choose an expedient transaction rather than a "correct" one and Enga are acutely aware of the alternatives. In short, there is an ambiguity of contradictory values in the tee system, which manifests itself in the options for courses of action open to an individual. To gain politically or to honor obligations regardless of the personal consequences is a choice confronting every transactor. Tombema see the choice as one between calculating, or "thinking" (*masingi*) which may lead to acts of expediency, versus an action which originates as part of a person's being (*petenge*—being, living inside); individual strategy versus social appropriateness.[2] Enga recognize and highly praise a "good tee man," one who is morally upright even at the risk of personal loss; a man who is always trustworthy in exchange dealings, a *katenge akali,* a "remaining man." It is apparent also that tee ideology stresses "morally correct" behavior. If we take Derek Freeman's point that value systems are the result of choices which have become encoded in human cultures, one could say that the tee is an institution in which morality has been encoded as the essential message, one which is continually reinforced by appropriate behavior despite ever present options of a contradictory sort.

My main aim here is to consider briefly some examples of Enga morality expressed and actively valued in tee exchange dealings. Some comparative remarks will follow as well as an attempt to discover the basis for Enga morality in exchange.

ENGA AND THE TEE

The Enga are the largest ethno-linguistic group in all of Papua New Guinea, numbering in excess of 170,000 people. They live in scattered, widely dispersed clan communities in the Western Highlands. Though differing in dialect and minor cultural detail, all Enga (and many neighboring non-Enga groups as well) are connected by the tee (exchange) system. The tee is a highly elaborate, intricate series of transactions, organized in three distinct phases, in which all groups throughout the area must participate (see Feil 1980, 1984, for details).[3] People give pigs and pearlshells to partners in one direction during the initiatory phase of debt-incurring payment called *saandi pingi*. These debts or loans (made for many reasons, for example: bridewealth, homicide compensation, death compensation, for pork to eat) are repaid during the main phase of giving called *tee pingi* which moves in the opposite direction to cover *saandi* debts. A further series of gifts of pork called *yae pingi* may flow back in the same direction as the opening initiatory phase which then sets up the ensuing saandi pingi phase, and ultimately foreshadows the new tee which reverses the directional flow of the previous tee phase. Tee chains of credit between individuals are often extremely long, involving many interpersonal "steps." Separate transactions for an influential man may number in the hundreds during any tee. Furthermore, in an environment marked by hostility,[4] one relied heavily on partners in neighboring, warring groups, to honor their debts. The tee is essentially exchange involving "kinsmen" linked by women whose groups are perpetual enemies.

Like other exchange systems in Melanesia the tee, at one level at least, can be analyzed as a system of social control in which transactions muted hostilities (for the tee could not proceed in an atmosphere of outright war) and fostered communication between groups. The Enga say that the tee involves everyone; it is universal, while warfare involves only two groups and associated allies, and is thus parochial and infinitely less significant than tee. Exchange is given higher cultural value than warfare. An early commentator on the tee noted just these aspects of it:

> the *te* has a much more elevated and noble aim, an aim rather social than commercial ... the *te* strengthens the feeling of solidar-ity and belonging to a single community ... it has created among these people an atmosphere of confidence and security ... and it is why the natives do not give themselves over neither to war nor head hunting and why they are not even given to the hatred of neighbouring tribes [Wirz 1952:71, translated by D. K. Feil].

This glowing assessment of the tee is no doubt overemphasized, but it is clear that if a tee is in progress, hostilities cease and attention focuses on an institution more important than warfare.[5]

INDIVIDUAL TEE DEALINGS

It is on individual decisions and individual relationships, however, that I want to dwell. The tee is predicated on individual transactions, and it is in them that we must seek the basis of the tee's overall meaning. The procedure for making a tee payment is nicely illustrated by the following:

A friend from a neighboring tribe would come to his (a tee partner's) house in the evening and after a brief and pleasant visit go
home again. During his stay his guest would unostentatiously place
a small package behind his back, and after the friend had left he
would open the package. Expertly bound up in the choicest leaves
and bound up in the tastiest spinach-like greens would be a small
cooked pig stuffed with the best seasonings and deliciously salted
[saandi pingi]. So delighted and honoured would he feel at this
splendid gesture that the next moring [sic] he would take his best
and biggest pig and cut a slit on its ear thus designating it as the
reurn [sic] payment [tee pingi] for his friends gift to him [Kleinig
1955:5–6].

This account relates the way in which tee transactions should proceed
(see also Elkin 1953:197–198). It stresses the personal side, perhaps less
tangible, of the spirit of tee alliance and the great respect shared by
partners. More recent writers on the tee and systems of exchange in the
Highlands have, in my view, neglected this aspect of the exchange process.
Furthermore, we need not deprecate the spirit of friendship because, even
as in the above example, self-interest is an element in the transaction. It
can be anticipated that the giver of the cooked pig would expect the return
payment set aside later for him, but his unpretentious generosity, privately
dispatched, reveals a deeper involvement between the two men than mere
self-seeking material reward. The personal, moral content of a tee partnership can never be overlooked. It is an important consideration in the
initiation and continuance of a partnership.

To say how the tee should proceed is not, of course, to say how it
always actually proceeds. Credits and agreements made during the initiatory phase may go awry. A pig, which should go to a person in the tee
because an appropriate saandi payment has been made for it, is instead
given elsewhere. This is a tee infraction known as *duna lakenge*, "bending
the end." As I shall point out, such infractions are relatively rare today and
were probably even rarer in the past among the Tombema, when compared to the overall number of transactions undertaken. The chain-like
character of the tee means, of course, that if a person is defaulted to, it
is possible that he might in turn default further to a linked partner, who
is preparing to receive from him (if he cannot supply the valuable, usually
a pig, from his own stock). Thus, a default in one dyadic pair can cause
repercussions all down the chain. This could mean the severing of many
partnerships although the fault occurred distantly. Tombema believe (and
it is encoded in tee rule) that a person should freely supply a replacement
pig so as not to break the linkage, but more importantly, so as not to give
an immediate partner any cause to feel that his partnership, his friendship,

is not highly valued. Tombema call this action *ndenge nyingi*, literally "supplying the corner"—giving a replacement pig from a "bent end" (see also Elkin 1953:198).[6] A person who supplies valuables even when another has defaulted to him is accorded high prestige among Tombema-Enga. He is one who has promoted the spirit of the tee, of honoring obligations to an exchange partner even when other partners have made it difficult to do so.

Tee dealings include not only the exchange of valuables, but a further range of expected behavior between partners which, importantly, has no parallel outside tee relationships. Men must protect visiting partners from clans who have come to discuss tee matters. This may mean an active defense against one's own "brothers" who recognize no tie of exchange to the alien visitor and may wish him harm. Also, public defamation of a partner during the course of tee speeches is highly unusual. A partnership is based on trust, and occasions of potential competitive one-upmanship between partners are virtually nonexistent. In the boastful oratory of successful tee makers, one's own partners are never the object of derision. Only those in other tee networks, including one's own clan brothers, are slated for ridicule.

When a linked partner is away "talking tee" and contracting negotiations far from home, a man may take over the domestic responsibilities of his partner, such as chopping firewood and fetching water for a friend's wife. These acts are done in the spirit of tee friendship and with the realization that pigs gained abroad will be given to a firm-staying friend who has seen to wider tee-related obligations. From what I have said, it is clear that the tee is an institution in which the exchange of valuables is highly embedded in a system of morality and friendship. The tee-maker is not merely a strategist, but a person fettered by the constraints of tee rule and custom.

Tee partnerships are remarkably stable and free of conflict. Elsewhere, I have estimated that approximately ninety percent of all persons with whom a man transacts in his lifetime will remain tee partners until they die (Feil 1984). Many of these partners will be inherited by future generations of descendants. Partnerships of some influential men number in the hundreds. In a system of exchange based essentially on the goodwill and integrity of individuals, and which lacks formal sanctions, this is indeed remarkable.

TRANSACTORS OR TRANSACTIONS?

The valuables transacted in any exchange system are a critical element of its structure. With concomitant social relations, they determine the character of any exchange configuration (Feil 1982). I do not want to downplay tee transactions themselves or the value of pigs and other valuables in Tombema-Enga eyes. It follows, however, from the presentation thus far, that Tombema emphasize exchange partnerships rather than products. Anybody can find pigs, Tombema say, but good partners are more scarce. Historically, the tee system was founded on pigs, their production equally open and accessible to all. Just as importantly, pigs are a valuable in which the investment of arduous human care and nurturance assured a continuing high value. Other items have entered the tee's ambit, and transactions have proliferated. But pigs remained the basis of the tee, known more properly as *mena tee*, "pig tee." A common complaint among tee-makers today is that the plethora of exchange items now circulating has shifted emphasis slightly from the quality of transactions (in pigs) to quantity (in other less valuable items) (see Kleinig 1955:8–9). Transactions in like items (in pigs here) reflect the equality of men and heighten relations between them. As freely accessible items, pigs remain a mere aspect of a valued partnership which includes much more.

The Enga tee (and perhaps much of the Enga area as well) has also been shielded from the most pernicious of colonial influences which distinctly altered other Highland societies and their exchange systems at an early date. The Melpa of Mount Hagen (and the moka system especially) were shattered by the introduction of large quantities of imported pearlshells by early colonial and mission personnel and then rapidly transformed by cash which, as Strathern has documented, took the place of pearlshells as a "stronger" valuable in Melpa eyes. It alone could be used in transactions with whites (Strathern 1982a).

In the precolonial setting, the moka and tee, so outwardly similar, appear to have differed in a fundamental premise of their exchange arrangements. In this way, they stand opposed as systems of ceremonial gift exchange. In the Melpa moka, the principle of "interest" (Strathern 1978) is its most striking feature, and indeed, this sets it apart from many other Highland exchange practices, most notably here, the Enga tee. Strathern considers this "principle of increment" to be an indigenous element of the system. Whether or not this is so, the moka's historic basis is less firmly centered on pigs than is the tee. Rather, pearlshells were always markers of inequality among men when pigs could not, for the reasons mentioned above, so serve. Pearlshells were a valuable of mystical foreign origin, not locally produced or subject to domestic production, and their scarcity was more firmly and easily controlled (Feil 1982).

My point of comparison here is that transactions in Melpa seem more prominent than the relations between men. Pearlshell inflation and the cash nexus, with ensuring anonymity and depersonalized transactions, have perhaps "fit" the indigenous moka pattern more than they ever could the tee. (This recalls Strathern's [1982b] earlier remark.) Money was never a part of the tee transactions I witnessed in the years between 1974–1980. Money belongs to a different sphere of activities much like gimwali. On the sole occasion when money was given in tee, it explicitly represented a pig that had died, the meat of which had been sold to outsiders at a patrol post market. The sum was passed on, as a valuable in itself, for it stood for a pig. It was given to the partner who was to have received the live pig. He duly passed the sum further on. It is, furthermore, virtually impossible to buy pigs in the Tombema area with cash, which is a further hedge on the inflation of tee valuables.

The Melpa moka, in the post-colonial period, has increasingly embraced money, but as a consequence, its status as a system of "gift exchange," as Mauss conceived the category, must surely be severely undermined. Money's many uses ensures that its standing as a moka valuable will be short-lived and eventually give way to its primary use, the purchase of commodities, and thereby so severely strain relations between givers and receivers that the system will crumble. Strathern (1982a:315) notes that "younger men frequently declare that they want to move out of moka altogether" and concentrate their efforts instead on making money in business. At this stage, gift exchange has given way to the kind of economy which Mauss found so lacking in social constraints and community process. The community control over the practice of exchange has been broken. The moral responsibilities of individuals are likely to be less evident than in former exchange contexts. Recent writings on the moka suggest this subtle change.

Thus, in the colonial and post-colonial periods, the moka has initially assimilated vast changes in its stride. These will be eventually too much for any "gift-exchange" system to incorporate. On the other hand, the tee has changed less significantly thus far. I would forecast its total demise as a system rather than the piecemeal incorporation of changes that the moka, beginning from different premises than tee, has managed up to now to weather.

In times past when the tee was suspended, it was substituted for in total terms (Feil 1983). During millenarian movements the whole system was done away with. Partnerships, pigs and the morality of tee dealings ceased; there were no slight alterations or modifications. When the Tombema do turn to business, and cash assumes a greater role in their lives, as increasingly it is doing, it will be at the expense of tee-making and the social trappings of partnerships that accompany it. Other choices will become available, and it is the critical element of choice in the formation of tee partnerships I will next explore as the basis for the morality of this exchange.

THE "HOLDERS OF THE WAY"

In his highly important and sensitive paper on morality among the Gahuku-Gama, Read wrote that "conduct which is moral is conduct which involves notions of duty and the ideal, of obligation and intrinsic desirability" (1955:254). The tee system, as I have briefly described it, embodies these values; it is a moral system. Reciprocity between friends, the duty to support and defend a tee ally, the obligations and trust which are shared by those who exchange are the highest ideals held by Tombema-Enga. Furthermore, the context in which these ideals are played out is a global one: a system recognized, however imperfectly, by individual Enga, that extends beyond local boundaries and narrow parochial interests. Thus the tee exchange system forms a community of interests beyond one's own. I have heard orators make just these points when suggesting that warfare and killings between rival local groups should cease. The tee belongs to everyone they say, and it is being blocked by our insular feud. "What will others say of our selfishness if we don't send the tee onward."

It has been pointed out that a person's most important exchange partners are members of other clans in areas far removed from the security of one's own, where a climate of hostility and suspicion exists. Although typically a man establishes exchange connections in these clans through affinal or matrilateral ties, there is nothing intrinsic in them which obliges exchange to proceed. If a person exchanges, he is a *kaita miningi*, a "holder of the way." If he does not, no connections will suffice to ensure such status. In other words, exchange partnerships have the critical element of choice in their formation and maintenance. This feature gives to these relationships a force beyond, even greater than, those predetermined by residence, kinship or common descent. A person's set of exchange partners in the tee system forms an unparalleled set of ties of his own making and of his own choice. A man freely seeks out other men as partners, and with the payment of a valuable counts them as friends, whose friendship grows to entail the important moral dimensions mentioned above. The tee is the significant institution in Enga where choice in relationships prevails. It is also the focus of society's highest moral ideals. Choice is a key factor in this Tombema morality.

That these relationships are special is symbolized foremost by the gift. The myriad social obligations, the protocol, the ceremonial trappings (Feil 1984) observed by men can only come about through acknowledgment of a relationship of exchange in the tee. With the choice of a relationship freely entered into, gift exchange becomes a "social contract," as many since Mauss have pointed out (for example, Sahlins 1972, Van Baal 1975). The heavy burdens on tee partners give these relationships high value; they are not fragile contracts. Other relationships in Tombema society are claustrophobic, ordinary and predetermined. Tee partnerships alone offer choice, and this especially sets them apart.

In the face of pressures which increasingly make gift exchange "irrational" in the logic of modern economics thinking, the Enga cling steadfastly to the tee, for nothing can replace it as a "total" institution. "The tee will only die when all men are dead," Tombema resolutely proclaim. In a way, they are right. When the gift exchange system of the tee is no more, as Mauss lamented, a new sort of man will be born.

Notes

1. Van Baal (for example, 1975:50) may wish to distinguish these types of communication as "trade" versus "real" gift exchange, but in many societies, such a distinction cannot be made so easily between them, or that "trade" is subsumed in gift exchange or carried out under its auspices.

2. This recalls a somewhat similar Melpa contrast between *noman* ("mind") and skin (visible resources). "No one can see into another's noman, only guess by his behaviour what his inclinations are ... do a person's words come from his noman and reveal his true intentions, or are they simply 'in the mouth?'" (A. M. Strathern 1979:250).

3. The tee traditionally operated on a 4–8 year cycle. Precise timing is a political fact and subject to innumerable delays and obstacles.

4. Warfare in many parts of the New Guinea Highlands, including the Enga Province, remains very much a reality today. After a period of *Pax Australiana*, old hostilities and enmities have re-emerged and heightened in intensity.

5. *Yanda tambungi*, literally the "fastening together of weapons" (of war), occurred when a tee neared and groups at war thought it prudent to make tee instead. Courageous individuals in the warring clans initiated yanda tambungi despite personal threats, by exchanging pigs that were precisely identical with each other, and challenging men in their own clans to try and do as well.

6. The Enga conceived the tee as a straight path along which pigs can easily find their way between linked partners. When the way is bent or crooked, pigs cannot so easily reach their destination, that is, find their proper courses and rightful recipient.

References

Elkins, A. P.
1953 Delayed Exchange in Wabag Sub-district, Central Highlands of New Guinea, with Notes on Social Organization. *Oceania* 23:162–201.

Feil, D. K.
1980 Symmetry and Complementarity: Patterns of Competition and Exchange in the Enga *Tee*. *Oceania* 51:20–39.

1982 From Pigs to Pearlshells: The Transformation of a New Guinea Highlands Exchange Economy. *American Ethnologist* 9:291–306.

1983 A World Without Exchange. *Anthropos* 78:89–106.

1984 *Ways of Exchange. The Enga* Tee *of Papua New Guinea*. St. Lucia: Queensland University Press.

Godelier, M.
1979 *Perspectives in Marxist Anthropology*. Cambridge: Cambridge University Press.

Kleinig, I. E.
1955 The Significance of the *Te* in Enga Culture. Unpublished manuscript.

Mauss, M.
1954 *The Gift*. (Translated by Ian Cunnison.) London: Cohen and West.

Read, K.
1955 Morality and the Concept of the Person Among the Gahuku-Gama. *Oceania* 25:234–282.

Sahlins, M.
1972 *Stone-Age Economics*. Chicago: Aldine.

Strathern, A. J.
1971 *The Rope of* Moka. Cambridge: Cambridge University Press.

1978 Finance and Production Revisited: In Pursuit of Comparison. *Research in Economic Anthropology* 1:73–104.

1979 Gender, Ideology and Money in Mount Hagen. *Man* 14:530–548.

1982a The Division of Labour and Processes of Social Change in Mount Hagen. *American Ethnologist* 9:307–319.

1982b Alienating the Inalienable (correspondence). *Man* 17:548–551.

Strathern, A. M.
1979 The Self in Self-Decoration. *Oceania* 49:241–257.

Van Baal, J.
1975 *Reciprocity and the Position of Women*. Amsterdam: Van Goraum.

Wirz, P.
1952 Quelques notes sur la ceremonie du Moka chez les tribes du Mount Hagen et du Wabaga sub-district, Nouvelle-Guinee du Nordest. *Bulletin de la societe Royale Belge d'anthropologie et de prehistorie* 63:65–71.

PART III

Filial Ambivalence and the Moral Order in Choice Behavior

5

Like Father, Like Son: Filial Ambivalence and the Death of Fathers in Kalauna

Michael W. Young

There needs no ghost, my lord, come from the grave
To tell us this.

—*HAMLET*, act I, sc. V.

Fathers, declared James Joyce (having written three great books to come to terms with his own), are a necessary evil. Since human societies vary greatly in the role they ascribe to fathers, this sad dictum may not always ring true, though it is certainly the case that no known human culture has managed without fatherhood altogether. The "principle of legitimacy"—the rule of indispensable social fatherhood—Malinowski declared to be a cultural universal (1930). While for Freud (1955), ambivalence, "the simultaneous existence of love and hate towards the same object," is as old as the reputed killing and eating of the primal father.

In a reasoned critique of *Totem and Taboo*, Derek Freeman demonstrated how, in the light of more recent ethological and anthropological evidence, Freud's ambitious and comprehensive theory requires substantial modification. On the particular issue of ambivalence, for example, Freeman suggests that the phylogenetic basis of the "jealous death wishes" that characterize the Oedipus complex "lies in the phenomena of rivalry, contention, and dominance which are intrinsic to the behaviour of most animals" (1969:6–7). He is careful to point out that "where there is marked variation in the structure of the family from one society to another, we may expect to find marked variations in the form of the Oedipus complex" (1969:78).

In 1973, Freeman addressed the problem of ambivalence from a different standpoint in his festschrift essay for Meyer Fortes. "The axiom of amity" or "the rule of prescriptive altruism," in Fortes's view, is intrinsic to all relations of kinship; but, as he observes, "many ties of close kinship ... subsume rivalries and latent hostilities that are as intrinsically built into the relationships as are the externally oriented amity and solidarity they present" (Fortes 1969:237, cited in Freeman 1973:115).[1] Adducing evidence on attachment behavior and the nature of the primary bond between mother and child, Freeman demonstrates how the latter "is always characterized by ambivalence," and suggests that it "tends to be transferred, in some degree, to all of the subsequent relationships into which an individual enters, and that, on this basis, each new relationship comes to develop, in the course of further interaction, its own ambivalent character." From this ontogenetic point of view, "one of the functions of 'the rule of amity' among kinsfolk is the containing of ambivalence within manageable bounds," and "only by actively valuing amity" Freeman concludes, "are we humans able to live together like good kinsmen" (1973:116–117).

The values of kinship, however, are by no means always compatible with the other value systems of a given society, and it is not uncommon to find them in conflict, such that ambivalence between kinsfolk is exacerbated. Father–son ambivalence is likely to be most problematic in those societies where sons succeed fathers, and fraternal ambivalence most in evidence where brothers compete for the same inheritance. In short, it is in societies with strong ideologies (beliefs and values) of patrilineal descent and succession that ambivalence between fathers and sons might be expected to flourish. In an early formulation of this viewpoint, Malinowski wrote:

> The father sees in the son his successor, the one who is to replace him in the family lineage and household. He becomes therefore all the more critical, and this influences his feelings in two directions: if the boy shows signs of mental or physical deficiency, if he is not up to the type of the ideal in which the father believes, he will be a source of bitter disappointment and hostility. On the other hand, even at this [early] stage, a certain amount of rivalry, the resentment of future supercession, and the melancholy of waning generation lead again to hostility. Repressed in both cases, this hostility hardens the father against the son and provokes by reaction a response in hostile feelings [1927:37–38].

Malinowski drew this picture to represent "patriarchal Europe" in order to contrast it with the situation in "matrilineal Melanesia," of which he took the Trobriand Islands to be typical. Even so, his formulation will serve to characterize "patriarchal" Kalauna, a community on eastern Goodenough Island, Papua, less than one hundred miles southwest of Trobriands. My intention in this essay is to indicate the social and cultural conditioning of father–son ambivalence in Kalauna, and to present two case studies which focus on the responses of two men to their fathers' deaths. The death of a father, Freud avowed, is "the most important event, the most poignant loss, of a man's life" (Freud 1953:xxvi). One might surmise, too, that it is an occasion for the most dramatic and revealing expression of filial ambivalence.

In Kalauna, patrilineal descent confers the most important attributes of social identity.[2] Through his or her father, a person gains membership of a particular patrilineage identified with a stone sitting platform within a particular hamlet, which is itself associated with a particular clan. Through his or her father, a person acquires the right to use or be identified by distinctive "customs" (names, taboos, decorations, songs, dances, and the like) common to the patrilineage or clan. Land, fruit trees and traditional values are also inherited patrilineally. An eldest son succeeds to his father's exchange partnerships and to his other political statuses; moreover, he inherits his father's debts and credits in pigs and food-wealth. Ideally, it is the eldest son who inherits his father's ritual property: his garden magic, sorcery, and other magical knowledge.

Residence is strongly patrivirilocal. Sons, Kalauna people say, are like "house posts" who stay to anchor the hamlet; daughters are "bouncing coconuts" who leave their fathers and brothers to marry into other hamlets. Men give this as a reason for wanting sons rather than daughters: "sons replace us, daughters do not." Clans—and therefore hamlets—are exogamous, but most marriages (86% in 1967) are between partners from within the village. Matrilateral kinship produces a web of cognatic ties, and there are few people in Kalauna who cannot trace a real or putative kinship link to everyone else in the community. Nevertheless, the formal structure of the village is based on the agnatic groups (clans, subclans, patrilineages) which constitute the local residence units, and it is to these that men owe primary allegiance. Clan hamlets are paired in food-exchanging partnerships and there are also countervailing ties of "traditional enemy" relationships between certain clans, such that the acephalous political organization of Kalauna entails a complex balance of forces. Food prestations (of yams, taro, and pigs) between groups provide the main idiom of contention and dispute. To give more than one receives is not only a matter of pride but a tacit claim to superiority, and however ephemeral it may be, such status betokens a moral ascendancy. As Marcel Mauss puts it, the giver is *magister* (1966:72).

Consequently, leadership in Kalauna is predominantly concerned with the production and management of food resources. Nominal clan or hamlet leaders are genealogically defined elders: senior male members of senior lineages by the rule of primogeniture. But such men may defer to more energetic "big men" within their groups who become locally renowned for their gardening prowess, their management skills, and their oratorical ability. There is yet another basis for leadership which, while not exclusive of the others, is ideologically the most important: ownership of the magical systems of prosperity and famine. These systems of ritual knowledge are traditionally the prerogative of a single clan, Lulauvile. Numerically and politically the dominant clan, Lulauvile might be said to enjoy "submerged rank," for the egalitarian ethos of Kalauna only grudgingly admits its pre-eminence. Accordingly, the elders of Lulauvile—a handful of men who have inherited the awesome magic of prosperity— are *toitavealata*, "guardians." They are the most respected—and feared— authority figures in the community, for ultimately it is upon them, so people believe, that everyone's livelihood depends.

The idiom of kinship in Kalauna is one of nurture by "feeding." A father must establish his full claim to paternity by feeding his wife during her pregnancy and while she is suckling their child. It is the food grown on his own land by his own efforts that is said to make the child's "bones strong." This is a fundamental principle of the ideology of agnatic descent, and the growth toward and eventual achievement of adulthood is likewise conceived as the tangible result of food-provisioning or fostering by fathers, whether real or classificatory. To say of someone, "He fed me," is to admit a binding and lifelong obligation to that person. One may suppose that this realm of food symbolism is so basic, so close to infantile oral concerns that it facilitates expressions of ambivalence. Instead of deflecting or disguising oral discontents, the idiom sharply focuses them and centers, as it were, the growing child's anxieties and ambitions in his belly.

Let us consider briefly the passionate emotional investment men make in their yams. Subsistence in Kalauna is based on the production of yams, taro, bananas, and sweet potato, but it is the yam gardening cycle that dominates the year and requires the greatest expenditure of labor. As among neighboring Dobuans (Fortune 1963), yams are believed to be quasi-human and sentient, animated by spirits under the magical control of master gardeners. Yam cultivation provides a man with the competitive means of achieving distinction, a personal renown that will long outlive him if his name is appended to the lists of illustrious yam growers chanted in gardening spells. Fame and the assurance of nominal immortality are the rewards of the successful; but for all Kalauna men, the quest conduces an identification with the objects of their endeavors. As among the Ilahita Arapesh (Tuzin 1972), yams are not only conscious symbols of male pride and preconscious symbols of the bodies of their growers, but possibly also unconscious symbols of the phallus. Hence, probably, the notion that debilitating sexual activity has adverse effects upon a man's competence as a yam grower. Conversely, successful yam cultivation is held to be evidence of sexual restraint, if not of celibacy. Competitive yam exchanges (*abutu*) to settle disputes arising from adultery are predicated wholly upon the supposed incompatibility between yam growing and philandering (Young 1971:212, 1987).

Having been taught from infancy that his father's biggest and best yams are not to be eaten, that they are "poisoned" by magic and hoarded for the day when they can be aggressively exchanged in abutu, a son eventually learns the rudiments of yam growing from his father, from whom he also receives his own seeds. Yams have their own lines of descent, so an inheritance lost or squandered—by eating the seed yams, for example—is not easily replaced. As a young man intensifies his gardening activities, he strives to produce the large yams (*dioscorea alata*) that will ineluctably draw him into the political arena of the village. As he does so, however, his father's efforts are likely to be waning. The rise of the son who wishes to succeed, and the decline of the father who resents being superseded, inevitably creates friction between them. During public food distributions, a vindictive device for provoking discord is to call the name of the son to receive his father's share: "You have already replaced your father ... We rely on *you* to repay us." While the father and head of the family may accept such jibes with a show of good grace, he is likely to be smarting at the public announcement of his failing powers. The father may withhold the transmission of his garden magic, suspecting that only this now stands between the deference and negligence of his son. Old men without knowledge to confer are often pathetic and solitary, neglected by their grown sons. In such cases recriminations rebound, charged by the hurtful idiom of "feeding": the aged father accuses the son of starving him, to which the son retorts that he is paying back for being poorly fed as a child. It does not always come to this, of course, and filial obligations more usually prevail; but the values that inhere in "feeding" permit the expression of grievances in this way.

A Kalauna folktale dramatizes this double bind in the father–son relationship:

> An orphan is gathering shellfish on the beach when a giant bird snatches him up and carries him to its nest. "O grandfather, perhaps you are going to eat me!" cries the boy. "No grandson," replies the bird, "I am going to feed you." And he flies hither and thither catching fish and fetching vegetable food for the boy. The child grows up, and one day he sees from the nest some children

playing in the distance. When the bird has gone in search of food for him the boy climbs down the tree and joins the children in their play. He does this day after day, sending the bird further and further afield for more and more exotic foods, until eventually he goes with the children to their village and does not return to the nest. The bird laments his loss. One day the boy is playing on the beach and the bird swoops down to him. He reproaches the boy bitterly for his ingratitude in tricking and abandoning him. He instructs the boy to build a pile of sticks and set fire to it. When he has done so the bird leaps into the flames and immolates himself. "I am resentful (*unuwewe*)!" he cries. "You did not love me after all I did for you, and you ran away." The bird dies and the youth mourns him.

In this sad tale the provider is patently a father figure. Thematically, the story is an inversion of a much longer and better known Goodenough myth in which two youthful brothers, abandoned by their father, hunt down and slay a giant "cannibal" bird who is terrorizing the island.[3] Whereas in this myth the "sons" vengefully slay the "bad father," in the above story the "good father" resentfully kills himself to punish the "son" with remorse. The two acts are facets of the same father-killing fantasy, however, and would appear to articulate the anxieties of both sons and fathers.

Father–son ambivalence, then, is pervasive in Kalauna society and more or less consciously acknowledged. Fraternal strife is also common, and brothers are prone to quarrel over their patrimonial inheritance: land, fruit trees, house sites, seed yams, valuables, and not least, magic.[4] As for the community authority figures (exemplified by the ritual "guardians" of the crops) one of their principal burdens is to endure people's animosity whenever misfortune befalls the village. Such leaders are colloquially "fathers," and they are frequently cast as scapegoats when there is drought, deluge, crop infestations, or other conditions of failed prosperity. Their response to such scapegoating is, as I have shown elsewhere (Young 1983), typically that of their mythical heroes. They threaten to abandon their "children" in resentment, and to punish them further with crop or weather sorcery. In this cultural scenario the community is brought to its knees in real or imagined hunger and begs the forgiveness of the "fathers," who then relent and attempt to make things right. The idiom of this scenario is thoroughly consistent in its oral mode. It is believed that the most terrible punishment of the "fathers" is to inflict *tufo'a*: an insatiable mass appetite and unrestrained greed that compels people to consume their own food reserves until famine forces them to exchange and cannibalize their children. A chilling fantasy indeed of social suicide and stilled time.

Although it has been to my purpose to sketch the wider "Oedipal" configuration of Kalauna culture in order to indicate how far-reaching is the theme of father–son ambivalence and how pervasive is the idiom of their contention in terms of nurture given and nurture denied, it is with the behavior—observed and reported—of particular fathers and sons that I am mainly concerned in this essay. Given that the father–son relationship in Kalauna receives particular cultural emphasis (one can regard it as the privileged genealogical dyad in any patrilineal society), then it can be supposed that the deaths of fathers are of profound significance for their sons, events both personally traumatic and socially consequential. Accordingly, the manner and timing of a father's death, his personal relationship with his son, the political or extra-familial circumstances of the status changes it entails—all might combine to precipitate a unique crisis in the son's own life. In short, his response to his father's death should reveal much about their relationship, both social and psychic, that is normally hidden or disguised.

It is a truism that death provokes grief which is "worked through" in customary mourning practices. Typically for the Kalauna man whose father has died, this is done in the following way. An eldest son generally takes on the role of "manager" of the funeral arrangements. He selects the gravediggers (*toifa'abi*, "the holders of the digging stick"), decides the immediate distribution of wealth to the mourners who attend the burial, and plans the subsequent—and often quite complex—mortuary and memorial feasts which are held during the ensuing year. Up to a dozen men and women perform the burial services: digging the grave, laying out the body on the stone sitting platform, wrapping and placing the corpse in the grave, building a rude shelter over it, and keeping alive a fire on the grave for three days and nights. The son's task is to supervise all of this—including the washing ceremony that follows the burial—and ensure that the members of the burial group are paid in food, wealth, and sometimes plots of land, for their "polluting" work. He must also organize the distribution of pigs, cash, and wealth objects which other mourners— usually maternal kinsmen and affines—come to ask for "in memory" of the dead man. The son feeds the mourners and members of the burial group with food from his own or his father's gardens, though he is forbidden by strict taboo to eat any of this himself. For a year the products of his own and his father's gardens are forbidden to him. To subsist, he is obliged to exchange some of this food for produce from others' gardens, but much of it he conserves to disburse at the mortuary distributions and memorial feasts. We note, then, that the son is obligated by convention to expend some of his patrimony and to adopt an abstemious regimen by denying himself the food of his patrimonial land.

If his father was a man of status—a big man—or if the son himself has aspirations to become one, he will commemorate his father's name after a year or so by staging a spectacular feast at which the whole community eats. The son, aided by his clansmen, is responsible for the funding and organization of this feast, and if it is a success (judged by the amount of food disbursed and the number of guests from other villages) people will say of him: "Truly, he has succeeded his father." On the same occasion he will destroy some personal belonging of his father (a knife, a pipe, a betel chewing gourd or spatula), a memento he will have cherished over the year as a reminder of his task and a spur to his ambition. The burning of this object signalizes the end of the mourning period, the fulfillment of all obligations to his father's memory, and his final release from mourning taboos. Henceforth he can enjoy the fruits of his patrimonial land.

Following this summary account of the customary role of a Kalauna man in managing his father's death, I now present my two case studies. The materials for each case were gathered over the fourteen-year-period (1966–1980) of my intermittent fieldwork in Kalauna. I was privileged to know the fathers (Iyahalina and Didiala) before their deaths, but I have come to know the sons (Adiyaleyale and Keyayala) much better. Each case is based on personal observation and testimonies of the principals.[5]

Adiyaleyale, a man of some thirty-five years when he recounted the following in 1977, was the second son of six children of Iyahalina. In middle age, Iyahalina had inherited magical systems that gave him a responsible position of leadership in Kalauna as one of the three "guardians" of the crops, and when I knew him in 1966–1968, he was a dignified and respected elder. His wife had died several years before. Iyahalina's eldest son, Bunaleya, was a somewhat retiring and diffident man with little inclination to learn the ritual duties his father performed. Rather, he embraced the Catholic Church and became a local parish leader, a role which earned him some respect yet enabled him to avoid becoming embroiled in village politics. His brother, Adiyaleyale (with whom he had quarrelled bitterly on a number of occasions), was a more forceful and ambitious personality. Highly intelligent, querulous and questing, he was a traditional big man in the making.

In 1973, two years after Iyahalina's death, Adiyaleyale told me a great deal about his relationship with his father and there could be no mistaking the love, respect, and admiration he felt for him. He had wept and fasted for three days when Iyahalina died, behavior that is by no means expected of a bereaved son. But he also admitted to an early hatred of him, and in his view, Iyahalina was a harsh and authoritarian parent.

When I was small he was always beating me and refusing me food. Once when I came home late from school he said: "Why does Bunaleya always arrive first? No food for you tonight!" And he told me to sit on the stone sitting platform. I sat there waiting, getting hungry and expecting him to call me inside the house. But I waited for two hours and he still didn't call me, so I began to cry. I said: "You are treating me like someone else's son, as if I did not come from my mother's womb." He got very angry and took a rope and tied me under the house. I stayed there until morning, just like a dog. He did this to me many times, not just once. Sometimes he tied me upside down, sometimes by the arm, sometimes by the leg. Everyone in Kalauna knew what a cruel father he was.

When in his teens, Adeyaleyale seized an opportunity to run away and join a newly established Catholic school in the north of the island. A Methodist by conversion, Iyahalina was incensed and dispatched Bunaleya to retrieve him. But Bunaleya took his brother's side ("You did not treat him properly, that's why he ran away") and later went to a Catholic school himself. Adiyaleyale harbored many other bitter memories of his father ("I wanted to pay him back for what he'd done to me"), but in his maturity he learned to forgive him ("When my mother died I felt sorry for him"). By the time of my own first visit to Kalauna, Adiyaleyale seemed to trust and confide in his father, and took a genuine pride in his father's incomparable understanding of Kalauna lore and custom. When Iyahalina remarried in 1969, Adiyaleyale was deeply touched at the way his father approached him, half-apologetically, to seek his approval.

Tragically, Adiyaleyale came to suspect his father's new wife of complicity in his death.

One day my father had no tobacco and he asked his wife. "Yes," she said, "I have a piece." And she gave him some that K. had prepared [i.e. doctored with sorcery]. When my father had smoked part of the cigarette, she took it back and gave it secretly to her brother ... My father was sick for three months. He guessed the cause of his suffering for he told us a Bible story. "Do you remember Samson?" he asked. "He was a very strong man. His enemies wanted to kill him but they couldn't find the secret of his strength. So they sent their sister to marry him, and she discovered the source of his power. She weakened him so that her brothers could kill him. That is why I am dying of the sickness now." Early one morning I awoke and heard my father calling me from his bed. My stepmother had brought a piece of ginger from her brother and put it between his lips. He had chewed a little then slept. Then he called out to me: "Look quickly! See that dog ... It came to bite me. I'm going to leave you this afternoon. I want you to go to Yaueda and clear the coconut plantation there, and when you return I shall be ready to die." I went to Yaueda with my wife. I was working when a black *buluwoi* bird alighted on a branch above my head. I threw a stone and it flew away. Then it cried and wheeled back again to the same tree. "Your father-in-law is dead," I said to my wife. "The dog bit him and took his spirit away, and now that bird has come to tell me his life had ended."

Adiyaleyale hurried to his father's house, but arrived too late to hear his last words ("His breath lingered, but his spirit had gone"). Next day he took charge of the burial arrangements (Bunaleya was abroad), and that night was visited—like Hamlet—by his father's spirit.

He had always told me: "Don't search for sorcerers. I will show you after you plant me in the grave." We had placed thorny branches over the grave to protect it. I was sleeping on my house step with my back to the doorpost when it seemed to burn me. It was my father's spirit. I stood up and looked at the grave. I could hear leaves rustling. I went down and saw that my father had moved the thorny branches to form a circle around his grave. It was like a fence, the shape of a widow's fence. [A bereaved widow dwells, for a matter of weeks nowadays but traditionally for much longer, under her brother's house in a space enclosed by a wall, or "fence," of woven coconut leaves.] A few days later I had to go to the patrol post for a local government council meeting [at this time Adiyaleyale was Kalauna's councillor], and there at the market I saw my father's widow with a hibiscus flower in her hair [i.e. flaunting herself when she should have worn the signs of mourning]. I boiled inside. I went to the government office and spoke to the district officer. "Can I kill the woman who killed my father?" "No," he said, . . . I returned to Kalauna, still angry. I got my bush knife and fishing spear. My younger brothers carried a spear and stones. I confronted that woman. "O my son . . ." she said. "I am not your son!" I shouted. "You killed my father with your brother's tricks. I saw that spirit dog. I saw my father's message from the grave, the circle of your widow's fence. And I saw your disrespect for him . . ." I was about to kill her, truly. But my brothers held me back, so I simply broke part of her house. . .

Adiyaleyale exploits a number of dramatic narrative conventions: the search for a scapegoat; the final dialogue with the deceased; the omens of death; the symbolic message from the grave; the rhetorical demand for vengeance. But there is a ring of authenticity in the bathos of his displaced aggression. Instead of assaulting his "mother," he "simply broke part of her house."

The real object of Adiyaleyale's vengeance, however, was his father's rival clansman, the notorious sorcerer K., toward whom Adiyaleyale had borne for many years an implacable hostility. In the months following his father's death, Adiyaleyale, acting with the presumed legal sanction of a local official, went on a veritable rampage through the village, denouncing K. and two other suspected sorcerers, ransacking their houses for "evidence" of their crimes, forcing them to eat the suspicious contents of their baskets, threatening them with exile or imprisonment, and finally marching them down to the government office to have them charged. Faced by a skeptical Australian magistrate, however, Adiyaleyale lost his nerve in pressing the charges and the three sorcerers were dismissed with a warning. Back in the village he somehow survived their enmity and with the help of his brothers managed to stage a fitting memorial festival for Iyahalina. By 1977 he had come to uneasy terms with the men he had persecuted; but having lost office as councillor he felt it prudent to remove himself and his household (including two wives and three children) and set up in an isolated and independent hamlet on his garden land.

Keyayala was the first born son of Didiala, another of the ritual leaders of Kalauna. A great man by local standards, Didiala was a master gardener as well as a respected "guardian" of the crops and a feared sorcerer of the sun. Like Iyahalina, he had had six children and was a stern and dominating father. In 1967, when I got to know him well, Didiala was in his late sixties, dim-sighted, lame, but still forceful in manner. Although he claimed to have "retired" from the leadership of his hamlet Anuana, this was in fact far from being the case, and he played a prominent advisory role in village affairs until his death in early 1970.

The following extracts from an autobiographical narrative I recorded from him reveal the degree to which, risking hubris, he boasted of his achievements and denigrated the abilities of his sons. One is tempted to observe that with a father like this, his sons need no enemies.

> When I was young I stood up and made abutu [competitive food exchange]. I orated powerfully and my [abutu] were amazing. People made huge prestations to me. I killed pigs and repaid them, and people were happy ... I, Didiala, was like that. But today I am old, as you see, and I have passed these ways to my children. They have taken my place and rule the hamlet, for now I am quiet and stay still ... My house is small like a child's. I have no valuables. I feed no pigs. I plant no yams ... But before my gardens were amazing ... I used to wear croton leaves and hornbill feathers for abutu challenges. I filled my big wooden dish with food so heavy that women tried to lift it in vain. They fingered the big yam which rested inside and said: "Oh, feel the size of this!" There was nothing

I did not do. I attempted and accomplished everything. Tongues wagged about me. People saw my hands, my gardener's hands, and the many gardens they made ... They swore at me because of my gardens and my wicked strength; they cursed my ability to hoard. But now I am old and have put aside many things. Some of them my children have pursued, but others they have neglected. Some of my children are weak, their work incomplete, their authority feeble. No matter; they can try. But now I am retired. I am short of energy and empty handed. My face is the face of no-one-in-particular ... Now I am a bald man. I am retired and my skills remain unused. I say now, "If you children are strong you will compete with one another." They may yet grow strong, but not as strong as I was. I was just one man, but my hands were too much for the others....

Didiala's sons were humble, unassertive men, very much in their father's shadow when it came to public demonstrations of leadership. In 1973, nearly four years after Didiala's death, I found Keyayala the nominal leader of his hamlet; finally, it seemed, he had taken his father's place. But there was something amiss. He bemoaned the "bad times" that had stricken Kalauna since Didiala had died (there had indeed been a serious drought early that year). He complained that someone was spoiling his yam garden with sorcery and that he could not find the wherewithal to make a memorial feast for his father. In 1977, when next I returned to Kalauna, Keyayala, now a widower, was the only man of his patrilineage to remain in the village; the others, including his real brothers, had founded a new hamlet on the grassy slopes below it. In that year, too, Keyayala lacked even a yam garden. He seemed a pathetic figure, prematurely stooped and balding, sad, wistful, and bitter in the belief that his enemies had withered his yams with magic. He was as far as ever from staging the memorial feast that was Didiala's due. His reason for staying in the virtually abandoned hamlet of Anuana was pure piety: "My father is buried here," he said, "and here I shall be buried." He devoted unusual attention to the grave in front of his house, a grave remarkable—considering that nearly eight years had elapsed since the old man's death—for its neat stone edging and colorful crotons. Most graves in Kalauna are neglected within the year and become indistinguishable from the bare, swept earth of the village. In short, it was as if Keyayala could not fully accept the fact of his father's death.

Predictably perhaps, Keyayala eulogized his father when I asked him to talk to me about him. He spoke of nothing but Didiala's grand provisioning exercises as a "guardian" of the crops and "feeder of the people" ("During his life there were good times and bad, but all lived well because he ensured there was enough of everything—food, pigs, fish"). When I prompted him to tell me about his father's death, he delivered an impromptu elegy, full of simple pathos, about how the old man had been ensorcelled while supervising the pig platform of a grand festival. "I knew my father," he concluded; "A real man. A leader of men. His death occurred, and now you can see how bad things are with us."

When I next visited Kalauna in June 1980, Keyayala was housebound with swollen legs and feet. A medical doctor who visited the village examined him at my request and diagnosed septic arthritis or, less likely, tuberculosis of the ankle joints, though he admitted puzzlement at the symmetrical affliction of both legs. He advised that Keyayala be carried down to the small hospital on the coast, admitted, and treated with aspirin. This was duly done, but for the weeks I remained in Kalauna he showed no improvement.

There was no dearth of explanations for Keyayala's affliction; indeed, in the Kalauna view it was heavily overdetermined. Unlike the scientific medical opinion of my Western colleague, however, the diagnoses of various village experts were rich in moral implications. Keyayala himself (perhaps hopefully) suspected he was the victim of *edaboda*, a bespelled stick placed upon the road by an unknown sorcerer. Alternatively, the swelling of his legs was a gathering of poisonous criticism, *talafou*, directed against him by malcontents in the village who deplored his failure to perform coconut-prospering magic for their copra-making enterprises, or by other malcontents among his clansmen who were impatient for him to stage his father's memorial feast (now nine years overdue). Still other explanations for his sickness concerned his supposed ineptness at performing the ritual duties bequeathed by Didiala: he had broken a taboo by lighting a fire with the wrong wood; he had used the wrong leaf in taro-prospering magic; he had made a grievous error in the magic of "stopping the sun," a rite that accompanies the yam-growing cycle. All of these explanations were offered with persuasive symbolisms as "evidence," such that, for example, the bedsheet with which he covered himself and incessantly agitated represented the wrong leaf "covering" the taro; or the stone on which he rested his swollen feet represented the stone he had improperly deployed in the magic of the sun. In short, there were so many possible causes of Keyayala's affliction that there could be no consensus among his kinsmen concerning whom to blame. "Who is doing this to me?" he lamented from his hospital bed.

But so many suspected that he was in some way to blame for his own misfortune that they avoided visiting him. The unspoken common denominator of their divergent diagnoses was that his sickness was due to a failure of leadership; a failure, that is, when measured against the supreme competence and outstanding accomplishments of his father. It is especially interesting that Keyayala's affliction entailed his immobiliza-tion. As Michael Jackson (1979) has shown, an inability to walk is a common if not natural symbol for prevented or delayed succession. Key-ayala's excessive filial piety and prolonged post-mortem identification with his powerful father are aptly expressed in the physical imagery of his useless legs. It is quite possible, therefore, that his affliction was psycho-somatic and self-induced. Unable fully to succeed his father, Keyayala wanted to regress to the "good times" of his father's protection and pro-visioning, and much of his behavior can be interpreted as an unconscious desire to annul if not reverse time. As Jackson has also suggested, there is a real and metaphorical connection between physical immobilization and social discontinuity (Jackson 1979:125–126).

It was a cruel irony indeed, then, that Keyayala, in late June of 1980, should suffer the worse conceivable loss: the death of his eldest son and heir. There is a Kalauna saying, *leuwa uwana leuwa* (literally, "banana sucker banana"), meaning "like father, like son." Another conventional image likens the bananas at the top of a bunch to fathers, and those at the bottom to sons; it is the top ones which should be plucked and eaten first, while those below are still ripening. Likewise, fathers should die before sons and it is a terrible tragedy for a father when this natural order is reverse. Apart from the personal grief involved, there is an interrupted succession, an "arrest of the progress of tie" (in Jackson's phrase) and hence social discontinuity.

It was, therefore, a dire event for all Kalauna when Keyayala's 21-year-old son, a prison warder in Wewak on the far side of New Guinea, was reported killed in a car accident. The villagers were dismayed and immediately feared for their crops. Keyayala's kinsmen carried him back to the village to await the return of his son's body. As an honorary member of his clan, I was permitted to attend a secret caucus of senior men at which they discussed, in prolix and veiled speech, the "punishment" they should or should not inflict upon Kalauna. Fearing for their children, most men were against taking vengeance; but Keyayala, numb and vindictive, advised that "something should happen." Bunaleya protested that it was unchristian to seek to punish the village thus for their loss; "It is God's work to do so, not ours." But Keyayala replied by alluding to Joseph's Biblical dream of seven fat cows and seven lean cows. They were all thinking of famine.

The days of waiting for the coffin to be flown from Wewak were electric with suspense. Men weighed down the roofs of their houses with heavy branches in expectation of hurricane winds. Portents were seen and heard. When the sealed coffin finally arrived, Kalauna people were terrified Keyayala would open it and vent his grief and anger by bespelling his son's corpse with sorcery of the sun. Didiala, too, people remember, had conjured a drought by the same means in 1943 following the death of his first-born daughter. Like father, like son. But the coffin remained sealed and, not without further dire omens, it was duly buried. People hung well back from the stone platform on which the coffin was laid for mourners to weep over; few dared approach while Keyayala prostrated himself on it. The members of the burial group, more agitated than I had ever seen them before, were alarmed to hear a knocking from inside the coffin as they lowered it into the grave. "It was not the boy's spirit trying to get out," one of them said to me later. "It was the knocking of hunger—like the bumping of an empty stomach." From this they deduced that, while he wept over it, Keyayala had bespelled the coffin with *tufo'a*, the dread sorcery of insatiable hunger. When I left Kalauna that same evening, people were convinced they were in for a difficult time.

The "death of fathers," Claudius reminds an inconsolable Hamlet, is nature's "common theme," and his mother the queen admonishes him: "Why seems it so particular with thee?" (Act I, sc. ii). Why, indeed, was it "so particular" with Adiyaleyale and Keyayala? Without presuming to understand the unconscious motivations of these men, I cannot resist one or two observations on their responses to their fathers' deaths, responses far in excess of—as Claudius puts it—"filial obligation for some term/To do obsequious sorrow."

Adiyaleyale's towering anger was directed toward those he believed responsible for Iyahalina's death. Whether such anger—fully characteristic of the earlier phases of mourning—attempts to recover the lost object, as Bowlby (1961) has argued, it was manifestly retaliatory in seeking to punish those Adiyaleyale believed has caused his loss. It is not uncommon in Kalauna for accusations of sorcery to be made following a death. Usually, however, such allegations are made covertly, and no public action is taken by the bereaved. In publicly prosecuting his scapegoats then, Adiyaleyale's behavior was highly unconventional and foolhardy. At great risk to his personal safety, he took a course that had the community breathless with suspense. While his official standing as councillor enabled him to gloss his persecution as a public-spirited attempt to root out evil, no one was under any illusion that his real motive was any other than to avenge his father. That the objects of anger were possibly innocent victims would not have occurred to him, so convinced was he of their culpability. Nor was he deterred by the certain knowledge that one day, having lost the protection of his "office," he would be persecuted in return. His act, therefore, although fuelled by impulsive anger, was one of considerable moral courage. Subsequently, while living under the threat of revenge of those he had humiliated, he never regretted what he had done, but remained proud (if somewhat surprised) at the audacity of the moral stand he had taken.

Adiyaleyale's ambivalence towards his father gives some clue to his extreme course of action. The three men he persecuted were all in the relationship of classificatory father to him. Being a fellow clansman, K. was the closest and bore the brunt of Adiyaleyale's enmity. Not only did he suspect K. of ensorcelling his father, but he was also convinced that K. had been responsible for his (Adiyaleyale's) wife's stillbirth several years before. In Adiyaleyale's mind, K. stood convicted of denying him a child; it was another instance of interrupted succession.[6] On that occasion, Adiyaleyale took no action (his suspicion that K. was to blame hardened slowly), but when his father died and his grief turned to anger, and after he had sought and found symbolic circumstantial "evidence" of K.'s guilt, Adiyaleyale's projective blame was unsullied by rational doubt. K. was the hated "bad father" upon whom the son could vent his righteous fury, while the beloved "good father," lyahalina, lay mourned in his grave. (Analogously, perhaps K.'s sister was the "bad mother," but I have too little information on Adiyaleyale's relationship with his real mother, long since dead, to substantiate this interpretation—despite Adiyaleyale's fierce rejection of his stepmother. It is interesting, however, that in Adiyaleyale's account of his father's death—as in Hamlet's first soliloquy—it is not the loss of his father he laments so much as the perfidy of his "mother.")

Keyayala's response to his father's death took quite a different, though equally extreme, course. His excessive filial piety and marked reluctance to succeed his father betokened a chronic melancholia. In his classic paper on "Mourning and Melancholia," Freud observed that this condition of profound dejection is characterized in particular by low self-regard and "a delusional expectation of punishment" (1957:244).[7] Keyayala's persistent bemoaning of "the bad times," his failed yam crop and impotent magic, the death of his wife, his brothers' abandonment of the hamlet, and finally the affliction that immobilized him, were like the self-fulfilling expectations of a melancholic. Keyayala seems to fit Freud's clinical picture in which the low self-evaluation of an "impoverished ego" is a disguised reproach against another—the object being mourned. If Keyayala ever reproached his father, he could not now admit it; his "mental constellation of revolt ... passed over into the crushed state of melancholia" (Freud 1957:248). The conflict of his ambivalence, it seems likely, led Keyayala to prolong his mourning for the heroically powerful father he could neither criticize nor supersede, and induced him instead to punish himself for his unworthy hostile feelings. In the circumstances of Didiala's death, Keyayala might well have secretly believed himself to have been responsible. His father was an old man and ostensibly retired, yet he died performing a dangerous ritual task—the anchoring of a pig platform for the climax of a festival. This was a task his mature son should have been ready to undertake as his successor.

Characteristically, Keyayala took no retaliatory action when his father died. He turned his anger upon himself with the result we have seen. It took the death of his first-born son (ironically, a "good provider" like his grandfather and one whose death must have seemed the most terrible punishment Keyayala could conceive) to make him assert himself in a way commensurate with community expectations. When he demanded, quietly but firmly, that "something must happen," he was, given the terms of Kalauna belief, acting positively, with the awesome privilege of a bereaved father. Whether Christian scruples checked him and he refrained from using the sorcery in his power, we do not know. To the extent that sorcery is a projective system of belief and an imaginary force it does not work directly upon the world, but only through the psyches and dispositions of actors in the system of social relationships. But it is significant that Kalauna people, in their acute apprehension, cast Keyayala in the role of a right-eously avenging father—in the same role, in fact, that his own father had assumed more than forty years earlier in response to an identical loss.

A more general problem is indicated here. We can understand how bereaved men seek vengeance (whether by violent or magical means) by attacking a scapegoat, but how are we to understand their retaliation against the collectivity of which they are a part? Why does the community acknowledge this resentful, even masochistic, course of action as a con-ventional, a "moral" response to death, though it flies in the face of the "axiom of amity"? Kalauna people otherwise relatively unaffected by the death of another's father or son *expect* to be made to suffer, to be pun-ished, moreover, in a way that affects their most vital concerns—the live-lihood they derive from their gardens.

One explanation lies in the nature of talion in a system of values that not only enjoins equality and reciprocity but ties them firmly to the pro-duction and exchange of food. The society of Kalauna is a delicately balanced network, an all-embracing web of debts and credits in foodstuffs. The death of an important man (or the death of the child of an important man) unbalances the network, collapses a segment of the web, and before it can be repaired, corresponding adjustments have to be made. In such cases, the production-limiting sorcery of the bereaved is a means of sus-pending activities until the web can be reconstituted. Generalized venge-ance, in this view, is a means of forcing a moratorium. It induces a fear-inspired diminution of production and exchange activities until the material disadvantages resulting from a death can be checked, and the group that suffered the loss can regain its position of equality in the network. The bereaved kinsmen retain the economic initiative during the mourning period by means of their taboos. They place interdicts upon their stone sitting circle, their fruit trees, their fishing streams, and sometimes even their very hamlet ground; anyone caught using them (inadvertently or otherwise) is charged with showing "disrespect" and made to pay compensation. The bereaved's self-imposed food taboos restrict, within the hamlet, the consumption of all "good" foods—yams, taro, pork, and fish; by this means can they accumulate surpluses and reserves. "We are afraid of men who wear beards," Kalauna people say, for the unshaven state of mourning signifies well-stocked gardens which the bereaved kinsmen will later use to shame and indebt other clans with their munificence. Taboos and the threat of generalized vengeance, then, serve similar ends.

But this explanation, while elucidating a social function of generalized vengeance, evades the behavioral issues: loss is painful, anger is real, and the demand for talion breeds vicious cycles. The community must suffer to atone for a death, and it goes on suffering as deaths succeed one another. It is a phenomenon of social values, certainly, but by what process does a personal loss come to be perceived as a communal threat? How does the anger of a bereaved father come to be translated into an expectation of punishment by a whole village? The process surely inheres in the realm of symbolic communication: the realm of rhetoric, of art, of mythology and other media for the transmission of social meanings. The power of art and myth to "move" people is of a similar order to the rhetorical power of magic and sorcery. All have their genesis in dream and the developed human capacity for fantasy, and all proceed, mysteriously, from private invention to public convention.

Tamaku tamaku	My father my father
Kwanuloveloveku	You abandoned me
Nabelita hinayena	Inside the grave
Dalukemuleya	I search for you
Tamaku tamaku	My father my father
Daludadaniya	I look everywhere in vain

Debalewa's father died some thirty years ago; his son composed this song when he saw that his grave had begun to collapse. The song conforms to the strict canon of lawako, a drum dance, and is one of hundreds sung by Kalauna men who no longer know whom they commemorate. In such songs, a personal emotion is translated into a public sentiment, a personal loss transmuted into a public gain, for every song enriches the culture of the community.

The ambivalence of father–son relationships fuels some of the most creative achievements in Kalauna: notably the sumptuary death feasts at which dance songs such as Debalewa's are performed. The most powerful myths, too, are concerned with paternal resentment and filial guilt. Indeed, there is a singularly important myth, an Oedipal drama, which has paradigmatic status for fathers and sons. It features an impotent old man, Honoyeta, who can doff his skin to reveal a shining youth beneath, in which guise he courts his own two wives. On discovering his secret, the women destroy his slough, but he abandons them in resentment (unu-wewe) and wanders the island in search of death. He finds his nemesis in the form of "sons" who butcher, cook, and try to eat him; but he is indestructible. When they have realized their error, Honoyeta bids them bury his pieces with solemn rites. They obey, but all die. Honoyeta then ascends to become identified with the sun, and it is as a sun deity that he continues to punish mankind by bringing drought and famine. Just as the hero is a "father" who punishes his "sons" for their original sin of trying to kill and eat him, so do the punishing "fathers" of Kalauna control Honoyeta's sun magic, periodically depriving their "children" of food. Honoyeta's curse works through the malign power of the sun, but there is a deeper interpretation. As one who is father to himself, Honoyeta's curse is also a denial of the promise of generational succession. His "secret" is immortality and the annulment of time.[8]

In this myth, with its echoes of *Totem and Taboo*, Kalauna men seem to deny themselves the consolation of atonement: they do not succeed in identification with the father. The myth speaks only of pitiless vengeance and failed communication. It is interesting that in parts of the island the cult of Honoyeta has been joined with Christianity. "Honoyeta," people declare, "was our Christ. We killed him, he went to God, and he continues to punish us for our sin." In the death of every father there is the mortification of every son. A redeeming feature is the creative achievement which may grow from this mortification. For all its melancholy content, the myth of Honoyeta is a remarkable product of the human imagination, a product precipitated by the troubled ambivalence of fathers and sons.

The ghost of Sigmund Freud has haunted this essay, and I shall conjure it once more in conclusion. It is a paradox that one who devoted his life to unmasking the myths by which men live should have encouraged the cultivation of so many myths about himself and his work. Twice in his lifetime, in 1885 and 1907, Freud burned all his private papers to obfuscate and confuse his biographers. "Freud actively sought to cultivate the unknown about himself to ensure that he, an intellectual hero, would not be devalued by an overly detailed understanding of his genius" (Sulloway 1979:7). But he might have guessed that the filial impiety of his intellectual descendants would have turned the tables on him, using the very psychoanalytical principles he propounded to unmask him. It is an odd kind of testimony to his influence that Parsons, for example, could assert that the Oedipal conflict provided the dynamic for Freud's remarkable creative achievement (1969:376). Again, Derek Freeman has trenchantly argued that Freud's Lamarckian "actual event hypothesis" of the primal parricide was grounded in the profound ambivalence Freud felt toward his own father (1969:68–74).

Freud himself testified to the "subjective significance" of his first major opus *The Interpretation of Dreams* (1953), a significance he only grasped after he had completed it: "It was, I found, a portion of my own self-analysis, my reaction to my father's death" (1953:xxvi). Freud's self-analysis, which began in earnest during the year following his father's death in October 1896, was to become one of the heroic founder myths of psychoanalysis, a myth used by his followers to legitimate their claim to an independent "pure psychology" and to nullify Freud's debt to biology (Sulloway 1979:207, 492). Yet in the words of another biographer, the "central and most disturbing element" of Freud's self-analysis was "his unconscious desire to disavow the Jewish father whom he held responsible for his taints, his poverty, and his social humiliation" (Robert 1974:98).

At the time of Jakob Freud's death, his son had still not plumbed the depths of his own hostility towards him. Freud managed to arrive late for his father's funeral, having been delayed by his barber, and he evidently distressed some of the family by arranging a more modest ceremony than they would have wished. On the night after the funeral Freud dreamed he was in his barber's shop where there was a notice saying: "You are requested to close the (your) eye(s)." In the analysis of this dream he communicated to Fliess, Freud noted the double meaning of the sign:

It means "one should do one's duty towards the dead" in two senses—an apology, as though I had not done my duty and my conduct needed overlooking, and the actual duty itself. The dream was thus an outlet for the feeling of self-reproach which a death generally leaves among the survivors [Letter of November 2, 1896, cited by Robert 1974:90–91].

Freud's interpretation does not exhaust the meanings of the phrase, however, if one recalls that he had a year earlier arranged for the cure of his father's glaucoma, and that Freud's prototype for the guilty son, Oedipus, blinded himself when his crimes were revealed to him. Freud's "weak" interpretation of this dream (an even more perfunctory interpretation of which he published in *The Interpretation of Dreams* [1953:318]), is clear evidence that he could not yet admit to himself the depth of his filial ambivalence. His interpretation begins by accusing himself of impiety, but then proceeds to absolve himself of it. As Robert points out (1974:91–92), Freud disposes of the keen sense of guilt aroused by his father's death by obeying the command to "close the eyes." Of significance, too, is the fact that in his published interpretation Freud misdates the dream by stating that it had occurred during the night *before* his father's funeral.[9] At all events, this "Darwin of the mind," as Ernest Jones was to refer to Freud, made his momentous discovery of the "Oedipean conflict" (as he first labelled the father complex) in the years immediately following his father's death.

Ricoeur has also noted a pertinent parallel between Freud's self–analysis and his particular appropriation of the Oedipus myth:[10]

> Being honest with oneself coincides with grasping a universal drama. The relation is reciprocal: self-analysis discloses the "gripping power," the "compulsion" of the Greek legend; the myth in turn is evidence of the fate—I mean the character of non-arbitrary destiny—that attaches to the singular experience [1970:189].

This "gripping power" of myth, I have suggested elsewhere, is at the root of Kalauna men's identification with their mythical hero Honoyeta (Young 1983). As the death of Keyayala's son shows, Kalauna people are also inclined to seek a coincidence between "singular experience" and social destiny. The relation between Keyayala's immediate response to his son's death in seeking to prosecute universal vengeance is analogous to Freud's delayed response to his father's death in seeking to promulgate a universal theory. This might seem far fetched, but it is the nexus not the analogy I want to stress. The nexus, that is, between ontogenetic experience and phylogenetic destiny, between the biologically-based emotion and the socially constructed sentiment, and between private loss and public discovery in art or science. These are problems which compel us to adopt, as Derek Freeman would have it, an "interactionist paradigm." It is the crux of a modern anthropology, neither mentalistic nor behavioristic, that would explore the relationship between what is given and what is possible for man, while admitting his capacity to invent (or "choose") himself through his value systems.

Notes

1. Initially a psychologist, Fortes was well aware of the ambivalence in relations between parents and children, and he made it a central feature of his interpretation of the ancestor cult among the Tallensi (see Fortes 1949:234–235; 1959).
2. Much of the material in this section has been presented in greater detail elsewhere. See Young (1971:Chapter 3, 1977, 1983:Chapter 2, 1986).
3. For a published version of this myth, see Jenness and Ballantyne (1928).
4. Fraternal ambivalence is peripheral to the focus of this essay, as is the relationship between mothers and sons, though to elucidate the total complexity

134   MICHAEL W. YOUNG

of father–son ambivalence in Kalauna these relationships would need to be taken into account. For some examples of conflict between brothers in Kalauna, see Young (1971:43–46).

5. I have presented detailed biographical interpretations of Didiala and Iyahalina in Young (1983:Chapters 6 and 7).

6. In 1979, K. was driven from the village by his clansmen following the death of a woman in childbirth. His persecutors (including Adiyaleyale) wrecked and burned his house, cut his yams into pieces, and killed, cooked, and devoured his pig. While under physical attack, he cried: "O, my children are killing me!"

7. See also Bowlby (1961). Clinically speaking, Hamlet's condition was an exemplary case of melancholia (see Lidz 1975).

8. For a more detailed presentation and analysis of this myth, see Young (1983:Chapter 3).

9. There is a nice parallel in Charles Darwin's response to his father's death. According to Greenacre (1963:66), Darwin, then age 41, was "too ill to attend the funeral," and years later he misstated the date of his father's death, "an error which he could never understand."

10. I say "particular" because many scholars have pointed out how one-sided and idiosyncratic was Freud's interpretation of Sophocles' Oedipus myth, the most glaring bias being his assumption of Laius' innocence. As Theodore Lidz poses the problem: "Does the cycle of patricidal and filicidal wishes and fears start with the father's wish to be rid of the son or with the son's desire to be rid of his father?" (1975:184). See also Devereux (1953), Girard (1972:190–192), and Stanner (1982).

References

Bowlby, J.
1961 Processes of Mourning. International Journal of Psycho-Analysis 42:317–340.

Devereux, G.
1953 Why Oedipus Killed Laius: A Note on the Complementary Oedipus Complex in Greek Drama. International Journal of Psycho-Analysis 34:132–141.

Fortes, M.
1949 The Web of Kinship Among the Tallensi. London: Oxford University Press.

1959 Oedipus and Job in West African Religion. Cambridge: Cambridge University Press.

1969 Kinship and the Social Order. London: Routledge & Kegan Paul.

Fortune, R. F.
1963 Sorcerers of Dobu. New York: Dutton. (Originally published in 1932.)

Freeman, Derek
1969 Totem and Taboo: A Reappraisal. In *Man and His Culture*, edited by W. Muensterberger. New York: Taplinger.

1973 Kinship, Attachment Behaviour and the Primary Bond. In *The Character of Kinship*, edited by J. Goody. Cambridge: Cambridge University Press.

Freud, S.
1953 The Interpretation of Dreams. In *The Standard Edition of the Complete Psychological Works of Sigmund Freud*, translated by J. Strachey. Volume 4. London: Hogarth Press. (Originally published in 1900.)

1955 Totem and Taboo. In *The Standard Edition of the Complete Psychological Works of Sigmund Freud*, translated by J. Strachey. Volume 13. London: Hogarth Press. (Originally published in 1913.)

1957 Mourning and Melancholia. In *The Standard Edition of the Complete Psychological Works of Sigmund Freud: Papers on Metapsychology*, translated by J. Strachey. Volume 14. London: Hogarth Press. (Originally published in 1917.)

Girard, R.
1972 *Violence and the Sacred*. Baltimore: John Hopkins University Press.

Greenacre, P.
1963 *The Quest for the Father*. New York: New York Psychoanalytical Institute, International Universities Press.

Jackson, M.
1979 Prevented Succession: A Commentary Upon a Kuranko Narrative. In *Fantasy and Symbol*, edited by R. H. Hook. London: Academic Press.

Jenness, D. and A. Ballantyne
1928 *Language, Mythology, and Songs of Bwaidoga*. New Plymouth, New Zealand: Avery & Sons.

Lidz, T.
1975 *Hamlet's Enemy: Madness and Myth in Hamlet*. London: Vision Press.

Malinowski, B.
1927 *Sex and Repression in Savage Society*. London: Kegan Paul.

1930 Kinship. *Man* 30:19–20.

Mauss, M.
1966 *The Gift*. (Translated by I. Cunnison.) London: Cohen & West.

Parsons, A.
1966 Is the Oedipus Complex Universal? In *Man and His Culture*, edited by W. Muensterberger. New York: Taplinger.

Ricoeur, P.
1970 *Freud and Philosophy: An Essay in Interpretation*. New Haven: Yale University Press.

Robert, M.
1974 *From Oedipus to Moses: Freud's Jewish Identity*. London: Routledge & Kegan Paul.

Stanner, W. E. H.
1982 On Freud's *Totem and Taboo*. *Canberra Anthropology* 5(1):1–7.

Sulloway, F. J.
1979 *Freud, Biologist of the Mind*. London: Burnett Books.

Tuzin, D.
1972 Yam Symbolism in the Sepik: An Interpretative Account. *Southwestern Journal of Anthropology* 28:230–254.

Young, M. W.
1971 *Fighting with Food*. Cambridge: Cambridge University Press.

1977 Bursting with Laughter: Obscenity, Values and Sexual Control in a Massim Society. *Canberra Anthropology* 1(1):75–87.

1983 *Magicians of Manumanua: Living Myth in Kalauna*. Berkeley: California University Press.

1986 The Worst Disease: The Cultural Definition of Hunger in Kalauna. In *Shared Wealth and Symbol: Food, Culture and Society in Oceania and Southeast Asia*, edited by Lenore Manderson. Cambridge: Cambridge University Press.

1987 Skirts, Yams, and Sexual Pollution: The Politics of Adultery in Kalauna. *Journal de la Société des Océanistes*, forthcoming.

6

The Son as Savior:
A Hindu View of Choice and
Morality*

T. N. MADAN

Krishna said ...

*Seek not to choose between various modes of
morality: come rather to Me for shelter and Self-
realization. You will thus be freed of the burden of
all your sins: rejoice!*

The Bhagavadgita 18.66

During the last forty years, Derek Freeman's research has been a
steadfast quest for an adequate paradigm for the understanding of mankind's ways: an understanding that may equip us all to face the future
with greater wisdom. To this intellectual endeavor he has brought a rare
combination of three precious gifts: fieldwork in Samoa and Sarawak that
is praiseworthy both for its depth and detail; scholarship that is remarkable
for its seriousness and range; and a critical faculty that is not only con-
structive, but also aimed at his own work as well as at the work of his
professional colleagues.[1] He has thus moved forward step by step, refuting
what he has considered on examination and reflection the mistaken con-
jectures of himself and others (in this respect Karl Popper has been one
of the major influences in his work), and ever pursuing the goal of a unified
science of man. He has blamed the social sciences in particular for their
retreat from such a goal into the exclusively narrow grooves of culture,
society or behavior in the manner of, for instance, Alfred Kroeber, Émile
Durkheim, and John Watson, respectively.

In a 1969 lecture on human nature and culture, Freeman recalled Wilhelm Dilthey's dream of 1894 in Silesia in which the naturalistic philosophers and the idealistic thinkers of Europe fell apart in hostile alienation, causing this sensitive German philosopher deep anxiety, as if the unity of his own being was being torn apart. "I have recounted this dread dream of Dilthey's," Freeman commented, "because it prophetically epitomizes what was indeed to happen to the sciences of man during the immediately ensuring decades, and points to consequences from which these sciences still suffer—some of them to the very marrow of their methodologies" (Freeman 1970:50).

Summing up what he considered the relevant discoveries of recent decades, Freeman recommended to the student of human behavior "*an interactionist paradigm* which gives recognition to genetical and environmental feedback and interaction both in the ontogeny of individual organisms and in the phylogeny of breeding populations" (1970:68). Freeman applied himself to the refinement of such a paradigm throughout the following decade (of the 1970s), producing a formulation which points in a direction that the present writer considers not only personally congenial but also, and more importantly, indicative of a concern with ethics and the mutual interpretation of cultures without which the so-called social sciences will remain both prescientific and antihumanistic. In other words, our study of "other" cultures should no longer be a "distant" enterprise of describing how these others live: it should also illumine our own way of life (see Madan 1982a).

In his presidential address to the anthropology, archaeology, and linguistic sections of the Australian and New Zealand Association for the Advancement of Science in 1979, Freeman, once again, rejected an exclusive reliance on culture or biology as the key to the correct understanding of human nature and emphasized the importance of exploring the linkages between these two domains. He asserted: "My thesis is that one of the most fundamental of these linkages is to be found in human choice behaviour which ... is both intrinsic to our biology and basic to the very formation of cultures" (Freeman 1979:3). He defined "choice" simply as the process of selecting between alternatives which help to bring about a new mode of behavior, "the survival of which depends not on any genetic adaptation but on the mechanisms of social learning"; but these mechanisms are also a part of nature. Man is thus embedded in nature with "a highly developed capacity for alternative action, and so is, to give a new twist to Aeschylus' words, a 'steersman of necessity'" (Freeman 1979:8). In this, man is helped by the important fact that all human languages "immensely facilitate the conceptualizing of possibilities not previously perceived and so generate new alternatives from which choices can be

Important

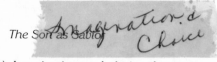

made" (Freeman 1979:11). Imagination and choice thus emerge as the twin mainsprings of cultural development.

The freedom to choose, Freeman quotes Kierkegaard as saying, is "the most tremendous thing which has been granted to man" (Freeman 1979:13); but this freedom entails the responsibility to choose wisely: the more the available choices, the greater the scope for good or bad and, therefore, the greater the need for ethics, rules, and laws—or, in other words, for defining what he calls "prohibited alternatives" (Freeman 1979:14). Recalling Aristotle's view that the "capacity to originate action by choice" is "the defining characteristic of human beings," and noting that in this endeavor of choosing to do or not to do something, one is guided by wisdom rather than demonstration and reason, Freeman concludes, "a culture is essentially a socially sanctioned accumulation of alternatives that have been selected from a vast range of human possibility. And this being so, it is always possible for those involved to change in some way, or even abandon, one or more of the alternatives of their culture" (Freeman 1979:17). From this conclusion he derives a definition of human values as the selected alternatives resulting from the exercise of choice. It is, therefore, open to any human society and, in fact, to mankind "to create our own worlds of meaning" through the "invigorating potentiality" for making choices (Freeman 1979:20).

I would like to suggest that the worlds of meaning are created from these possibilities of choices through the interaction of human relationships. What is more, the domain of these choices includes the most basic of all human relationships; namely, that between parents and children. In the 1979 address mentioned above, Freeman referred to the nature and importance of the "primary bond" (between mother and child), emphasizing the role of both biological and cultural factors in its making. He had attended to this theme in an earlier paper (see Freeman 1973), in which he had argued that kinship is not adequately understood in terms of genealogical linkages alone: that the predominantly autogenous behavior in the first year of life and the overlay of jural and moral principles on its subsequently, which acquires depth as the child grows, must both be given adequate recognition. It is only then that the ambivalence of the primary bond—"the simultaneous presence in kinship bonds of love and hate"—may be comprehended (Freeman 1973:116–117). The early irate feelings of the infant generated by the postponement or denial of the gratification of appetites are gradually overcome by attachment and amity, but they leave their scars.

What adulthood expressions such ambivalence will find depends of course on the actual experiences of an individual as the legatee of a culture and as one particular human being. Thus, every Hindu son may present his own version of what it has meant to him to have been his mother's son; the framework of norms and values within which he evaluates his personal experience is not, however, created by himself but available to him as part of his culture. It is in this interplay between cultural tradition and individual life experience that choice making emerges as the condition and guarantor of human freedom and dignity.

MOTHERS AND SONS IN HINDU SOCIETY

The position of the son in the Hindu family, particularly among the so-called "twice-born" upper castes, is one of high privilege and heavy responsibility: The very word for son in Sanskrit—*putra*—proclaims both. According to the ancient text Manusmriti (?B.C. 600 – ?A.D. 300), "Because the son protects his ancestors from the hell called *put*, he has been called *putra*" (ix.138).[2] This text gives a preeminent position to the first son, for through him does the father continue the lineage, ensure that offerings will be made to gods and ancestors, and contribute to the maintenance of the social (which is part and parcel of the cosmic) order. He is, therefore, called the son born of and for *dharma* or righteous conduct; the children that follow are said to be the fruit of *kāma* or erotic desire. Sons are always preferred to daughters, though in themselves the latter are said to embody auspiciousness and prosperity, as stated in the great Hindu epic *Mahābhārata*, the earliest extant manuscript, 500 A.D.

Like the traditional texts, ethnographic and sociological studies of Hindu society have brought out in great detail the intimacy between mothers and sons, which is of a different character than the closeness of fathers and sons. In an account of these relationships among the Pandits, a Brahman community of Kashmir (in north India), I have pointed out that, while the father–son relationship is the very foundation of the Pandit kinship system, the genetic and moral relationship between mother and child, and the emotional intensity that characterizes it, are without parallel. Among children the privileged position of sons is beyond any doubt and expressed in many ways including such sayings as the following: "whereas a daughter's birth makes even a philosophic man (who has cultivated detachment) gloomy, a son's birth is like sunrise in the god's own temple" (see Madan 1965:77–79, 87–89, et passim). In this regard the Pandits are typical upper caste Hindus.

Urbanization does not seem to bring about a radical change in the mother–son relationship in Hindu society. A study conducted in South India (in the 1950s) revealed that the mother–son relationship was most often mentioned by the interviewees as being "close and affectionate." Moreover, "sons often maintained veneration for their mothers even as older men" (Ross 1961:147). Similar conclusions have been arrived at in other studies of the Hindu family in the urban setting.

In an authoritative summing up of the ethnographic literature, David Mandelbaum observed:

> Between mother and son there is everywhere in India a strong, tender, unchanging, dependable bond. The bond is celebrated in sacred writing, romanticized in popular tale, upheld in the actuality of family life. A mother is respected; motherhood is revered. Sons give abundantly of both the tokens and the substance of esteem. She is not the aloof person a father is suppose to be. She is everlastingly loving and caring, certainly in ideal, often in reality. This is particularly true of a woman in a wealthy family who has little more to do than to care for her children. In that care lies her greatest fulfillment as a person [1970:62].

Psychoanalysts also have dwelt upon the theme of the mother–son relationship in upper-caste Hindu society. Ashis Nandy describes it as "the basic nexus and the ultimate paradigm of human social relationships in India" (1980:37). He adds, "To an extent this is true of all cultures, but only in a few cultures have the loneliness and self-abnegation of woman as a social being found such elaborate justification in her symbolic status as a mother" (Nandy 1980:37). The loving and supportive character of the mother vis-à-vis her children, sons particularly, is further emphasized when it is noted that the Hindu father is "one of a number of remote disciplinary male figures" (Carstairs 1967:76). The mother–son relationship is not, however, without its emotional complications, for the mother "has to repulse the child in order to resume her sexual relations with the father" (Carstairs 1967:76)—or so the psychoanalysts believe.

Probing deeper into this relationship, Sudhir Kakar has drawn pointed attention to the fact that the idealized image of the "good," benign, and nurturing mother is "largely a male construction." He adds (on the basis of clinical data) that only an "infinitesimally small" proportion of Indian men "express or experience an active dislike, fear or contempt for their mothers at the conscious level" (1978:83). On her side—and here ethnographic and psychoanalytic data reinforce each other explicitly—"an Indian mother," Kakar asserts, "preconsciously experiences her newborn infant, especially a son, as the means by which her 'motherly' identity is crystallized, her role and status in family and society established. She tends to perceive *a son as a* kind of *savior* and to nurture him with gratitude and even reverence as well as with affection and care" (Kakar 1978:88–89 emphasis added). According to Kakar, the Hindu mother, however, experiences the contrary pulls of nurturing and demanding, of loving her son and expecting from him the fulfillment of "her own unfulfilled desires and wishes." In short, she treats him as both subject and object and in the process creates confusion in his mind vis-à-vis herself. Thus, while he may feel compelled to "*act* as her savior," "her unconscious intimations and demands" may generate in his fantasies "the ominous image of the 'bad mother'" (Kakar 1978:89).

The ambivalence in the mother–son relationship which Kakar highlights is identified by Freeman as a cultural universal. Kakar notes, however, that the images of the "bad mother" are culturally specific. He adds that, while the aggressive aspect of maternal feeling towards the son is comparatively weak in Hindu society, the possibility of "disturbance" arises from her "unsatisfied erotic needs" and her "seductive restlessness" (Kakar 1978:90). From this he concludes: "Thus, underlying the conscious ideal of womanly purity, innocence and fidelity, and interwoven with the unconscious belief in a safeguarding maternal beneficence is a secret conviction among many Hindu men that the feminine principle is really the opposite— treacherous, lustful and rampant with an insatiable, contaminating sexuality" (Kakar 1978:93).

These psychoanalytic insights echo ethnographic observations, such as my own among the Pandits of rural Kashmir, who declare that a daughter-in-law "becomes visible" and proves her worth when she bears the first child—and what could be better than the birth of a son which illumines even the god's own temple? Motherhood is, therefore, defined as the destiny of womanhood. Generally speaking, the Pandits deny that there ever could be a "bad mother" (*kumata*), but "bad sons" (*kuputra*) are indeed born (see Madan 1982a:231). If the notion of the "bad mother" is at all admitted by the Pandits, it is invariably either as the stepmother or as the sexually vagrant mother (*vyabhacharini*). It is the son more than the daughter who is shamed and polluted by such a mother, for the daughter is protected by her own marriage which incorporates her into the domestic and ritual life of another family, often in another village.

For a particularly insightful interpretation of the mother–son relationship, when the son is cast by a strong-willed mother in the role of her savior, I now turn to a contemporary Tamil novel, *The Sins of Appu's Mother*, by T. Janakiraman (1972).[3]

In treating the novelist as an informant, I am following a procedure which is unusual, though not unknown, for an anthropologist.[4] I should, therefore, like to clarify briefly that, taking the cue from Roland Barthes, I simply exercise my right as a reader to bend the chosen text to my purpose, which in the present case is to fill a gap in ethnographic literature. In doing so the novelist's obvious intentions or latent motives are not my concern, nor is the narrative *qua* story. I am looking for what the novelist has to say about the cultural norms and values that enable us to assess the relations between a particular woman and her son. When we deal with literate societies, the "insider" novelist might well be considered a special informant who provides us with "second order interpretations" of a kind not totally dissimilar to the "first order interpretations" we receive from informants in the course of ethnographic fieldwork. The novelist, unlike the ordinary informant, poses his own questions—he has an artistic purpose which is also social and may harbor a strong ideological bias—and answers them in an articulate manner, combining personal experience with creative imagination. It is, however, a naive view of the novel which considers it "false" because it is "fiction." The novelist may invent or imagine characters and incidents, and the details in the lives of the people he writes about, but he does not invent a culture; his point of reference is the real world. It seems to me that if a novel appeals to a wide variety of readers, it must tell them something that is of general and deep concern to them: the novelist's literary genius does not by itself explain such wide interest. A novelist and his "insider" readers share an understanding of a common social and cultural background, besides a concern with the human predicament in its universal dimensions. Moreover, the novelist is often able to achieve a holistic view of a human situation better than the anthropologist because of his freedom to be creative; the latter must proceed cautiously as he is limited by the data he is able to gather. Freud stated this most felicitously when he wrote somewhere: "Wherever I go, I find a poet has been there before me."

Needless to say, however, the two kinds of study are complementary and neither is mutually substitutable or opposed to each other. If a novel helps us immediately to fill a gap in the ethnography of a people, it should do so in the long-run too by inviting anthropologists to study the neglected themes. Meanwhile, the novelist's data must be examined critically to assess their consonance with what is known about the ethos of the society depicted. *Appu's Mother*, which is a story about contemporary India, does not in any way contradict what anthropological or sociological accounts have to tell us about the mother–son relationship in upper-caste Hindu society. The novel does, however, deal with certain kinds of moral issues involving choice making which have not been taken up for study by anthropologists or sociologists generally—at any rate not by those specializing in India. The reason for this lacuna may well be that the actual moral choices are not available to the scrutiny of the student who would seek to understand them externally, independent of the cultural constructs of the people. This is not to deny the existence of cross-cultural moral imperatives, but that is not what I am concerned with here.

Turning to the novel *Appu's Mother*, then, we learn that Appu is his mother's third and last legitimate child. Alankaram—for that is her name—

has three more children, but their father is not the same as Appu's, namely Dandapani, but a client of his called Sivasu. Dandapani is an astrologer and a scholar of ancient texts. He is a nondescript Brahman who lives a humdrum life, makes a living as a proofreader at a printing press, and teaches Sanskrit texts to elderly and retired city gentlemen. He lives with his wife and children in a tenement situated in a lane in the city of Madras (in South India). Performing ablutions, offering prayers, eating, and working—these appear to be the activities that consume him. In his youth he had known conjugal pleasures too, but these had later been taken away from him irrevocably by Alankaram who had preferred Sivasu. Dandapani chose to put up with this liaison and the children born of it.

Alankaram is a rather extraordinary character, aptly named, for the word means "ornament." Somehow her parents had not given her the name of a Hindu goddess which is the common practice among orthodox Brahmans. Alankaram is a tall, well-built, physically attractive woman, and, though not well-read, a person of imagination and strong will. There is a touch of the arrogant and even the regal about her, and she dominates the scene wherever she is by her natural grace and poise. Moreover, she is endowed with a rich imagination.

> She sat majestically in her chair, in that tenement, in that cattle-yard lane, like a queen on her throne. In her smile and speech and the way she turned and walked she was regal. She never pleaded and she never bargained. And she never spoke at needless length [p. 102].

> She would look in wonder at the stars and see in their constellations shapes that he could never make out clearly no matter how explicitly she pointed them out [to Dandapani, lying beside her on the terrace of their house]. There was something child-like in her wonder at the stars, the shapes she could see in them, even in the way she lay still on her back staring at them. . . . It was not only her star-gazing; her dreams too were extraordinary; vivid, colourful and detailed. They were peopled by strange characters and beings and mythological figures with everything larger than life. His own [Dandapani's] dreams seemed so mundane and poverty-stricken by comparison . . . [p. 72].

Appu was Alankaram's favorite child and she paid special attention to his upbringing. When he was eight years old and in school, Alankaram revealed to her husband her "deep wish to give him a real education" (p. 75). Dandapani agreed and spoke of Appu going to the university and becoming a teacher or an engineer, but she dismisses such ideas as commonplace.

He must learn the Vedas. He must study them intensely and shine with their effulgence. Like fire he should burn up all pettiness and dross that come near him and should stand like a god; like Brihaspati.[5]

Dandapani's pleas that a Vedic scholar cannot hope to make a decent living are brushed aside. Appu can acquire a more utilitarian education later—but first the Vedas. Sixteen years later, Appu, adept in Vedic scholarship, was back from the village where he had studied the sacred texts and looking for work. He expresses doubts about the self-sufficiency of such knowledge. Alankaram admonishes him in reply:

If one reads the Vedas one's mind and body are purified and acquire an effulgence. No illness or anxiety can touch such a person for he becomes like a flower—an undying, ever fresh flower.... Nobody will let a [Vedic scholar become just a mean beggarly priest]. Don't go grubbing for money and your study will look after you [pp. 102–103].

This high idealism and faith in the Vedas are, in fact, a cover for a very personal motive. Having chosen the life of pleasure (*kāma*) outside the framework of righteous conduct (*dharma*), Alankaram had also chosen a way to atone for her sins by choosing that Appu become a Vedic scholar. As she confesses to him, when he prepares to go back to the village on hearing that the old woman, who had provided him both home and school for sixteen years, is ill (Alankaram is afraid Appu will not come back to her):

You are someone very special to me, Appu. It is by my concern for you that I must atone for everything. You are my last son. I tortured myself thinking how I could find atonement. Violent suicide could only mean my death and the end of me. Finally I decided to put you into the *pāthashāla* [traditional Brahmanical school]. These who learn the Vedas become *rishis* [singers of sacred hymns, sagas]. They are ageless and pure as fire. I hoped you would return like that and I could fall at your feet... [p. 123].

Alankaram had hoped to atone for her moral lapse by identifying herself with her son and thus becoming purified. She made her choices selfishly and, therefore, they were not wise. Not that a parent in upper-caste Hindu society would be blamed for dedicating one of the sons to the study of the Vedas; but her choice of the life of a Vedic scholar for her son had less to do with his good and more with her own atonement. A son is by definition the savior—putra—one who delivers his parents and ancestors from the tortures of hell.[6] This obligation is an *absolute value*: the essence of sonship is filial piety. But when an errant mother (or father) looks upon the son as the instrument of her (or his) salvation, the relationship becomes perverted and the parental purpose is defeated.

Appu does indeed decide to stay on in the village: he chooses to do so, repelled by a morally amorphous city ("I don't like anything about Madras" [p. 147]), and alienated from a home where he has suffered the most grievous emotional trauma that a son may have to experience—a mother and a father both of whom must be judged as morally weak. Alankaram's arrogance and Dandapani's cowardice weigh ultimately the same in the scale of moral values. Appu's discovery of Alankaram's truth, on his return from the village school after a sixteen-year absence, made him see her in a new light. "Why could she not be ordinary, like other people's mothers? Why did she have this imperious bearing and form, this arrogance on her face . . ." (p. 109)? As for Dandapani, "Why did he not leave the house and become a *sanyasi* (renouncer, renunciation being the last stage of life according to Brahmanical tradition)? Why was he still eating the food she cooked and served, indifferent to disgrace" (p. 114)? Appu had indeed wanted to tell his father that "he ought to be driven away from home." In putting up with a wife who was unfaithful to him, we could say that Dandapani was unfaithful to his own truly begotten children.

Realizing that Appu would not come home, Alankaram visits him in the village, only to have her fears confirmed: He is not going back for there is no "home" to go back to—just a house. The home is a moral place marked by conjugal fidelity and filial piety. She must now make her *final* choice which she does, firmly as before and also wisely. She tells Appu she is going north, far away from Madras, to the sacred city of Kashi, to await her death there.

> It is sound sense [she says]. A woman must die in front of her son—or in Kashi. I thought of you as my only son [she actually had three] and I thought you had become a *rishi* and at your feet I hoped to burn my soul; my all. But you have become a mother's son [the reference is to the benefactress of the village Vedic school] . . . I am going to Kashi and live there . . . There is no other way. Many old women go to Kashi to die. I, too, shall go there and wait [p. 165].

It may be pointed out here that, according to traditional Hindu belief, dying in Kashi not only absolves one of all one's sins but—and this is so much more significant from the Hindu point of view—also ensures *moksha*, liberation from rebirth through union with the Absolute. This becomes possible as God grants knowledge to the devotee at the very moment of his death in Kashi, destroying the fruits of all past actions—good and bad (see Eck 1982 and Parry 1982).

So, Alankaram goes to Kashi; her pursuit of Kāma (Eros) entails for her the pursuit of Kāla (Thanatos). Or shall we say that she goes there to begin a new life, as an autonomous moral agent, cutting off all her worldly attachments, including the bond with her favorite son? She will be her own savior by her act of renunciation and through divine grace. When taking leave of the school benefactress (who had called Appu back to the village), she had sought the latter's blessing so that she might gain "knowledge and enlightenment." The old lady had assured her: "God will give everything. If one abandons oneself to him, there is nothing he will not give" (p. 164).

Appu had met and known two women at the village Vedic school— its benefactress Bhavaniammal and her brother's daughter, Indu, who is a few years younger than Appu. Finding herself a childless widow at thirty, but in possession of an estate in land, Bhavaniammal had endowed most of it to establish the school. She brought her brother there to teach, and Indu was his daughter. His wife and he died within a couple of years of each other, leaving little Indu an orphan. Bhavaniammal arranged Indu's marriage, but her husband also died three years later. Meanwhile Appu had arrived at the school even before Indu's marriage. Bhavaniammal was thus a kind of foster mother for both the boy and the girl.

When Appu was grappling with his home and the city, after having returned there on the completion of his Vedic studies as a matter of familial obligation, about which his father had always kept reminding him, Bhavaniammal suffers from a paralytic stroke. Informed about it, Appu rushes back to the village. Though Bhavaniammal is better by the time he gets there, she is not sure of the future. Besides, the old teacher in the school, who had taken her brother's place, also is not well. Bhavaniammal had, in fact, asked Appu to stay on in the school when he had finished his studies, but he had declined, though the village school had been like a home to him. She now repeats her invitation and Appu accepts it, disillusioned as he is with his own home and his parents.

Bhavaniammal is a very humane and practical woman. Her "mind is like the Kaveri [which flows beside the village]. It rolls along broad and majestic, with affection and compassion in its swell" (p. 153). She gets the land deed altered to ensure that Appu and Indu will be provided for even if no more pupils come to learn the Vedas. She is afraid that many villagers will be jealous of Appu and that the orthodox among them will not approve of Appu living under the same roof as the young widow; and Bhavaniammal surely knows that Indu has always been in love with Appu and he with her. And yet she alters her will in their favor because, as she

says, her affection for the two of them is greater than her reverence for
Vedas. She recalls that she had endowed the school thirty years earlier to
enable some people to learn the Vedas—and one hundred and four pupils
had done so already.

> [But] why count the heads? Is that not mere pride? The Vedas will
> survive even without us. They are eternal . . . If you can [she tells
> Appu], continue to teach the Vedas. And if you cannot, give food
> and shelter to a few boys, then send them to some Tamil or Eng-
> lish school. Let them have a free choice. What does it matter
> whether one learns the Vedas or something else? A few boys who
> are destitute must be fed. But it is necessary to be aware of God
> and he is there in the shape of hunger. If you remember that, for
> my sake it shall be sufficient [pp. 148–149].

Bhavaniammal is Appu's second mother, and Alankaram realizes this
when she visits the village in the hope of reclaiming her son and learns
what Bhavaniammal has done. Alankaram's love for Appu and the choice
she made on his behalf was rooted in her concern with herself—her pursuit
of pleasure and the wish to atone for her sins both stemmed from this
preoccupation. There is, however, sarcasm as well as sorrow in Alankaram's speech when she tells Appu that he has become "a mother's son"
instead of a rishi. The reference is to his own fall, as it were, for she alleges
that he has been ensnared by Bhavaniammal's will. Alankaram had hoped
that he would be free of worldly entanglements—that redeemed by the
Vedas, he would deliver others from sin and the bitter fruits of sin.

It seems that Bhavaniammal alone emerges unsullied from her self-
conscious involvement with mundane affairs. She lives for others and uses
her worldly possessions for their good and happiness. She cares for them
for their own sake; she loves Appu for his own sake first and only then
for the sake of the Vedas. She is the mother who gives and does not
demand, and makes her choices wisely: she is a *true* mother. Though a
widow, she by no means betokens inauspiciousness. Like women *bhakta*
(devotees of god), she has cast away her human husband, as it were, to
devote herself to god's creatures. She has traversed half the way to divinity.

Human mothers may be foolish or wise, but motherhood remains a
supreme value in Hindu thought. In the myths and symbols of Hindu
civilization, bountiful, nourishing motherhood is represented by rivers; in
Janakiraman's novel it is represented by the Kaveri.[7] In fact, when Appu
has to say to Indu that Bhavaniammal is affectionate and compassionate,
he compares her to the Kaveri's broad and majestic role. The reader is
introduced to the Kaveri even before to Appu (or anybody else) in the
opening paragraph of the novel, which speaks of his having become

possessed, as it were, by the river, during his sixteen years in the village on its bank. He has been frightened by his first encounter with the Kaveri, the morning after his arrival in the village, when his father took him there for bathing. The river was in flood, turbulent, rolling by like "some great sighing snake" (p. 7). He had also been vouched on that very first encounter with a sight of the bounty of the river: a kingfisher plunging for its prey and emerging with something to eat in its beak. Ever afterwards, Appu had found a mother in the Kaveri in whom he could confide—to whom he could speak his heart and then listen. While his Vedic teacher taught him to sing the hymns and recite the texts loud and clear, perhaps bending his ear to detect and correct any mispronunciation, the Kaveri taught him to listen and speak in silence. It spoke to him of the same truth as the Vedas—of the Eternal and the Absolute. When Bhavaniammal tells Appu why she has altered her will and what she envisages the future might be like, he makes

> his way to the Kaveri—whatever emotion moved him it was always, and only, to the river that he could speak his heart . . . He remembered the evening he had come here just after finishing his studies, shortly before leaving for home. Today he felt just as he had that day—a sense of seeing the river anew and a strong reluctance to go away from it [pp. 150–151].

There is a kind of mysterious primary bond of attachment between Appu and the Kaveri—like that of a child to its mother, rooted in the depths of his being, but finding in culture the tongue with which to express it. It is noteworthy that not only do we take leave of Appu in the village on the bank of the Kaveri—the Ganga of the South, so-called—we also remember that Alankaram is on her way to Kashi to live and die on the bank of the Ganga itself—the holiest of India's rivers. These rivers of India, according to the Hindu tradition, wash away not only human sins but also the imperfections of being and understanding that necessitate the making of choices.[8] Though an elemental part of nature, the river here emerges as a key cultural symbol, while Alankaram, by an interesting reversal, symbolizes nature in the form of human appetites. Bhavaniammal bridges nature and culture and points to the human potential for moral perfection.

Appu remains unfree—or so it seems to me—as his choices are made for him by others, though he does not abide by all of them. Alankaram's choice makes of him a Vedic scholar, but he alone could have made himself a rishi. His father's exhortations take him back to home from the village—a father who, he comes to believe in the end, should himself have been driven away from home. Bhavaniammal recalls him to the village. He resists Indu's love for him, for he thinks that he is expected by his culture and society to treat another man's wife or widow as his mother or sister, but this moral posture he also finds difficult to maintain. He has to confess to himself that he has always been in love with Indu without having had the courage to admit it. In fact, he had rebuked Indu for declaring her love for him, and beseeching him on the eve of his departure from the village, on completion of his studies, not to go away. He had told her that her face reminded him of his mother's look, that he hoped to go back to his mother "clean in body and clean in mind"—an adept in the Vedas—without "smearing" himself with the "mud" of an illegitimate erotic relationship. "When you return after a bath in the holy Kaveri you shouldn't drop into a roadside tavern" (p. 42). His final appeal to her had been: "Send me home safe"—and home he went as a dutiful son, only to discover the bitter truth about his mother and father.

Finally, on his return to the village, having yielded to Bhavaniammal's persuasion to stay on, he meekly accepts Indu's invitation to share his burdens with her—"if ever anything bothers you tell it to me whatever it is; you can't bear it alone" (p. 143)—which is itself not a clear choice, only an acquiescence. What could the sharing of burdens between them mean, for Brahman widows do not remarry? In this sense, though the novel ends, the moral discourse contained in it does not come to a satisfactory conclusion. Appu's moral dilemmas—arising out of his relations with the three women in his life—remain unresolved. In opting to live in the village with Indu, does he really surrender to Alankaram? Does his decision never to marry, conveyed to Alankaram during her fateful visit to the village, constitute a vow of celibacy? If so, will he have the moral courage to adhere to it in the presence of Indu's passion for him? When she had first declared her love for him, he had sought to silence her by pronouncing physical love between them sinful. Her retort had been: "It doesn't seem to me. What is a sin? To do and say things against one's conscience" (p. 40). Appu had no answer to that.

Appu perhaps never listened carefully enough to the Kaveri, who would have liberated him, but only to the human mothers, who bind him to the wheel of karma. Bhavaniammal, the "good" mother does this no less than Alankaram, the "bad" mother. In fact, the former binds him fast to this world in a three-stranded bond of attachment (like the three-stranded holy thread symbolizing a Brahman's worldly obligations) consisting of the land, the school, and Indu. The flowing river would have spoken to Appu of the Brahmanical quest for the dissolution of worldly attachments and obligations and the supreme value of transcendence in the context of moral choices. The ideal is to overcome the agony of making choices by attaining a level of self-awareness at which one acts morally, as a matter of course, spontaneously.

CONCLUSION

I have made an attempt in this essay to delineate the mother–son relationship on the basis of T. Janakiraman's novel, *The Sins of Appu's Mother*, in the light of the relevant ethnographic and psychoanalytic literature. I have not been concerned with an examination of the literary merits of *Appu's Mother* nor with an analysis of its narrative structure. In other words, I have not been concerned with the novel per se. I have brought in only such details of the plot as seemed essential to the construction and interpretation of the text as a moral discourse. I have thus treated the novel simply as a contemporary commentary, generated from within Hindu culture, on the making of moral choices. In doing so I have perhaps read more into the novel than there is. Thus, the emphasis I have placed upon the symbolism of the river in my essay is not quite warranted by the story in which the Kaveri flows in the background, literally and metaphorically. From my special point of view the novel may be seen as being concerned with certain aspects of the mother–son relationship in upper-caste Hindu society, which have not been so far examined in any great depth or detail by anthropologists or sociologists.

A reading of *Appu's Mother* suggests that the well-defined moral order of the mother–son relationship does not make it immune to the impact of choice making by actors, which can involve a repudiation (or a denial) of this moral bond. The flowering of "primary bonding" into what, following Meyer Fortes (1969), we may call "axiomatic amity" is neither smooth nor assured of lifelong durability. In fact, the novel suggests that the domains of the most basic of all human relationships—namely parental and conjugal love—constantly present human actors with situations calling for the making of critical choices. If these choices are not made wisely, the consequences turn out to be very costly, if not unbearable, from both the moral and practical points of view. To use the words quoted by Freeman (1979:15) from Hierocils' "Golden Verses" of Pythgoras, "the evils that devour men are the fruits of their choice." The choices that Appu's mother Alankaram makes in respect to her conjugal life and in relation to her son inevitably lead her to seek a tryst with death—a choice beyond which there are no further choices to make. But at every crucial step she could have made other choices that were less egotistical and more altruistic and she could have gone forth to meet her death with a sense of fulfillment—a cherished Hindu ideal (see Madan 1982c)—rather than with repentance and sorrow. Unless she is *moved* by altruistic love, the mother fails to love truly; and if she is motivated by the expectation of returns, whatever these may be, she only succeeds in debasing maternal love and may fail to achieve her heart's desire. Appu's ambivalence towards his mother is not the result of his unwillingness to give love but of his

152

inability to respond to the mother–son relationship when the mother herself has not provided selfless love for her son—has not lived up to the ideal mother. Alankaram is excessively demanding in her relation with her son, and thereby generates ambivalent feeling toward herself in him. She is the "bad" mother of psychoanalytic literature, and her destructiveness arises from her erotic needs.

In other words, Janakiraman's novel points to an ever-present moral infirmity in everyday life, just as it points to the possibility of wise selfless choices. This infirmity may consist of making the kind of choices that finally devour the one who makes them, and perhaps others too, or in abandoning the responsibility for oneself. Appu's life is not only affected by the choices his mother makes but also by his own decision to abide by the choices others make on his behalf. His kind of a state of choicelessness—if it may be called so—only highlights the Brahmanical cultural ideal of freedom from the making of choices through the cultivation of "choiceless awareness." This notion is central to Hindu traditional (upanishadic) thought but the phrase used here is that of J. Krishnamurti.[9] To quote his own words (see Lutyens 1970:70–71):

> What is important, surely, is to be aware without choice, because choice brings about conflict. The chooser is in confusion, therefore he chooses; if he is not in confusion there is no choice. . . . Action based on an idea is obviously the action of choice and such action is not liberating: on the contrary it only creates further resistance, further conflict, according to that conditioned thinking.[10]

While the postulation of such a state of total awareness does not appear to the Hindus to be a kind of casuistry, as it well might from the perspectives of some other cultures, yet it would be acknowledged that it is hard to achieve and, therefore, not a common condition.

Choiceless awareness does, however, imply, it seems to me, that self-conscious actors should try to cultivate a bent for ethical conduct so that, gradually, acting ethically becomes one's second nature—nature is grafted upon nurture—and consequently wise choices are made spontaneously. If one has to *force* oneself to act wisely, and subsequently keep oneself under check *forcibly* to ensure that the choice made is not abandoned, then one may be judged to have chosen without achieving genuine mastery over choice making and over oneself. Alternatives which are prohibited externally alone, by law or the fear of social opprobrium, without first being rooted in inner conviction are to that extent always present, lurking in the shadows as it were, as a potential threat to one's induced moral tranquility. The assumption of full responsibility for one's actions is, therefore, a widely acknowledged cultural ideal in Hindu (Brahmanical) tradition, and one of its best-known and oft-quoted expressions is the following exhortation from the *Bhagavadgītā*, the most widely read and recited Hindu scripture: "Action alone is your entitlement, never its reward as well. Work not for the fruits of action, but do not cease to be active" (2.47).

Notes

* I owe thanks to George Appell, Veena Das, Ashis Nandy, Meenakshi Thapan, and J. P. S. Uberoi for their comments on an earlier draft of this essay.

1. In the course of the last twenty years, Professor Freeman has written to me on more than one occasion criticizing some of his own earlier writings for what he came to consider later as an overly narrow approach. Thus, as early as in 1962, he sent me an offprint of his Curl Bequest Prize Essay, "On the Concept of the Kindred," and wrote in the accompanying letter that he did not expect to be doing "that kind of work" any more. This was said at a time when "that kind of work" was, in fact, highly regarded. In 1975 I sent him a copy of a paper of mine, "On Living Intimately with Strangers" (see Madan 1975), recording, among other things, the heavy emphasis he used to place upon the structural-functional approach during the years 1956–59 when he was supervising my doctoral studies. He wrote in acknowledgement: "The depiction of my theoretical stance as it was in 1956 is certainly exact, though I scarcely recognize my erstwhile self. How structurally obtuse I was!"

2. Hell (*naraka*) is a place of post-mortuary torture for sinners and for those whose post-mortuary rites have not been performed properly. There are a number of naraka and put is one of them. The deliverance of those consigned to a naraka for want of proper post-mortuary rites, and the prevention of one's manes (*pitri*) being so condemned, is achieved through oblations, particularly the biannual food offerings called the *shrāddha*. The person who makes these offerings need not be a man's (or woman's) biological son but anyone else eligible to perform the rite. On the occasion of the shrāddha for one's deceased father, water and food are offered in his name and in the name of his five lineal ascendants in the male line. Similarly, alone with one's deceased mother, at least her father and father's father receives oblations. For details see Kane 1941:iv, 334ff.

3. The novel was originally written in Tamil but, since I do not read this language, I have relied upon an English translation (see Janakiraman 1972).

4. Among others, Professor Freeman himself has often drawn upon literary sources—novels, plays, poems—for information and insights. I have found his use of the Greek classics and Shakespeare particularly felicitous.

5. Brihaspati is the preceptor, counsellor, and chief priest of the Vedic gods.

6. See footnote 2 above.

7. After I had written this essay, I came across the following observation about the villagers of Kumbapettai in the Thanjavur district of Tamilnadu: "The River Kaveri and its irrigation channels were thought of as the villagers' mother. The muddy water in mid-July was her menstruation, and flood tide in early August her pregnancy, and the harvest her children" (Gough 1981:170; also see 225–226).

8. The rich symbolism of the redeeming rivers (and rain) is familiar to the

students of Hindu mythology, art, and architecture. It has also found its way into contemporary fiction. A notable example is Herman Hesse's fine novel *Siddhārtha*, which is not merely about India but, more significantly, about "the quest and yearning of nature for new forms and new possibilities." Incidentally, Professor Freeman has a high opinion of *Siddhārtha* as a work of creative imagination.

9. I was introduced to the thought of J. Krishnamurti (b. 1895) by Professor Freeman in 1956. Commenting on it in a letter to Ms. Meenakshi Thapan, a student of mine, Professor Freeman wrote in April 1980: "I remain profoundly interested in the notion of human beings as potentially self-defining; i.e., in the notion that given the requisite technical knowledge and skill (right knowledge joined with right action) an individual may reconstruct his, or her, own character and *dasein*."

10. I have elsewhere drawn upon three other celebrated works of contemporary Indian fiction to try to show that the Indian ideal is to recognize and then overcome binary oppositions, such as the one between asceticism and eroticism (see Madan 1980). I have also tried to bring out in the same essay that, according to Hindu thought, a major source of moral perplexity is the egoistic preoccupation with one's self, with the fulfillment of one's desires—with kāma (pleasure) divorced from dharma (righteous conduct)—which leads the human actor to look upon other human beings in instrumental terms and ultimately results in his own moral collapse.

References

Carstairs, G. Morris
1967 *The Twice Born: A Study of a Community of High Caste Hindus.* Bloomington: Indiana University Press.

Eck, Diana
1982 *Benaras: The City of Light.* New York: A. Knopf.

Fortes, Meyer
1969 *Kinship and Social Order.* Chicago: Aldine.

Freeman, Derek
1970 Human Nature and Culture. In *Man and Biology,* edited by R. O. Slatyer, et al. Canberra: The Australian National University Press.

1973 Kinship, Attachment Behaviour and the Primary Bond. In *The Character of Kinship,* edited by Jack Goody. Cambridge: Cambridge University Press.

1979 The Anthropology of Choice. Presidential Address, Anthropology, Archaeology, and Linguistic Section, Australian and New Zealand Association for the Advancement of Science, 49th Congress, Auckland, New Zealand. Duplicated.

Gough, Kathleen
1981 *Rural Society in Southeast India.* Cambridge: Cambridge University Press.

Hesse, Hermann
1954 *Siddhartha*. (Translated from German by Hilda Rosner.) London: Peter Owen Ltd. (Originally published in 1922.)

Janakiraman, T.
1972 *The Sins of Appu's Mother*. (Translated by M. Krishnan.) Delhi: Hind Pocket Books.

Kakar, Sudhir
1978 *The Inner World: A Psycho-analytic Study Childhood and Society in India*. Delhi: Oxford University Press.

Kane, P. V.
1941 *History of Dharmashastra*. Vol. IV. Poona: Bhandarkar Oriental Research Institute.

Lutyens, Mary (ed.)
1970 *The Penguin Krishnamurti Reader*. Harmondsworth: Penguin Books.

Madan, T. N.
1965 *Family and Kinship: A Study of the Pandits of Rural Kashmir*. Bombay: Asia.

1975 On Living Intimately with Strangers. In *Encounter and Experience: Personal Accounts of Fieldwork*, edited by Andre Beteille and T. N. Madan. New Delhi: Vikas. Honolulu: University of Hawaii Press.

1981 Moral Choices: An Essay on the Unity of Asceticism and Eroticism. In *Culture and Morality: Essays in Honour of C. Von Furer-Haimendorf*, edited by A. C. Mayer. Delhi: Oxford Univeristy Press.

1982a Anthropology as the Mutual Interpretation of Cultures. In *Indigenous Anthropology in Non-Western Countries*, edited by H. Fahim. Durham, N.C.: Carolina Academic.

1982b The Ideology of the Householder Among the Pandits of Rural Kashmir. In *Way of Life: King, Householder, Renouncer: Essays in Honour of Louis Dumont*, edited by T. N. Madan. New Delhi: Vikas. Paris: Maison des Sciences de l'Homme.

1982c Death in the Family: An Essay on Hindu Attitudes to Dying. Paper presented to a Seminar on Order and Anomie in South Asian Society and Culture. Duplicated.

Mandelbaum, David G.
1970 *Society in India*. Two Volumes. Berkeley: University of California Press.

Nandy, Ashis
1980 *At the Edge of Psychology*. Delhi: Oxford University Press.

Parry, J. P.
1982 Death and Cosmogony in Kashi. In *Way of Life: King, Householder, Ren-ouncer: Essays in Honour of Louis Dumont*, edited by T. N. Madan. New Delhi: Vikas. Paris: Maison des Sciences de l'Homme.

Ross, Aileen D.
1961 *The Hindu Family in Its Urban Setting*. Toronto: University of Toronto Press.

PART IV

The Dialectic Between Destiny and Decision: Nomothetic and Ideographic Conceptions of Anthropology

7

The Ethnographer's Choices

GILBERT H. HERDT

A story is told that an American philosopher, touring Japan after a conference, grew increasingly exasperated as he travelled from one temple to the next. Finally, with American impatience, he demanded of a Shinto priest, "But where is your philosophy? Your theology?" The priest, after thinking hard, broadly grinned: "We have no philosophy ... we don't practice theology. We *dance.*"

Most of us have probably experienced this distinction in everyday life: what can't be said is "danced." If we could say all we felt, dance, song, and daydream wouldn't be drawn on in the same way; our imaginative participation in poetry and plays, painting and theater, would alter, the joys or pain in our relationships would differ; and searches for discovery of ourselves—through work and play, science and art, at home and abroad—would take different courses, each with different consequences. Many such wonders, so difficult to say, are harder to write. Perhaps it matters not, except for novelists or the famous who write their autobiographies, for otherwise our experience does not belong in the public domain.

In some human sciences such as anthropology and psychoanalysis, however, the choices are not so simple. Because we researchers shape, interpret, and then write of our experiences—being parties to, and objects of, the same communications in which our subjects took part—it is unclear what parts are public or private, science or nonscience. Ethnographers face unique intrepretive problems. For the special task of ethnography is something like the converse of Shinto praxis: the writer must put "it," experience in another culture, into the words of a cultural discourse other than that of the natives, since readers have never done their "dance." More than in other disciplines, psychoanalysis included, the ethnographer struggles with the distinction between multitudinous human experiences and their translation into written texts. This task, I believe, involves the ethnographer's successive experiences and his or her choices in the field far more than anthropology accord in the past.

159

How do we ethnographers transform a dance or any multi-layered human experience into words, substituting a text for the original perceptions and sensations? How is the reader to know and trust in the participants' or observers' reports? How will empathy be drawn on? The pitfalls are many: saying too little, saying too much; schematization, mechanization, cute style, formal style—many maneuvers to avoid revealing who we were, and are, in our reports. The list could go on and on—there are many ways of letting the frameworks and abstractions of theory, the refinements of methodology and impressiveness of statistics, style, jargon, and so forth, ultimately replace the words that substitute for the experience of seeing or sensing the "dance."[1]

The essay that follows is unconventional, a first-person informal account of fieldwork among the Sambia, a horticultural and hunting people of the Eastern Highlands, Papua New Guinea.[2] I describe a trivial but perplexing moment, on singing, not dancing, that illumines a pervasive identity theme in Sambia culture, showing how my responses to that moment, and a more general theme, were affected by my theoretical views and personality.

I offer this essay in honor of Derek Freeman, an unconventional anthropologist who remains an original thinker. It is fitting to do so, since, in large measure, his extraordinary intellect and stimulus to my first New Guinea fieldwork have led me to the methodological and theoretical issues discussed below. For, if Derek conveyed anything, it was that the universe is complex, not simple; that human universes are interactions between historical traditions and the individuals—in all their complexity—who purvey them; that these systems of values and beliefs were created and can be changed by the choices of individuals complexly constrained by their experience and circumstances; that anthropologists' interpretations are as value-laden as the cultures we study; and that the search for scientific discovery should proceed in oneself, as much as in another culture. Such principles concern our capacity as *Homo sapiens* to transcend the restrictions of perceived "human nature" and "culture" and seek a greater image of human freedom and potentiality (see Freeman 1970). The ethnographer's choices in field praxis and writing are but an instance of these principles. I will argue, using myself as a subject, that the ethnographer's experience conditions "knowing" another culture, and, thereby, self-knowledge. Choosing to place oneself in an ethnographic account is a moral choice that influences interpretation—so is keeping one's presence invisible. In either case the consequences for the craft of ethnography are great, though, in the case of conventional normative ethnography, it was assumed that no moral choice was involved either way. The difficult step of placing the writer's presence back in the scene from which a text originated, rather than being edited out, makes us, in this sense, more fully—publicly—accountable for our presence in the field and its effects on our product, ethnography.

The reader must know that I did not select the singing focus for its exotic surface. I am not a singer; most Sambia men are not much better. Nor does my love of song at all match that of Sambia, who wrap themselves in it. Indeed, studying the events, name-songs, song-ropes, esoteric words, and singing contexts, depicted below was perplexing and was not at the center of my primary research. Nor do these subjects figure prominently in other writings—my own or those of other New Guineasts.[3] Ethnomusicologists seldom study the symbolic meaning of such phenomena.[4] But the ethnographer must, when—in spite of his or her own stumbling reluctance, blindfolds, boredom, whatever—it emerges that such an expressive medium is a powerful or subtle means through which one's hosts create interpersonal relationships, social and personal identity; and when the ethnographer's acceptance—in experience, not just in words—means that a people "sang him" to create inside themselves an image of him to feel with, hold on to, and trust; or else, send him packing: literally, or figuratively—in the case of those anthropological strangers who back home unpack their data only from field notes, not from their insides. The point is not whether I or any of us ethnographers were loved and accepted or hated and shoved away—and no number of optimistic vignettes can disguise those extremes—or probably something in-between them. My thesis is that ethnographers should study the intersubjective processes of those experiences, as, for example, by interpreting of whom and what it was those other selves knew and sang, for such interpretations offer clues into culture *qua* mind. Another story would have served as well from my own work, but this one, which contains a story in a story, illustrates that the ethnographer's identity mediates how much of another culture's "dance" readers can see.

It still surprises me, the memory of that first time I saw a gruff older warrior openly sob in a songfest. It was during a crowded gathering in our hamlet, Nilangu, amid his male comrades—when the last thing a man should do is cry, especially when he, Soluwulu, was the lead singer. Let me take the story of that incident and its ramifications as an example for understanding how the study of culture entails the study of individuals, and how we must also study the ethnographer's methodological choices to bridge the gap of information (intimate communications) otherwise missed.

The singing grew spontaneously in the men's house early one evening. It was cool out—one of those crisp brilliant nights of a dry-season day that had been so sunny—as only Sambia, who annually see nine months of miserable rain, can appreciate. A stiff north wind had swept away sunset fog revealing a sky of diamonds. Children were still playing outside in the dazzling moonlight when the singing began. I stepped out on my verandah; in the hamlet, slightly below, an orange glow shown here and there from doorways of the other, thirty-odd huts. Passed them, far beyond the hamlet's sharp ridge, one could dimly see a mile off in the darkness the faint outlines of our neighbor hamlets brooding on their own shadowy mountainside. The singing rang through this stillness. While songfests are ordinary, they were new to me, for after two months I still felt like a tourist. I was a bit curious, besides having had enough of that disciplined aloneness called "writing notes" for the night. Duty called, and I was glad for the distraction. So the singing lured me out into the night.

The men's house was just a minute's walk away from my house, and it was already alive with an assortment of its inhabitants, most of the older bachelors and younger initiates. Singing, like other social activities, is age-graded and has a ritual hierarchy based on the authority of the elders, which here inhibits boys and youths till they are older, and excludes women and children. A few married men had also joined in, as usual, having left their women and children to take a place in the all-male quarters. The igloo-shaped men's house was warm from a blazing hearth. After only a few weeks everything seemed so familiar: the smokey smell of burning oak, dirty bamboo walls, brown and tan bark cloth and feathers on brown and black bodies, bows and arrows, sweet potatoes and sugar cane peelings strewn on the floor or ready to be cooked. But what grips you are the friendly faces: bright and wide-open with hungry smiles through teeth stained red from chewing betel nut, raised voices and laughter, and looks that embrace, not drawn back—in this safe refuge—on faces young and old, taut and weather-beaten, the old ones proud of having made it this far against life's dangers and their enemies, and prouder still of being in charge of their families and their destinies. A couple of youths smiled at me, and I sat down in a place which my friends, Weiyu and Moondi, cleared for me, glad for the company. More men arrived. Then unceremoniously Soluwulu walked in, tall and stately—a near middle-aged fighter who later captured my attention.

The crowd grew as more married men pushed in. The singing progressed until a little later (around 10:00 p.m.), when the elders filed in. In Nilangu there are a half dozen of those wizards, ranging in age from 50 to 70 years; all of them made it that night except old Bangeratwo, who is senile, but sometimes comes along. Their leader, Kanteilo—my sponsor—entered, not greeting me or anyone else as is his fashion. He matter-of-factly plunged in. Having attended to the day's business and seen to it that their houses were in order, the elders always entered last with some aplomb, thus marking an entrance befitting their highest social status. (Kanteilo, in particular, had four homes: his regular residential hut in

Nilangu; a garden house; another house in a new settlement by the river; and my own house, where he slept many a night, during my first two years in Nilangu.)

Younger men were moved aside as the others took their places at choice spots around the hearth fire, towards which the circle of eyes trained. Soluwulu sat among them. Greetings were exchanged. One of the elders leaned into the next, muffling a confidence. Bamboo pipes and tobacco were passed around; betel nut was brought out and shared. The hut was soon fogged up with smoke. Meanwhile, the singing had momentarily broken off. But soon it grew and was stronger.

There was a special intimacy in the crowd of singers that night. I don't think I am romanticizing their mood, for it crops up again, from time to time, though seldom does it radiate as it did that night through a songfest. Perhaps it was a contagious effect of their own spontaneity, since there was no particular reason to celebrate. Perhaps the singing reflected lucky providence—the bright weather, general health and prosperity of the community, and their being safe together—blessings appreciated by those who have suffered long wars, epidemics, and even famine. The crowd's homogeneity helped, for only villagers were present: no need to stage a singing contest with competitive neighbors or to impress pompous visitors, since none were among us. And perhaps, too, my own presence added to the camaraderie, for I was another sign of good fortune: a lifeline (money, medical care, a radio) previously lacking to an outside world that increasingly pushed inwards. In that way I had become a go-between with the outside: a new audience for the men.

But whether for these reasons or not, no special event that night or on the morrow should have created the oneness which thickened their singing, and I doubt that we should search further for cause. Sambia love to sing, as individuals, and in groups. They will use most any excuse, aside from the ceremonial situations requiring it, to raise song, even fabricating a reason if necessary to stage a songfest: a noisy, smoked-up session made simply for the enjoyment of whiling away an evening in good company. By the time I had moved in the village, some things in traditional Sambia life had changed after pacification, but the songfest was not one of them. The singers were still around.

That ancient tradition was still foreign to me. I didn't understand the significance of songs or their words yet. I was especially green to their language. People knew that, and while at times it caused problems, they did their best to teach me. That is true despite the fact that there was safety for them in my ignorance: they were still hiding ritual secrets from me. Friends helped me out in the songfests, patiently pronouncing the words so I could parrot the phrases. Curiosity was my supporter in these frustrating lessons, but even that weakened after the long hours of dull, monotonous chords seemed to merge, growing muddier from the men's slurred refrains. One grows positively saturated with it, this singing that goes on and on and seems timeless, the singers transfixed for long hours.

I was tired but stayed on; and I have never ceased to marvel at how the men (who rise at dawn) can fend off sleep so with their paltry stimulants—tobacco and betel nut. The initiates, pushed back against the walls, grew bored and tired, many dozing off seated upwards, knees pushed into their jaws.

Not so with the elders and men, who sang on: sometimes low, baritone, even drab; sometimes stronger, lighter, exuberant; sometimes stiff; sometimes with greater harmony—especially when the bachelors, who were still not manly enough, and had to overcome embarrassment to sing in their elders' presence, felt brave enough to lead; and sometimes in lonely stillness, as a lead singer would raise solo chords to which his fellows responded in collective refrain. As the hours ticked by, it seemed the men would go on till dawn, as sometimes happened, oblivious to the body's need for sleep, the demands of their jobs tomorrow, their wives or the rest of the world.

Sometime then—was it midnight or after?—another vocal quality, so unpredictable yet characteristic of the do-or-die stance Sambia men learn to endure, crept into their singing. On the surface this affect first looks like dogged determination, and then stoicism. The pace of singing quickens, becoming melodiously higher pitched. The singing grows more intense and steadfast, and the singers more self-assured, smoking more and straightening up to stay awake. That late-night pitch has always seemed to me a sort of broadcasting—that one is master of, not slave to, the forces that challenge—inside and around. (But who or what is the audience for that signal? Peers? Women? The spirits? The other hamlets? Oneself? Now me? Or all of these resonating against each other?) Yes, bullheadedness. But waiting in the wings backstage of this hard and fast endurance test is a surprising guest at these nocturnal and very masculine parties that postpones dreams: displays of sorrow and sometimes weeping.

When first sensing the sorrow, I found myself moved by the thought that the songfest was not just a buffooning circus, that the men were sentimentally moved. (Many times they are a circus.) What kind of sentiment involved the communal chanting or the sorrowful attentions of a lone lead singer who sang proudly alone, obviously connected to some inner images of the songs? In the following minutes I spontaneously fell in with this reverie, not consciously searching for the memories that returned of friendly nights spent singing by campfires in Kansas when friendship was less complicated, of afternoons idled away in moody California concerts during the late sixties and early seventies. The singing shifted; the crowd's mood thickened. An hour had thus passed by as if in moments;

I had drifted also and was drowsy. The singing turned melancholy. Those currents were neither clearly apart from me, nor from the others. Then a vague uneasiness slowly grew and overtook me. I shot awake.

It was then that I focussed on Soluwulu—the lead singer—and became aware that something in his voice had minutes before sent me slumbering with the crowd, remembering boyhood and college as if they were yesterday, not a thousand years ago, until my drifting changed into uneasiness. Soluwulu's voice grew fainter, though he still glared ahead. But as he continued singing his face suddenly blazed two streaks of firelight matching those of the orange flames—like tiny streams of molten lava down a mountain. Tear tracks: he was crying. I could hardly believe my eyes. There in the spartan men's house, its high ceiling rafters smoked-filled, cold and empty looking down on walls beaming with the armaments of a proud warriorhood, the crowded audience unmoved and chanting round the hearth, Soluwulu broke off and bent slight forward, silently sobbing amid his old cronies. Now a part of me stepped back, puzzled and disconcerted: Why was that man, alone—the one there across the fire from us—crying?

The other men merely seemed to "ignore" Soluwulu. Though another elder spontaneously took the lead, and, in a moment, the singing actually picked up, as if to compensate for that one less voice. No one spoke; no one touched him or seemed to mind; no one (except me) looked around. (Two other times I have seen such a crying in songfests. On one occasion at this moment, I did see a married man—the old shaman Gambakutu—say: "Oh cousin..," and then reach out and warmly pat a man's side.) The two older men seated beside him, which included Kanteilo, raised their voices—staring straight ahead, staring with half-closed eyes past the fire, and beyond us, fixed towards the wall. They sang on. The elders' faces were in clear view and I watched carefully, expecting some reaction— be it care, anger, or shame—to this utterly uncharacteristic and "unmanly" action. But to no avail: they were unchangingly calm. There was, though, a trace of benign smile on Kanteilo's lips—as if he possessed some secret about this sobbing. I wanted to ask why, what the crying meant, for that was the first time I had ever seen it in a Sambian man, who generally disguise their emotions in public. Certainly, pain and crying were shameful reactions publicly hidden by men, especially older warriors. Since no one else moved, I adopted the "carry on" (not disinterested) posture of my hosts. In a minute, Soluwulu straightened up, and it was clear that we had been privy to his outpouring until he resumed his lead.

Although I looked at my friends again, they glared ahead, ignoring me, saying nothing, singing. I wondered if they had even noticed. In a couple of minutes though, Moondi and Kwinko began a new tack. Again they began correcting my faulty singing. Moondi carefully enunciated words of refrains so I could try learning some more. Some other initiates nearby, amused by my attempts, turned away to laugh so they wouldn't shame me, and hence, themselves: the Sambia way. There was some relaxation in that quiet clowning. Yet no mention of Soluwulu. (Nor would there ever have been unless I hadn't asked.) By now, Soluwulu was "himself" again, smoking and singing; things were back to normal. The crowd became expansive and carried on the singing.

Finally, in a fit moment, I whispered to Weiyu, "Why was he crying?" "Who?" (As if he hadn't noticed.) "Soluwulu." "Oh . . . He was singing his brother's song, who's dead." Weiyu continued, "It was his brother's song, he was crying for [the memory of] him." It was just a matter-of-fact.

It would be a long time until I understood more about the songs, the sorrow in Soluwulu's singing, or Weiyu's words. Or about these happenings—what they meant to Sambia—and how they are constructed around the "song-ropes" (ndaat-oolu) of men, as Sambia refer to them. Weiyu's remark seemed like all the answer necessary—at first—and it was enough to quell my curiosity. But it didn't tell what Soluwulu had felt, nor why his crying was so cozily accepted. Nevertheless, the singing didn't matter that much.

There were more pressing interests—such as the ritual initiations—and I set the singing aside. But I could never quite forget that episode and the look on Soluwulu's face.

Any visitor to a Sambia hamlet could not help but notice how much people enjoy singing. Those who stayed longer would soon see, moreover, that men love convening songfests—events that punctuate so much of daily, and especially, ceremonial life. Singing is a creative expression of joy, personal celebration, contentment, triumph—feelings we associate with "happiness." My informant, Moondi, described the importance of the songfests: "We feel happy when we go . . . Plenty of men have come together. They joke around; there's fun. They chew betel and there's lots of good tobacco. And they tell lots of stories and the singing is strong . . . We feel some excitement there: it's because many men have come together."

The songfest is also a ceremonial event used to bring folk together, to encircle and solidify them, as it were—shutting out the cold, sickness, ghosts, strangers and enemies, and death. So it is used defensively, too, in healing rites and at the mortuary wake. But whether in joy or with sorrow, Sambia songs are individually known, named, and particularized: identified with real persons, entities, or things in the world. Songs are metaphors for the many ways of being Sambian. They link the living with the dead, society and nature, individual and group. Songs are pieces of identity.

From the start I sensed this special significance in the singing. For example, on initial reconnaissance patrols in the area—trying to locate a field site—I noticed how often the men spontaneously broke into song, sharing lyrics and little refrains. Unknown and unnamed they were to me, those chants, but they had good uses: to bolster their spirits when tired and climbing that last mountain at the day's close, or when together, at nightfall, relaxing after dinner. Even on the first night of my arrival in Nilangu there was a celebratory songfest. (Rich European innocent opens holiday retreat in these wilds: why him, why here?) Many other songfests followed over the coming months. I often joined in at the men's house, and no other experience runs so much with the grain of Sambia life as do they—those cozy, sexually segregated gatherings.

My own house provided for change in those customary arrangements, but I didn't understand it until later. I was white and different: that's how people initially accepted me and my study of their "customs." My house was large, indeed huge, by Sambia standards, and I wanted it that way. The American in me needed space to spread out; the dismal weather makes one's dwelling a sanctuary for weeks on end; and it became, in time—without planning it that way—a neutral meeting place the whole village used.[5] The result was that my house soon became a gathering place for public songfests in which men, and later women, children, and initiates—all of whom never otherwise mixed (and even in my house the initiates covered themselves in the corner) due to strict ritual taboos—could be together and sing. Thus my house mediated their ancient divisions. Even the women joined in, and the men would abide them a voice, usually with good humor, though privately men said the women's weak and disorganized choruses—which were usually sang only during female ceremonies—proved once and for all that women were inept, even in singing, which could not be failed at except by women. In time, however, seasonal events pulled people in different directions, and the novelty wore off.

The men went back to their segregated men's house songfests. Occasionally, when the need arose, a healing ceremony would be performed in a family house. A shaman would perform, and of course the women and children joined in. Singing occurred in mixed company, then, but the women sang very little. I never again saw the same attempts as those before: women singing while males made up an audience.[6]

The singing among individuals was just as impressive and intriguing. I'd see a man singing quietly to himself as he walked up the forest path for gardening. The small initiates, pushed out into the night to fetch water from the creek for their seniors, would bundle themselves up and carry a bamboo torch, loudly singing together—braving against ghosts and other evil powers in the darkness, and the men would traipse off at dawn on a hunt, singing till they entered the forest, where only silence reigns.[7]

But none impressed me as much as old Kanteilo, who made me

grudgingly recognize that singing had a personality of great depth. For the first weeks, when I usually lived alone, he'd come warm himself by the stomachless barrel that served as my stove, eating and sleeping there— away from his fourth wife—so I "wouldn't be alone." (He experienced this as a friendly, status-filled protective gesture, to let others know that he sponsored me. Yet at times it got too cold in my house, and it was a sacrifice, except when he *wanted* to be away from his wife, fearing that sleeping near her too much would "weaken" him quickly, while not wanting to admit that to her, or suffer the ordinary discomforts of simply sleeping in the plain old flea-infested men's house.) He'd rise at dawn as was his habit, but not quietly. He'd build a fire, noisily splitting wood, loudly yodeling (as do the most exhibitionist senior men), and then settle down to baking some tubers. For an hour or so, he'd sit alone, demonstratively singing the same monotonous chants, merrily self-contained. He amused and annoyed me: I never woke as early as him—until he moved in. In late afternoon, his gardening and visiting on a remarkable set of daily rounds done—no one his age could match him—he'd return again, moving back in. He'd hand me some taro or choice sugar cane or some such morsel and then ask for coffee. So his singing would begin again at dusk, only it was more quiet and relaxed, hummed over and over and interspersed with bits of news, until his low voice disappeared into a drowse before the stove.

Not until months later, during the collective initiation rites of 1975, did I see the grander version of singing in great dance-ground ceremonial *sing-sings*. These, staged out-of-doors in public on those fabulous ceremonious occasions, are not to be confused with the indoor songfests, which are usually segregated affairs. The singing of song-ropes only occurs in the men's house setting, which is more private and exclusively male. Hundreds of men and women collect at those events, decked out in their finest ritual plumes and garb. Men circle in large groups round the dance-ground, singing war-ritual chants. Those chants are different from the songs I've described, for they belong to no one in particular, and belong to the group only by virtue of their harmonic style. But that singing also belongs to group identity: the sense of proud, honorable manhood— stampeding masculinity that is powerful and can get things done—which every Sambia recalls from initiation events seen since earliest childhood.

Somewhere in that early period I asked a few questions about the songs. There were many more important issues to investigate, for my assignment was ritual experience, time was precious, and my interest in singing was low. Still, armed with a lengthy checklist of questions on subjects as diverse as pig herding, politics, and categories of pollution, I got around with a few glib queries to singing. What I wanted to know, and didn't yet even know how to ask, was what the devil Soluwulu had felt that night when his singing lead to sobs. I thought no one (perhaps not even Soluwulu, whom I didn't know) could tell me that. And in those days anthropologists, including Malinowski's inheritors, largely avoided such subjective matters. They were too private. Besides, no one else, as far as I could see, ever talked about men crying. That wasn't what men do in singing. That wasn't even what men *do*. So I followed my questionnaire, and Weiyu or Moondi said a little about the songs.

Their answers would have heartened Durkheim. Every Sambia male has not one but several "individual" songs that "belong" to their names and thereby mark off their social personhood, and every man has several names. The first one, the childhood name, is bestowed sometime following birth. (Sambia wait until several months after birth to name a baby, for they say they fear its death: naming the baby makes people more easily attached to it, and if it dies prematurely they feel "so sad"—an attitude that gains plausibility from the high rate of infant mortality.) The second name, which is a sort of nickname used only by age-mates, replaces the first one, and this "initiate name" is bestowed at a boy's first initiation. The third and usually the last name—the adult, proper name—is also awarded then, but it is seldom used, except by women in formal reference at a distance, till the third-stage initiation at social maturity: pubescent bachelorhood, warrior status, and the marriageable situations its status brings. Each name, even the baby name, has a song identified publicly with it. The song has a simple lyric and refrain, the refrain being repeated three and four times, harmoniously, whereupon the whole is repeated. Here is a simple example:

Oorumbiundunmo   — andumouwuno:
("Man's name"—"mine")   (He is there)

awei, awei   — awei, awei.
... (refrain)   ... (repeat)

There are also more complex name songs than this one (see below).

Most names are inherited. A boy may receive the name of a deceased (never living) father or uncle or brother, even a grandfather, usually patrilateral, but male matrilateral names are also chosen. Both one's father and mother may have a hand in naming children, but others, like shamans, may be involved in it too. Sometimes, at the death of his father, a boy or youth will discard his adult name and assume his father's name when the latter dies. If a man has several sons, however, the rule seems to be that a much older, already married and established son will not usually change his name; instead, a younger son, again—usually but not always the last born male—will adopt his father's name, so long as the son has been initiated. This naming custom forms part of the Sambia kinship system, and it is borne of respect for social heritage. One's name and therefore a piece of one's very selfhood is a social product that has a collective seal stamped into it.

Not only people, but most of the animals, important plants and forces in the Sambia world are also named, and thus identified with songs. It is a kind of musical totemism: songs for the cassowary and possum and other salient animals; songs for the sun, moon, and stars; those for sugar cane, cordylines—red and green types—and for taro, yam, tobacco, betel nut, and banana; a song to scare away ghosts. Even the wind and some insects, like the preying mantis, ants, bees, and such, have songs. There are silly songs that make children laugh, like that of body lice. But there are formal and proud songs—like that one identified with the Harpy Eagle—great clan totem/spirit familiar of Nilangu hamlet. Nothing is too great or too insignificant to have escaped being hitched to the system of songs.

Each of a man's name songs are connected with one another by virtue of his self and social identity as a particular Sambia person. Those songs are interconnected with many others that are inherited and handed down from father to son in what I call the song-rope. Sambia say that these "ropes"—the idiom conveys a sense of continuity physically, from past to present generations—have come down from their ancestors. A rope is comprised of a long sequence of songs associated with a man, his father's clan, cognatic kin group, forest territory, property marks, and particular spirit familiars known and counted as integral to a family line for generations. The extensiveness of these ropes vary, some with a score of songs, others with hundreds. It is usually the eldest son who has the right to lead his father's song-rope during songfests in the men's house. There is a practical reason for this right. Each rope encompasses many songs, some of them esoteric, some of them cloaked in archaic language, and the whole of which is sufficiently complex that a man must teach his son the sequence over a long period of time.[8] In plain terms there may be only several others—usually elders, who have heard the ropes over a lifetime and who correctly "know" a man's particular sequence of songs.

It took a long time to understand that these ropes are an invariable structure of songs oriented in four ways: by tradition, by time, by geographic space, and by virtue of the particular singer's identity. Tradition imposes a conventional way in which one is taught that the songs follow a certain order, rhythm, and musical pattern, inherited from the ancestors. Chronological time is another dimension, for, in general, the songs are sung from present to past, from the living singer back to bygone, faceless generations. Spatially, the songs also follow an imaginary course—the fantasied trajectory of the "rope" extending from the speaker's location to particular water marks, garden patches, groves of bamboo, especially liked groves of individual, ritually efficacious, trees, up to the peaks of the mountain ridges.[9] These special spots have their own names (e.g., *Tar-owultangu*, a taro patch growing near a high mountain pandanus grove). Thus, these locations (place names) have songs too. Lastly, there is the singer himself, his own name songs, those of his father and direct ancestors, as well as those associated with his and his father's particular spirit familiars (*numelyu*) gained through initiation ceremonies or his own dreams (see Herdt 1977). So the song-ropes embody a wealth of information about oneself, one's social network and genealogical ancestry, one's property and its jural boundary, and a sense of being firmly centered in a universe the songs chart out by time and space. The act of singing, which on its surface appears so simple, actually bathes a man in the fullness of his existence.

In short, a Sambia man's songs carve out his social world and personal history, quaintly and exhaustively demarcating—even beyond that of Lévi-Strauss's fictitious *bricoleur*—a circle of symbols we could appropriately label his personhood. That social labelling seems obvious, is important, and more could be said of it; but that is not my special interest here. The discourse that followed my glib questions helped. I had learned some "social facts." But far more remained to be known. For instance, what was the "personal function" or meanings of these song-ropes? Especially, I had learned nothing about the topic that had initiated my probe and still stuck in me—Soluwulu crying that night, a performance that hadn't recurred during the ensuing months of other songfests.

What I had discovered was that virtually everything in the Sambia world is named and everything of importance has its own song—a certitude of identity signs. All, that is, except the aliens, e.g., government patrol officers—and that included me.

It is not precisely clear when I first heard others "singing" me, but it was several months later. The memory was of walking along the path in our hamlet, as usual, returning from a trip to another village. Some women greeted me as they sat outside making grass skirts and chatting, easily distracted because they were simply enjoying themselves. They welcomed me by breaking into a song as if they had done it their whole lives. I didn't think much about it. It seemed expectable; nothing seemed out of place. Sambia commonly greet others, especially male kinsmen to whom they wanted to draw attention or who have been away, with a little demonstration like that. It is a fond greeting. "The women are just amusing themselves," I thought to myself with a smile. (Still, in looking back, I realize that a momentary combination of subtle embarrassment and pleasure overtook me; their song had hugged me.) I thought no more about it.

The same kind of song greeting came later, but from a different group of women.

Again, one afternoon, a while later, the initiates did it inside my house. It happened like this. I discovered that someone had eaten all the taro in my larder, and when I showed my irritation, chiding them like their mothers but still half-faking, they turned away, chuckling. Whereupon they began "singing me," Moondi leading this beguiling ploy, drowning out my scold and making me laugh.

So it went for another week, possibly two—my swimming in the usual scenes with only subliminal awareness of the singing—until one afternoon, when another sense of their singing crystallized for me. Some young women passed my yard, quietly stepping by but then halting to stare at me, giggling. Even then I suspected they were flirting. They began singing; again some embarrassment. But when I asked them, demandingly smiling, "What are you singing?", they ran off, noisily laughing down the creek path. They were singing *at* me, as if I were a Sambia bachelor.[10]

I found Weiyu and Moondi later, asking them—with some consternation—"Do people have a song for me?" They smiled, "Yes," rather matter-of-factly, and seemed amused that I would ask. It had never occurred to me that that would happen. I was thrilled and honored, for I "knew" intuitively people's singing signalled some additional recognition of me as a social person and a "self" among themselves. Yet, in an instant, my feeling changed back to puzzlement. How could I, a stranger without Sambia ancestry, have been given a name song?

My two friends weren't of much help in that department. After asking them where the song had come from, they vaguely replied that "some women" had started singing it. That is all they knew. It seemed a sufficient explanation.

In fact, the "singing of me" occurred so subtly that I took little notice. It was gradual and informal. It seemed to happen in situations as a spontaneous response to me on people's part. But I did sense a feeling of being in better contact with others, intersubjectively, as a result of being sung. That idea is worth pondering.

After six months' living with Sambia, the singing, like so much else, was just another part of a great thick soup, as fascinatingly exotic and perplexing as were the language and rituals and feelings behind the names. But for me, the singing was insignificant: just singing, "having fun," musical entertainment, an insignificant part of ceremonies. Singing didn't seem serious enough to take seriously. Besides, who had ever said that song systems or interpersonal singing had had much importance in New Guinea? It was all too esoteric and humorous, and I had come to study serious things that books taught, like initiation rites, which I intellectually *knew* to be important. And another thing—and here I must confess an acceptance of the men's smug chauvinism on this score—it was the *women and children* who were "singing me," with their unserious smiles and giggles.[11]

I knew, at least I thought I knew, that it was the men who could teach me important things. It wasn't to be until later that the men stamped formality into the women's and initiates' casual acts by singing my song with their usual seriousness in a men's house songfest. In a very real sense, then, I didn't go looking for the songs. They found me. I had no reason to examine singing or its meaning, at least until I had asked the standard checklist questions, for it seemed unrelated to anything important, just a distraction.

Ironically, it was my sociological checklist that helped me resist making conscious the significance of the interpersonal change that people were "singing me." The songs were a product of the *group*, a synthesis of its cultural heritage. No one, at least not the living, had *created* them, as they were a product of the ancestors. Yet, their living effects were to categorize people, stereotyping them into age sets, status groups, persons and nonpersons (e.g., women). The songs were tied to a naming system that celebrated formally male maturity: being male, being initiated, having a family and estate—all the social trappings that solidified men as a clan group with property and politico-jural rights to defend. The song-ropes seemed to convey that fullness of male personhood in a closed system. Men were named, tagged with songs, and counted in the songfests. Taken together, the songs were threaded into genealogical lines, and the ropes of clans crisscrossed to weave a larger rope for the community as a bounded, property-based, local descent group. One need not account for oneself; society did that—reassuringly—for all its various selves.

That is the view I adopted; social theory had dictated it, and it *was* reassuring, at first. The group had taken me in. Society, no individual Sambia or myself, in particular, had been responsible for the singing of me. Perhaps it was a short-sighted view, but no one seemed to have insight about the song system or my song: an unwitting, nonconscious group process had been responsible for what I had experienced. Of course, there were problems with this view. What is Soluwulu's anomalous crying? Why had the women—not the men—started my singing? Who had gotten it into their heads to do that to me, and why, in the first place?

The answers might lie in the structure of the song system itself, as if that object could reflect back to me insights. So that is where I next looked. For a few days—it stands out vividly because it was frustrating— I wedged questions into my conversations with the men and initiates. I searched for clues, some rule, a hidden cultural code, some kind of symbolic calculus that would clarify how the song-ropes took their general ordering. I asked, *in general*, who, what, when, where, and how men sang. People said, "We think of that place," "that thing" (tree, animal, and so forth), "that man" (objects of the songs). Beyond that, men would say glibly that the songs were their "custom" and had been "made by the ancestors." All that work hadn't helped much in finding a social logic for unraveling the symbolic system in which the songs were wrapped.[12] Friends seemed perplexed by my perplexity. Several younger men, for example, said they could not understand the archaic words and obscure names in the lyrics of older songs. The elders were worse. When asked about the songs' root meanings (*kablu*; base, kernel)—which was appropriate to ask, though no one ever did so vis-à-vis songs—they gave me the same line: it is "custom," it is "what we (men) do." (Every social anthropologist recognizes this in working with individuals. That is why social structure and nonconscious ideology supply the observer with missing interpretive links.) Even Moondi, my younger translator, said on one occasion that the song-ropes were very hard to explain in everyday language, especially the language of Pidgin. Moondi compared the difficulty to explaining the idea of numelyu, which remains partially untranslatable because of its religious undertones. He said the song-ropes would be as hard as learning the whole language, an unreassuring statement coming from my most articulate informant. In despair I went back to the more productive study of ritual.

Meanwhile, my name song would pop up here and there. I grew accustomed to it. I also got more adept at singing, listening to the words and refrains. I spontaneously fell into the Sambia style of singing my friends' names. I could do it with Kanteilo and several others. Intellectually, I didn't know what I was doing, except parroting words, and singing-teasing-honoring as a way of being with them. A couple of times, as I said, the men actually sang the song identified with me in the songfests, and someone would preface it with: "They all want to sing your song now." It seemed natural, another way of being with them. Then the initiations began in mid-1975, lasting four months. Afterwards, I began focused studies of the boys who had been initiated. That took two more months.

By then I had lived in Nilangu a year, and I was to take a break back to Australia and America. The women began singing of me differently—this time sadly—and it was sort of painful. People accused me of wanting to go away and never coming back. Kanteilo got depressed and disappeared from my house. When I found him, he said he felt sad that I was leaving, so he didn't want to live with me now, for it would make him sadder to see me go. I kept saying that this fuss was unnecessary, that I would be back. But people said they had heard that story before.

I don't think anything I had done had had such an effect on people as when I did return two months later. Some were incredulous; others said, "I told you so." I told Kanteilo that I hadn't lied to him after all, and he had seen for himself that my things—including field notes—had stayed behind (an insurance of my return). The shamans held a healing ceremony for me before and after I left, their way of magically protecting my person in transit, and then again welcoming me back. People were "singing me" more than ever. Nothing seemed to have changed except a knowledge that I had been good to my word.

My relationships deepened. I began case studies of individuals—Moondi, Weiyu, Nilutwo, other men, like Tali, the ritual expert, and some initiates too, in no small measure due to Derek Freeman's encouragement (see Herdt 1981, 1982a, 1982b). I went to work with the shamans. I got more interested in sexuality. I began studying Nilutwo's dreams. I also got to know Soluwulu, Tali's older half brother. Working with individuals was not entirely new to me. A few years earlier I had studied social transactions, especially those of psychotherapy in a California psychiatric ward. Sambia interviews were much different than that, of course, but there were certain kinds of experiences—communications—that were like familiar faces. That work was, and still remains, more exciting to me than is conventional ethnography focused on normative observations of social relationships and cultural institutions. This is still vital and necessary as a baseline for individual case studies. But it lacks the personal involvement of one-on-one interchanges of awareness—wanting to know what other persons see and feel and think, and not just what they "think with"—that led me to anthropology. That work was entirely exploratory: there had been no manual written on how to do clinical ethnography. I made mistakes, and some were painful: for instance, laughing behind Kalutwo's back with the other men at his deviance, his failed marriages, his homosexuality. Then he approached me to work on his shamanism and wore me out with his unconscious resistance, so I wrote him off, only returning three years later to find him in as much desperation as ever to talk with someone (see Herdt 1980). But the failures were as instructive as the successes, even though ethnographers, like other researchers, seldom publish them. It was from this disparate mien of ethnographies of individual lives that I began to see the "singing of me" in a different light.

It seems remarkable, in looking back, that I, besides being an ethnographer, could have gone so long without "recognizing" the fact that interpersonal singing is one of *the* fundamental ways (expressive modes, channels of information, cultural discourses, projective techniques, and so forth) through which Sambia subliminally communicated and create identity. More than that: the singing of me had evolved *my* identity—had presented an important change in people's feelings, responses, being with me—and I had not gotten it. There is the rub: "important" in whose eyes, defined and compared as a "change" in who or in what? It was all too damn subjective—my embarrassment in being sung had told me that. But that was my problem: Soluwulu had not felt that the night he cried.

To understand the full load of experience that Soluwulu carried that night, we have to go back a number of years before my arrival on the scene (1974) to the period around 1940, when Soluwulu was born in Nilangu—which was then a far smaller hamlet. It was an important period in Sambia history—a full two decades before pacification reached the valley in 1964–65.[13]

Only shortly before his birth (c.1939), Nilangu had been founded, an event that changed the political complexion of the Sambia Valley. Six or eight generations before, ancestors of the first Sambia pioneers had left the Papuan hinterland to the southwest and penetrated into the southeastern Kratke Mountains. They were Papuans, fierce warriors, and most probably—if we are to judge by the intermediate Vailala people—cannibals. (Sambia, themselves, are not cannibals; and cannibalistic figures do not appear in Sambia stories, folklore or myths either, except in the form of enemy tribes, animals (e.g., pythons) or spirits (e.g., ghosts, bogs).

The vast stretches of Sambia territory were probably uninhabited, save for scattered hunters and gatherers. Three generations later pioneers forged into the Sambia Valley itself, invading and overcoming the indigenous Kumundi people, one of these scattered groups. The whole belt of this territory is rugged and thinly populated. Even now Sambia are small in numbers and politically insignificant compared to the steaming Eastern Highlands groups that live just the other side of the Great River, a natural ecological barrier. Hamlets were established, settlers gradually moving northward till reaching present-day Nilangu, which was still being expanded into the roughest virgin rain forest in Soluwulu's youth.

Theirs was a hard life, those pioneers. In many ways it still is. Sambia live in a hard land. Isolated, land-locked, amidst a broken landscape, high in elevation, the hamlets are virtual island fortresses, only recently unbarricaded after pacification, where one has a feeling of living in a windswept bird's nest that nature threatens to topple any day. You would have to search a good bit to find a more ruthlessly beautiful habitat perfect for the stockading of a warrior band. In sunny season the weather is beyond perfection. But most of the year it is worse than ugly with heavy rain to light rain that turns into fog—a patrol officer once called it Frankenstein's country—miserable fog that shifts from cold to warm, actually seeping through the huts. One is chilled to the very bones by that cold damp fog, but in it, people must eke out subsistence as best they can. The rain forest had to be cleared with stone tools until the 1960s, when the Australians came. A single large tree took days to fell; a garden patch required months. Nature didn't yield easily; it still doesn't.

The hamlet was staked out and settled. The total village was little more than 200 by 200 square yards. It was bounded by small creeks on either side of its ridge and, far below in the valley, by the stormy Sambia River. Gardens extended in many directions. This tight-knit fortress was virtually impenetrable to attack. It wasn't long before it was a political power in the whole valley, for it contained a group of ambitious men—warriors, war leaders, a couple of shamans, and some young bucks—the present elders of Nilangu, including Kanteilo. Soluwulu's father was among them. He was a warrior, a minor shaman, and some say he was a strong man. He also had three wives and many children. He was an outsider, as was his clan, which had splintered during a previous fight, years later settling in Nilangu. Nilangu's leaders took them in but never quite trusted them. Back in those days you could never completely trust anyone, except your closest biological brothers and children. But the deciding factor was the need for manpower: warriors and hunters, and their women and female children, to work gardens and secure wives for the up-and-coming youths. The needs for defense came first.

Theirs was a warrior society, it had to be, for the world seemed at war with itself. It is hard for us to imagine it, to summon up that ghost without overdramatizing its harsh cruelty hammering into everyday existence, or without dismissing it by a few glib sentences that must stand for the reality of man-to-man stone-age combat that could cut, tear, and decapitate human bodies—men, women, children—the victims of quasi-enemies across the river, or true enemies in the next valley. The fear and horror and glory of it got stained into everything, filtering everyone's way of gardening or playing or making love, because it was always so close and so possible, that ugly death. That dreaded warfare more than anything else moved Sambia social relationships and their other cultural institutions.

Take marriage, for instance. Incest taboos made the contracting for wives a trade between different hamlets who could also fight with one another, and had. There was no choice in it. None could be permitted. What women would willingly leave hearth and home and loved one to take up squatter's rights with a stranger in a hostile hamlet? The elders made the arrangements by infant betrothal or brother–sister exchange. It was an awkward business, those marriages. The men were taught to fear women and their bodies, a kind of "antagonism" that invaded sexual relationships, and far more. Parenting, eating, gardening—everything was infected by the arrangements into which spouses were thrown. At best it was compatible; at worst it was hell: arguments and beatings, anxieties about menstrual pollution, sorcery, or semen depletion, and suicide. The children were part to it; they were why it was to work and they made it bearable. They were the inheritors.

Religion—what else could such a world spawn except, at best, protective hamlet spirits and fearsome forest spirits, who were capricious, but not as angry or carnivorous as the hated ghosts of Sambia—who hover about vengeful and envious, and must be formally cast out with screaming bullroarers and long song-filled wakes, cast as far away as possible to ensure safety for the living? (Sir Maurice Bowra was wrong; people don't always get the gods they deserve.)

Overseeing it all was the men's secret society, a ritual cult generating initiations, age-sets, status-ranked relationships between males, wholly aimed at creating the warriors needed to run a society that was—and is—based on the idea that "strength" (*jerungdu*) is the only means for surviving and winning in the battle, the hunt, in making babies, in being honorable.

Soluwulu was initiated into this warriorhood when he was seven or eight. Like his father he had no choice. Every male in such a small world is vital and is counted; must count. He left a household where he favored his mother and was probably spoiled by her; knew his father less, admired and feared him more. Good parents would have prepared and encouraged him for the fearsome ordeals that lay ahead; so he would have cried and possibly held on to them, but could stomach the hard rituals, fasts, beatings, and teachings, emerging more like a man, the warrior his father was. Initiation went on for months.

Its greatest secret was the revelation that he had to suck the bachelors' penises to get their semen and grow strong. Those homosexual activities were necessary, the elders said, because his body could not make its own semen, and that substance was the only thing that could physically mature him. So he did as his father did, and it was unbelievably filled with panic and shame, at least at first. Those homosexual contacts went on for years, all the time. They were carefully hidden from his mother and all other women and children. To ensure that secrecy, boys were entrusted with another secret: that the strange sounds said to be the power-filled cries of the old female hamlet spirits, which the men could direct and the women feared, were really only the flutes men blew at times of ritual. It was a great secret; death awaited any that revealed it.

There were other initiations, six of them in all, which directed and matured Soluwulu, from childhood to manhood, over some fifteen years. His life was lived as a warrior only in the spartan men's house after initiation. Taboos hemmed in his daily life—eating, drinking, moving around—and especially he could never talk or be with women, including his mother and sisters, who remained in his father's household, a world apart. All the while, war was going on.

By puberty, third-stage initiation—bachelorhood—came more fiercely than had his two previous initiations, but he was stronger and ready for them. More nosebleeding, endurance tests, and more glory, too: dressing up in a true warrior's outfit, his own now; marching in public—being seen formally for the first time in years by those he loved and whom he knew admired him. His parents had fed and clothed him his whole life; now it was his turn to help them in return. (In a year or so his father would die and he would have no choice in supporting his mother and younger siblings anyway.) He got to sing, too; could be addressed now by his adult name and start to be counted in the songfests. It was his right.

Coming of age at that initiation allowed, indeed forced him to take the dominant sexual role with younger initiates in homosexual activities. He became the fellated: finally he was out from under the thumbs of the older males (at least sexually), and it was exciting and risky, too, for he would begin "losing" semen through sex with boys. He was still roped off from women. Even casual heterosexual relations were forbidden, and sex with women was punished by death. The boys were his sexual outlet; they were available, wanted semen, and needed him and his age-mates to get it, so homosexual intercourse was easy to have. It could be rough and cruel, but it didn't matter: his fellators were usually "strangers" from the other hamlets. (All homosexual activity is tabooed with all relatives: most of one's fellow hamleteers.) It was manly, and was a duty. But there was far more to it than that (a part of him knew): he desired the boys, at least some of them, whom he could control and were more like himself than the dangerous, mysterious women the men kept for themselves. He used the fellators; they used him. There was one who would even sing his name song, teasing and honoring him, poking fun at him: the boy got away with it because Soluwulu favored him for awhile. Thus it went for years until marriage. After awhile the novelty wore off and he would tire of it sometimes, for his semen was being drained off to no benefit for himself. It was all a game, but it was an important game.

His brothers were among the men's house gang. Tuvunu, his oldest brother, had helped initiate him. And Soluwulu had helped initiate Tali later. He and Tuvunu had not been very close for years, had avoided each other in public. He never understood until initiation. Before then, as it had been with his father, there were hidden areas—ritual secrets, the avoidance taboos (namely women), the homosexual play—that put awkwardness in their relationship. Even after initiation they belonged to different status groups empowered by dominant/submissive rights and duties, as was true of men and women—who were even more walled-off by secrecy and pollution taboos.

Soluwulu's biggest status change came from being accepted as big enough to go on war raids with the men. Some of the treks were to far-off places of which he had heard. After third-stage initiation, he went on one. He was expected to earn his mark by killing someone, that was the ideal. Whether or not he did, it was status-filled just to be on the raid, returning with a new kind of experience the initiates and women lacked. He was a warrior: they would have to respect—even fear—him now. Tuvunu respected him more, and they were closer. There were other bow fights with the neighboring hamlets, too, yet they were more for show. Warclubs and axes were not used with them, only bows and arrows, and usually from a distance. It was part of a contest: Who was the strongest? Who had grown up quickest? Who could outfight us or outdo us in masculinizing boys or producing babies? He was compared with his age-mates in being a war leader or a rubbish man. His brother became a war leader and was married. War was also a game, but a deadly one.

Several years later he got a wife from Kwoli hamlet. She had been marked for him at birth and had come of age. He was anxious to marry, wanted his own house, and some children. They had no sex until her menarche, though he had heard rumors that some of his age-mates had fellatio with their premenarchal brides. He still had homosexual intercourse sometimes on the side. But that stopped soon, after his wife had her first menses and they began coitus, a totally different kind of sex than with the boys: genital-to-genital, more dangerous, more exciting, more uncontrollable and adult. It was all a bit overwhelming at first, but he couldn't let his bride see that; the elders had told him to stay composed, in command, and not get too involved—by avoiding looking at her during intercourse, and by keeping bitter bark in his mouth so he wouldn't say much or swallow his saliva, for that would contaminate him. In two years a child came. Sex was now forbidden till the baby was weaned. It was a hard transition to make: no sexual contacts at all. The sacrifice hardened him more. He went on long hunts and a trading expedition; went on a war raid; had wet dreams; and remembered that Numboolyu, the ancestral culture hero, had had to endure all this too, so the elders had said in their secret myth.

Two years before (c.1957) word reached Nilangu that some strange and powerful "red-skinned" men in weird garb entered Kaim hamlet over the mountains. They had forged the Great River passing over from Indoowi (Fore) country. They had strange sticks that had killed a pig and could make booming sounds greater than the bullroarer, people said. They stole food, too. The Kaim people fled into the forest, and some of the warriors later tried to ambush them but failed. It was a weird sound, the booms, like the ones the elders said were heard over the valley just after Soluwulu's birth (c.1942), flying things—the elders called them "great white birds"—up there swooping around, booming at each other.[14]

During that period a war began with the Northern Wantuki'u tribe. It was over some stolen pandanus nuts on the same old disputed boundary up in the mountains. There were raids. The sporadic pot shots went on more than two years.

In between these periods, Soluwulu's parents had both died. Several more initiation cycles were staged. There had been a big sickness for awhile, especially over in the Green River hamlets, where a lot of people died. That was their tough luck. Our shamans had blocked it out, only a couple of old people died over on the other side of the river. Tali was first initiated (c.1955), and later initiated as a bachelor (c.1962), which responsibility fell upon Tuvunu and Soluwulu, now that his father was dead. Arrangements had already been made to exchange younger sisters for women from other hamlets for their youngest brothers, Tali and Yawutyu. After the next initiations, around 1960, a great songfest was held, for the men had decided to launch a large war raid into the Wantuki'u and put them in their place, once and for all. The war leaders wanted blood. The new bachelors would be tested to see who among them would become the new fighters.

That songfest was special, it belonged to the all-night preparatory ceremonial preceding a war raid. There was even some hooting and dancing over on the village dance ground. The shamans all came and expurgated the men, removing the traces of women from their bodies that attracted arrows like a magnet, magically blessing them for a safe journey. There were war chants. But the songs were brought out, too, the song-ropes of the old ones. After his father died, he took his name, so Soluwulu sang his father's song. His brother Tuvunu was older and did not take the name; his brother sat in the crowd and joined in. At dawn they all left for the mountains.

The raid was launched and a Wantuki'u hamlet was attacked. There were no deaths and the raid wasn't very successful. The party was chased back. Their enemies counterattacked. That war dragged on for months.

Meanwhile another argument flared up and bow fighting began with the Wunyu-Sambia phratry across the river. One bow fight lasted for days. The Wantuki'u could have attacked at any time, inflicting a heavy blow, for the valley was itself divided; but they didn't. The bow fighting dragged on.

In one of those bow fights Tuvunu, Soluwulu's brother, was wounded. A few days later he died. He had lead in the fighting. Soluwulu wept, wanted blood revenge, and eventually Nilangu got it. Tuvunu's body was wailed over and put atop some trees in customary fashion. Wakes were held; the flutes and bullroarers mourned. At least it was a warrior's death.

It went on like that: there were a lot of battles. The "red skins" were sighted twice more. Word had it that the "great white birds" had landed in Baruya territory.[15] The red men fought with the Baruya and won; good for them. The Baruya were the worst of enemies.

A few months later the "red skins" came again but this time they went through the Sambia Valley itself. The women were terrified and fled to the forest. So did most of the men. A couple of war leaders stood up though—from a distance—and launched arrows. Kanteilo was one. The trespassers left. Another battle flared up, this time between Nilangu and Moonunkwambi—a hamlet on a neighboring ridge.[16] Shortly before, the initiations were held again. Weiyu's age-set was made a part of the cult. No sooner was it done than another battle began, this time Nilangu torn apart because its men took sides over an argument involving an eel stolen from a river trap.

That incident led to the last great battle. Many men were wounded. It seemed as though it would turn into an all-out war when the "red skins"— the government patrol officer—appeared. He seemed to ignore the fighting and went away. But in a few days he returned with a great line of black-skinned police. He built a hut over near Kwoli hamlet and made a speech. A distant Kaimeru man—a Sambia—who had gotten to be a government interpreter translated. They said they wanted to put the men's names in a book, so they were all to assemble the next day. But they were tricked; the police circled the men, took their weapons, and put them in handcuffs. It was terribly humiliating. Two score men, including Soluwulu, were marched off in chains to Mountain Patrol Station and jailed. They were treated as—what is the right metaphor?—savages? Animals? In a few weeks they were released and warned never to fight again. That was in 1964. War was done with.

Two years later a missionary came. He settled not far from the village down in the valley, and left us alone. They were strange, wanted to learn the language. They lived down by the river, made a settlement of their own (KwatSambia) in time. People mistrusted them at first, but soon came to like them: they never hurt anyone. Two years later Mountain Patrol Station was built. Some Sambia helped level the airstrip.

Six years later I arrived. Nilangu seemed idyllic; people were friendly. War was a living memory, and Sambia were glad it was gone. In between that time, two more initiation cycles had been held; Moondi's was the first. The next year (1975), the last full initiation was performed, and it lasted weeks. It wore me out. New Guinea was decolonized that year. It became Papua New Guinea, an independent state. Four years later in 1979, and again in 1981, I returned to the Sambia. Their society was changing faster than ever, and I had changed too.

What we call Sambia culture is the accumulated product of these generations of change compressed into the impact of Western "contact"— pacification drilling backwards and forwards unevenly and building this tiny outpost of a broader world itself divided—as measured, negotiated, in the lifetimes of its individual members. Their acts, words, and thoughts contain that experience, at many levels of awareness, which has dramatically changed over the past twenty years. History has transmuted their identities, a fact that convenient fiction, the "ethnographic present," ignores. Any moment of it is registered—microdotted[17]—in events like that night of Soluwulu's singing.

It is precisely because men share in their knowledge and experience of this remarkable history that Soluwulu's crying that night made "sense" to them. Life is harsh; war could kill; it took Tuvunu: they knew all that. It was obvious. It is precisely because the songs are *of* male identity and *for* their songfest (sexually segregated in the men's house) that Soluwulu could proudly sob as a most intensely masculine act. Take away the men's house context and place women and children in the audience, and he probably would not have allowed his feeling to become weeping: that would be shameful, unmanly. But the all-male situation and the fact of his dead brother's song might still not have produced that rare act in another man.

Is it coincidence that I have only seen the most masculine of warriors weep—in a very noble manner, at that—in songfests? No: "a quiet" man probably would not do that, and a rubbish man might be dismissed (or even scoffed at: "same old weakness") for it. Soluwulu did it because of who knows what motives and dynamics and because he is Soluwulu, the fine and respected warrior people know to be the embodiment of all that is idealized as Sambian masculinity. The ethnographer—the outsider— cannot know that until he learns. By sensing and then knowing it, we see a different side of Sambian men that is richer and more complex than their behavior "speaks" in public.

Sambia used my name (or versions of it) to interact with me. But they *gave* me a song because they had to in order to have me around. Perhaps someone else could have been taken in but not given a song, I don't know. Perhaps if I had come now (1982), under the throes of massive cultural change, no song would have been necessary, for people sing far less. The songfests are a thing of the past. In 1974, though, I—the ethnographer I am—because of my personality, was not adopted and entrusted by Sambia without my self having a song they could keep inside themselves and hold onto, even when I was gone.

I didn't understand that until years later. I knew how they named me: Gilbert was corrupted to "Gimbo" (pronounced Gëm-bo), or "Gimba-two";[18] later on people called me Gilberto and my friends used Gil (in 1981). In 1979 it came out—or so I thought—that my song had been borrowed from my friend Kokwai, a young married man. But that was wrong: our names, as modified in song, just sound alike. Then I thought that perhaps the shamans had invented my song; they used to astonish me by coining new names and songs from their dreams and who knows what else. But that was wrong too. Someone or group—I'll never know just who—created my song. It has three key phrases that go like this:

1. *Weiyatmeilo . . . Weiyatmelio . . . Weiatmei . . .* (corruption of *Weiyapu* — "red-skinned one"? . . . mine)

2. *Gimbatmeilo* ... *Gimbatmeilo* ... *Gimbatwo* (Gilbert, mine ... etc.)

3. *Bwanjatmeilo* ... *Bwanjatmeilo* ... *Bwanjatwo* (Harpy Eagle, mine ... etc.)

Awei, awei ... *Awei, awei* ... etc.

The order is then reversed, and the refrain sung again.

The etiology of *"Weiyatmeilo"* is vague, but it is probably a form of *Weiyaapu*, which Sambia use for whites. *Bwanju*—The Harpy Eagle—is the great clan totem and spirit familiar of Nilangu, a highly prized, aggressive-protective symbol: it is forbidden to kill or eat this bird. For several reasons I am identified with it.[19] The three phrases rhyme and are harmonized. When sung, they sound similar to those of Kokwai's song, though the words are all different. When my song is sung in some ordinary setting as a greeting, only the *"Gimbatmeilo"* chord is sung. Sometimes, bwanju was used as a metaphor for me, and people have said: "You've come to be with us and you have the spirit familiar of the bwanju; that bwanju must stay here."

There *is* something special about this way Sambia have of being with people by singing their songs. Only now am I conscious of it. Everything important is named and has a song. These songs are strung together to link past and present in so many ways. But, men do not sing of women (although the reverse is true). Only older men have the status and self-esteem to sing their own songs in the songfests, and only the most masculine men have been seen to weep on rare occasions. What is in a song? The identity that Sambia "say" with their behavior: the full-blown identity of esteemed masculine personhood. I can add two other obser-vations. First, of all that is named and has songs, none includes the body or body parts. Second, a strict taboo forbids anyone ever to say their own name—*except when singing their own song*. Likewise, it is forbidden ever to say one's childhood name or sing that song, except in songfests. Obviously some older, and perhaps deeper, parts of selfhood are sum-moned up as guests to men's private songfests. Why should that be?

I remind you that Sambia is a technologically simple society without our electronics, buildings, bombs, and supermarkets. They have no mir-rors, and nothing, not even water pools, in which to see their reflections. That means that Sambia never saw their own faces—images or reflections of their bodies—before recent. People now have mirrors from tradeposts, and some Sambians—particularly the younger generation—enjoy looking at themselves.

What would it be like to have lived one's whole life without ever having seen your own face? Think on that thought a moment. One *can* see the products of one's labor in gardens or hunting; or see one's trappings—

clothes, exuviae (fingernails, hair, spittle), and waste products (feces, urine). But one cannot see fully what we Westerners call the self, the primary referent of which is our face. Sambia see themselves only in the responses of others: smiles, body posture, grimaces, gestures, interactions. In a society like America, the "me" society, a "culture of narcissism," as Lasch (1979) refers to it, we have surrounded ourselves with mirrors, photographs, portraits. We seem to be in love with ourselves.[20] Yet so many seem so alone, so diminished of self. Certainly, we seldom sing together; our radios blast songs anonymously to anonymous selves. Sambia had none of that. Their world stopped at the top of their mountain ridges. Everyone was named, known, and sung. Their songs are mirrors, reflecting their selves to and from themselves and others. But because they are also songs taught, learned, and sung together with the only significant others there are, they define a selfhood that seems to be equally public and private, and is no way anonymous. Singing expresses the very life force of Sambia society, the existence of separate but interlocking selves.

Anthropologists achieve professional status by first doing fieldwork. Since ethnography is both a process and a product (see Agar 1980), our professional lives are embedded in field experience and in its effects upon our awareness when interpreting retrospectively and writing. These hermeneutic processes, no matter how systematic or rigorous, always involve personal experience; so there is a moral dimension—made explicit or not—in all anthropological writing. Our fieldwork approach, daily interactions with natives, what we see (insights) or don't see (blindspots) in observing and interviewing, all involve choices, at many levels and at all stages leading to publication, on the ethnographer's part. If we place ourselves on the ethnographic scene, another interpretive dimension is opened. Choosing not to do so (even choosing not to report a datum or misunderstanding) is a choice. All that editing is also ethnography (see Devereux 1967): the praxis of fieldwork and writing. But praxis is just a fancy word to cover field techniques, interpersonal communications, operations in one's interpretations, and, of course, the ultimately moral image of ourselves that we project to readers in our writing. There never has been a complete description of such praxis in anthropology, even for a cultural episode, including the one above. The difficulties obstructing such an account are immense; perhaps we are not wise enough yet to be accountable for the full consequences of such. But our awareness of the challenge is growing (see LeVine 1982, Chapter nineteen). When, someday, others (following Read 1965) take up the challenge, ethnography will make anthropology more of a science, with the added benefit, as Derek Freeman (1983) recently argued, of separating facts from fiction in our theories and their moral consequences for Homo sapiens.

Every society provides an ethos and its own distinctive discourses through which people communicate with others. The human spectrum includes directives that one should be warm or cold, friendly or suspicious, calm or pitched in dealing with strangers or friends, through such diverse activities as work, play, ritual, fishing, sex, mountain climbing, basket weaving, watching television, picnics, teas, beer bursts, speechmaking, lying, subterfuge, secrecy, coronations, revolutions—you name it. These cultural designs produce different phenomenologies and behavioral outcomes. For they can bring people together or keep them apart, each providing distinctive meanings for being human, or a group member, or an alien, thereby communicating, directly and indirectly, who we are, what we are worth, how others feel towards us, and how we feel about ourselves. Sambia do this communicating through their singing, but they have other ways (ritual, gossip, myth, warfare, taboos), too. No anthropologist ignores such distinctive signposts of how people live together and invest their selves with meaning. But neither should we shun describing how we responded to through the same basic processes, whatever that entails and wherever it occurs, in ethnography.

Perhaps it is comforting to believe that what transpires in a tribal society like that of Sambia is dictated by group custom or determined by the impersonal forces of history, economy, or psyche. Such a belief has led, often enough, to the search for the Symbol, the Cultural Code, the Political Economy, or the Unconscious, keys to understanding the Deep Structure of a Society, not its people. What a pity. For in that instance, the ethnographer chooses to ignore innovations, insights, personal meanings, real political decisions, consciousness, and the logic and capriciousness of human minds. In other words, all that is distinctively human. But we know—Two Crows (see Sapir 1938) alerted us long ago—that that stance is specious. What a comforting rationalization for ignoring why and how an ethnographer lived with a people when reporting on them. I would add that my personality and cultural orientation defended me against the insight that Sambia were internalizing an image of me and making my selfhood conform to their way of knowing self. My initial avoidance of topics like singing, and my belief that it was trivial, were intellectualizations and rationalizations that kept me from truly understanding what was going on in me and in my friends. But I see this now and didn't know it then. Sometimes insight, like age, grows slowly. (See Lévi-Strauss 1970 for a somewhat different view.)

Thus in the ethnographic account removed from the field experience, the author's field tactics and experience can remain invisible. Meanwhile, as he reaps academic honors or pelts in the Ivory Tower, another skeleton rattles in its moral dungeon. Impersonal methodological approaches permit impersonalized—no—depersonalized accounts.

Anthropology has afforded me the best of two worlds: a very privileged Western education and research training, and the wonderful experience of living with a non-Western people full and rich with life in a forgotten corner, untrampled until recently by our more sophisticated corruptions. It has also provided a lifestyle that well suits me: direct contact with the wholeness of people, which I need and enjoy; and, through my field data and thoughts about them, reflection upon another culture, hence philosophizing about humankind, leading back to reflection upon myself. Our ethnographies comment not only upon other cultures, theory and method, but on the choices we made in and on behalf of our own cultures, and ourselves—silent subjects of reflection. Thus, in anthropology we proceed from outside of ourselves, via another culture, to return to self-discovery.

We anthropologists are—notwithstanding our critics' divertisements—largely a powerless, poorly paid lot, as professions go. But we are lucky to have had that great intellectual experience—fieldwork—which, of all other training experiences, only the psychoanalysis matches in depth and complexity and far-reaching discovery of self. Nevertheless, where the anthropologist works through another society back to cultural insight, the psychoanalyst works through past and present experience to personal insight (see Habermas 1971:228). The process of discovery in both is similar, but analysis is more focused on self-insight as its chief product. What psychoanalysis needs is our cross-cultural experience; what we need is its insights into self. They must go together, for they are of a piece, and one is damaged without the other. Have we—anthropologists and psychoanalysts—not reached a cul-de-sac without the other? Have we not concluded but merely begun the exploration of our true object: the possibilities in human existence? Derek Freeman has helped us to say yes. Will we also have the courage to look more deeply at ourselves, even when, in public, it is sometimes painful to do so? Do we in our disciplines know this: if we do not take courage in that scientific discovery of insight, who will?

It seems, in ending this essay, that we are only slightly further along in understanding how to translate others' experience into words. I fear that I have simply raised more problems for those who would be ethnographers. Stories and fine rhetoric are no solvent for the moral choices confronting fieldworkers. I would also be dishonest if I denied my uneasiness in making public the autobiographical materials herein. We all live in glass houses; I would hate to have mine stoned. Yet, perhaps, the personalized ethnography of Sambia singing helps us see a bit better the advantages and difficulties of using one's experience to interpret social life. In my case, I was led from a seemingly trivial incident into many facets of Sambia culture, both profound and trivial, that led from experience back to ethnohistory and then to the social field, the ins and outs of which disclose my approach and my self, explicitly and subliminally, and show, more than another method would, what singing means for Sambia, as known through me. It will never be easy to translate experience between cultures and discourses. For readers will have only words (rarely photographs or films) to know what the ethnographer knows—of Africa, New Guinea, South Carolina, southern France or wherever—and had they been there, they would still not know what you know, for they did not see, feel, think, hear, and touch what you did. And the natives, being humans, would respond somewhat differently to anyone else. All the while, everything is changing, as must the ethnography. Thus, we have not danced their dance or sung their songs. Only your past, present, and future ethnographers will do that through your choices, and those keys to their lives are in you.

Notes

1. The fuller logic and demonstration of these ideas will appear in a forthcoming book (Herdt and Stoller n.d.).

2. For fieldwork support, I thank The Australian National University, The Australian-American Education Foundation, the National Institute of Mental Health, The Department of Psychiatry at the University of California, Los Angeles, the Wenner-Gren Foundation for Anthropological Research, and Stanford University. I wish also to repeat here my great debt to Derek Freeman for facilitating my original fieldwork and supervising my dissertation.

3. That is not quite correct. There are scattered references in the literature to similar phenomena, like those of Malinowski (1929) on Trobriand love songs, Nilles (1950) on the songs of Chimbu courting parties, and many references on ceremonial singing (e.g., Williams 1936, 1940). A. Strathern (1974) has added a piece on Melpa love songs, and since I left the field Schieffelin has well written on the ceremonial singing of Kaluli (1976, 1979). But, as far as I know, there is little on the interpersonal meanings of singing or song systems, the latter of which is scarcely reported for Melanesia, but is common in Australia (see Berndt and Berndt 1951). While I am at it, I cannot help wondering aloud what was going on in Malinowski's fieldwork that led to his being called "The Man of Songs" by Trobrianders?

4. But see the marvelous recent work of Feld (1982).

5. My house was used for everything from local council meetings, neutral ground for dispute settlements, marriage negotiations, and ritual planning (by the men), long afternoons of storytelling by elders among themselves, village cooking and feasting, babysitting, gossiping, a way-station and lodge for village visitors as well as songfests. I was also allowed to live there.

6. Perhaps we can see, in this example, one of the changes anthropologists unwittingly produce in their hosts. I could plead that I was at first innocent of the meaning of these mixed songfests in my house. But they were not an accident:

something was propelling people together, overcoming traditional barriers, into the unprecedented arena of an alien's abode. That something was increasing social change—of which my presence was a major sign indicating that: "here is an opportunity to try out a change we [Sambia] can control." It was their experiment. After several weeks I sensed that, and realized better what was occurring. Then I was not an innocent. I was complicit conspirator in their innovation. Scores of other examples—seemingly trivial, but taken together they add up—could be adduced to underline the same point: ethnographers do introduce or facilitate significant changes in their hosts.

7. Men never sing in the forest, which is the preserve of the forest and hamlet spirits, even ghosts. Singing arouses their attention, inviting trouble: being struck with an invisible ghostly arrow, or having a tree pushed over on me. But Sambia are warriors, too. It is considered bad luck, even dangerous, to sing while out of the hamlet fortress, since one never knows who is waiting to attack.

8. This archaic language is Sambian, but some of the morphemes and infinitives occur only in the songs and are probably survivals of a parent language; namely, Menyamya-area languages like those belonging to Sambia-like neighbors and their ancestors, whom Sambia say they are descended from.

9. In one of the few pieces on traditional singing in Melanesia, Schieffelin (1979:133) insightfully notes of the Kaluli, a people of the Southern Highlands:

In effect, as one moves along tracks and pathways through successive areas of different kinds of forest, one passes sites representing a history of houses and gardens and the people who made them over the previous fifty years. These sites mark to people the various contexts of their own past experience.

The Kaluli identify themselves with their lands because they are reflected in them. And this, in turn, is in part the source of the nostalgia with which people react to place names in ceremonial songs.

Here we see a striking parallel with Sambia use of geographical signs in their song system.

10. I realize belatedly that women's gestures were the first sign of a change, as is true of other social changes in Sambia hamlets. In ordinary, nonsecret discourse, it is the women (and less so children, who sometimes act as go-betweens for women), who may themselves serve as go-betweens for men (cf. M. Strathern 1972), and have license to informally move around and push the men into action on matters like arranging feasts, marriage prestations, garden corvée work, and the discipline of children or misbehaving men. In interpersonal relations among adults, women are sometimes "in the know" about domestic news before men.

11. Such staring is considered a form of sexual looking among Sambia: if a woman had been alone and done that—blinking both eyes at me—it would have been the signal men and women illicitly use to communicate erotic desire. But in that case they would not have sang. Women only sing about men like this; men never sing about women. That is unheard of, and would be rude, like a man patting a woman's behind in America. Nor do women—except rarely in groups— ever sing a lone bachelor's song. It is too risqué. I have only seen it happen a

couple of times nowadays. It used to never happen. More commonly, sisters, mothers, cross-cousins may sing a man's song—a microdot expression of fondness, dramatic heroizing—such as upon his return from a successful hunt or trading party or a long patrol away. I think, now, that there was another reason for my embarrassment, aside from the teasing. That gentle, innocent singing was so naive, and awareness of that naiveté can make me awkward about my power, i.e., to harm. But I consciously knew that six years later, not then.

12. I cannot take up the whole range of anthropological problems that are involved here, which would detract from the main argument. The symbolic inter-linkages still perplex me, though: I believe that the *individual* creative element, as in the elaborate instance of the symbolic system Sambia use for dream inter-pretation, is sufficiently large, complex, and has been at play for generations, such that the song system has transmuted far beyond its original form, retaining linguistic archaisms with it.

13. What follows is ethnohistory, i.e., people's versions of social change as I have pieced them together from oral traditions, elders' memories, legends, and genealogies, with special reference to Soluwulu's history, elicited from him and Tali. No historical records exist before the 1960s, when the first exploratory patrols reached the Sambia Valley, and even these reports are crude.

14. Sambia memories and Australian reports from World War II campaigns indicated that Allied bombers flew over the Sambia territory several times, engaging Japanese planes in aerial combat at least once.

15. Cf. Godelier (1971).

16. Moonunkwambi was abandoned in 1971. Its people, including Soluwulu's clan, then moved into Nilangu.

17. The concept is Stoller's (1979).

18. The old people still call me Gimbatwo; one old man calls me "Toopeikwi," a nonsense name he dreamed up which people think ridiculous.

19. These include the politics of my belonging to Nilangu's clan group; dreams shamans have reports in which they believed I was identified with the eagle; and an odd incident that occurred in 1976 in which an eagle killed my pet cockatoo. Though I was sad about the latter and felt people would see it as a bad omen, it was quite the contrary: they saw it as a protective sign of my power, for reasons that are too complex to describe here.

20. Cf. Lasch (1979). Pardon my pseudophilosophical social criticism, for I do not mean to imply that Sambia are not in love with themselves: only that the way in which our industrialized, capitalist system, with its ideology (in many ways mystifying) of individualism, institutionalizes narcissism more, and in more atomistic ways, than do Sambia.

REFERENCES

Agar, M. H.
1980 *The Professional Stranger.* New York: Academic Press.

Berndt, R. M. and C. Berndt
1951 *Sexual Behavior in Western Arnhem Land*. New York: Viking Fund Publication No. 16.

Devereux, G.
1967 *From Anxiety to Method in the Behavioral Sciences*. Paris: Mouton.

Feld, S.
1982 *Sound and Sentiment*. Philadelphia: University of Pennsylvania Press.

Freeman, J. D.
1970 Human Nature and Culture. In *Man and the New Biology*, edited by D. Slatyer. Canberra: Australian National University.

1983 *Margaret Mead and Samoa: The Making and Unmaking of an Anthropological Myth*. Cambridge: Harvard University Press.

Godelier, M.
1971 "Salt Currency" and the Circulation of Commodities Among the Baruya of New Guinea. In *Studies in Economic Anthropology*. Washington: American Anthropological Association.

Habermas, J.
1971 *Knowledge and Human Interests*. (Translated by J. Shapiro.) Boston: Beacon.

Herdt, G. H.
1977 The Shaman's "Calling" Among the Sambia of New Guinea. *Journal of Soc. Oceanistes* 56–57:153–167.

1980 Semen Depletion and the Sense of Maleness. *Ethnopsychiatrica* 3:79–116.

1981 *Guardians of the Flutes: Idioms of Masculinity*. New York: McGraw-Hill.

1982a Fetish and Fantasy in Sambia Initiation. In *Rituals of Manhood: Male Initiation in Papua New Guinea*, edited by G. H. Herdt. Berkeley: University of California Press.

1982b Sambia Nose-Bleeding Rites and Male Proximity to Women. *Ethos* 10:189–231.

Herdt, G. H. and R. J. Stoller
n.d. Intimate Communications. Unpublished manuscript.

Lasch, C.
1979 *The Culture of Narcissism*. New York: Warner Books.

LeVine, R. A.
1982 *Culture, Behavior, and Personality*. Second Edition. Chicago: Aldine.

Lévi-Strauss, C.
1970 *Tristes Tropiques*. (Translated by J. Russell.) New York: Atheneum.

Malinowski, B.
1929 *The Sexual Life of Savages in North-western Melanesia.* (Preface by H. Ellis.) New York: Harcourt, Brace and World.

Nilles, J.
1950 The Kuman of the Chimbu Region, Central Highlands, New Guinea. *Oceania* 21:25–65.

Read, K. E.
1965 *The High Valley.* London: George Allen and Unwin.

Sapir, E.
1938 Why Cultural Anthropology Needs the Psychiatrist. *Psychiatry* 1:7–12.

Schieffelin, E.
1976 *The Sorrow of the Lonely and the Burning of the Dancers.* New York: St. Martin's Press.

1979 Mediators as Metaphors: Moving a Man to Tears in Papua New Guinea. In *The Imagination of Reality,* edited by A. Becker and A. Yengoyan. New York: Ablex Press.

Stoller, R. J.
1979 *Sexual Excitement: Dynamics of Erotic Life.* New York: Pantheon.

Strathern, A.
1974 *Melpa Love Songs.* Boroko: Institute of Papua New Guinea Studies.

Strathern, M.
1972 *Women in Between.* London: Seminar Press.

Williams, F. E.
1936 *Papuans of the Trans-Fly.* Oxford: Clarendon Press.

1940 *Drama of Orokolo.* London: Oxford University Press.

8

In the Thrown World: Destiny and Decision in the Thought of Traditional Africa

MICHAEL JACKSON

What then is freedom? To be born is both to be born of the world and to be born into the world. The world is already constituted, but also never completely constituted; in the first case we are acted upon, in the second we are open to an infinite number of possibilities. But this analysis is still abstract, for we exist in both ways at once. There is, therefore, never determinism and never absolute choice.

(Merleau-Ponty 1962:453)

If he is lucky, an anthropologist will carry out fieldwork in a society that assists new understandings, both personal and scholarly, which he may not have arrived at anywhere else. Fortuity may likewise guide him towards thinkers whose preoccupations are similar and whose views help shape his own. My years among the Kuranko of Sierra Leone have provided me with the first kind of milieu, and among thinkers I have been singularly fortunate in my friendship with Derek Freeman.

When I began casting around for a subject that might adequately reflect the significance I attach to his original contributions to the anthropology of choice, I found myself drawn back to a topic which has been central to all my anthropological writing; namely, the relationship between what is given and what is chosen in social existence: between destiny and decision.[1] I have always felt uneasy with explanations which reduce lived experience to some immanent factor—nature or nurture, innate structures

193

of the mind, jural codifications, modal personality, economic infrastructures, and so forth—because such explanations seem to me to confuse analytical abstractions with empirical realities as well as producing a false dichotomy between the part and the whole. A basic problem for me has always been to find a way of reconciling nomothetic and idiographic conceptions of anthropology. The first seeks abstract explanatory principles, but often destroys the texture of immediate experience and actual events; the second seeks to locate meaning at the level of biography and subjectivity, but at the risk of phenomenological naivety and at the cost of elucidating general laws. In trying to reconcile these two conceptions of anthropology, I have returned often to Sartre's later work where Marxism and psychoanalysis are made to stand for these dual aspects of our understanding. Sartre shows that *both* perspectives are necessary, and that existence is a dialectical interplay between impersonal and given forces of history that define the conditions of existence, and individual projects and choices which simultaneously reveal these prior conditions and surpass them. Man is never identical with the conditions that bear upon him; human existence is a vital relationship with such conditions, and it is the character of the *relationship* which it is our task to fathom.[2]

Sartre (1969) speaks of the "dialectical irreducibility" of lived experience (*le vecu*), by which he means that the special character of human existence cannot be dissolved into general forms or formulae without serious distortions.[3] Reductionism denies the perennially unique interplay between the given and the possible because it insists that man is determined either from within or without. For Sartre, we are a synthetic unity of what we make out of what we are made (1963a:49). This view is so like the view implied in many West African cosmologies that I have often had occasion to explore one through the other. In this essay I hope to trace some of these philosophical parallels by showing how the dialectic between destiny and decision is expressed in Africa, and how it gives rise to a particular conception of human being as well as to particular ethical concerns.

There is a Kuranko adage—*dunia toge ma dunia; a toge le a dununia*—which, translated literally, means "the name of the world is not world; its name is load." The adage exploits oxymoron and pun (*dunia*—"world"—and *dununia*—"load"—are near homophones) and implies that the world is like a head-load, the weight of which depends on the way one chooses to carry it. The Kuranko view of life is thus comparable to an existentialist view: "World is never something static, something merely given which the person then 'accepts' or 'adjusts to' or 'fights.' It is rather a dynamic pattern which, so long as I possess self-consciousness, I am in the process of forming and designing" (May 1958:60).

Let us now see how the interplay between givenness and choice is expressed in various West African societies. According to the Yoruba, each person is said to make a choice about his preferred destiny before he is born. A divinity called *Ajala*—"The potter who makes heads"—molds heads from clay, fires them, and places them in a storehouse. Because Ajala is an incorrigible debtor whose mind is seldom on his work, many of the heads are badly thrown or overfired. The act of selecting one's *ori* (which means "head" in both literal and figurative senses) is regarded as one of free choice. But because of Ajala's irresponsible handiwork, many heads chosen prove to be defective. Nevertheless, as soon as the choice of a head has been made, the person is free to travel to earth where his success or failure in life will depend to a large extent on the ori he picked up in Ajala's storehouse.

Ori is, however, only one aspect of human being. *Emi* (which means both the physical heart and the soul) is the imperishable aspect of the person which continues to be reincarnated. Emi is given by Olodumare, the supreme being, after Orisanla, the creator god, has formed the physical body of a person out of clay. The third aspect of a person is called *ese* ("leg"). Wande Abimbola notes that while a person's destiny is derived from his ori, the *realization* of that destiny depends on ese, the legs (1973:85). A Yoruba tale nicely illustrates this complementarity of ori and ese. All the ori meet together to deliberate on a project they want to bring to fruition. But they fail to invite ese. Having made their resolutions, the ori find that without ese they do not have the means to carry out their designs. As Abimbola puts it, "the point of the story is that even if one is predestined to success by the choice of a good ori, one cannot actually achieve success without the use of one's ese, which is the symbol of power and activity" (Abimbola 1973:86).[4]

The Yoruba conception of ese is reminiscent of Merleau-Ponty's notion of *comportement* (1965) which implies that ideas should not be studied apart from their actual embodiments. For Merleau-Ponty, human behavior is neither a series of blind reactions to external stimuli nor an outcome of disembodied mind. It is neither exclusively subjective nor exclusively objective, but a dialectical *interchange* between men and the world which cannot be adequately described in traditional causal terms.[5] Thus, meanings are neither passively assimilated from an external, cosmic order that is already fixed, as the realists have it, nor constructed *de novo* by a creative mind, as the idealists suppose (Wild 1965:xiv–xv passim).

The notion that a prenatal choice influences the course of a person's destiny is prevalent in West Africa (Fortes 1959). It is also widely held that a person may be ignorant of this choice and find his conscious aspirations in conflict with the deeper intentionality of his destiny.[6] Among the Igbo, *chi* is the incorporeal aspect of a person which presides over the prenatal choice of destiny. One's lot or portion on earth reflect a primordial bargain with one's chi. But once a person is thrown into the world, he and his chi may find themselves in disagreement. Thus, a person may find himself at the mercy of an intransigent chi, or he may become locked into a struggle to revoke his prenatal choice (Achebe 1975). Among the Kalabari an "immaterial agency" known as the *teme* utters a person's destiny before joining the body on earth. Robin Horton notes that the teme is a kind of "steersman of the personality" whose inclinations often baffle and prove inaccessible to the conscious mind (the *biomgbo*). In this way the teme may be likened to the psychoanalytic notion of the unconscious; it is a force which may move darkly against a person's conscious aspirations (Horton 1961:113).[7]

How are these conflicts, between prenatal decisions and worldly wishes, between unconscious and conscious intentions, resolved? In answering this question from the African viewpoint we have to consider the kinds of complementary forces which may offset or countermand the prenatal destiny, providing room for intelligent purpose and conscious control in the actual working out of one's social destiny on earth. Edo ideas on this subject are particularly illuminating.

It is believed that before birth each individual predestines himself (*hi*) by making a declaration before Osanobua, the creator, setting out a life program and asking for everything needed to carry it out successfully. One's *ehi* ("destiny") acts as a kind of prompt at this time, and will remain in the spirit world as a guide and intermediary with Osanobua. Misfortune in life is explained as a failure to keep to the chosen program or a result of having a "bad ehi." A person may implore his ehi to intervene and improve his lot. R. E. Bradbury notes that ehi "represents the innate potentialities for social achievement with which each individual is believed to be endowed" (1973:263).

But while ehi implies the absence of personal control over one's fortunes, the head (*uhumwu*) "admits a greater degree of responsibility" (Bradbury 1973:263). The head is the seat of thought, judgment, will or character, of hearing, seeing and speaking. It therefore complements ehi, and in the past was the focus of a cult concerned with the headship of families and the rule of the state.

The second force which complements ehi is the hand (*ikegobo*) which connotes manual skill and successful enterprise. Also the focus of a cult, the hand symbolizes a person's vigor and industry in farming, trading, craftwork, and other undertakings. "It implies personal responsibility and self-reliance in a highly competitive and relatively individualistic society" (Bradbury 1973:265). The English phrase, "your fate is in your own hands," translates readily into Edo.

Like other West African peoples, the Edo regard the chosen destiny as something whose realization depends on a person's understanding and actions. But proper understanding and correct action must be learned from others in the course of a person's social existence. The prenatal destiny is therefore like "a field of instrumental possibilities," to use Sartre's phrase, which, though not infinitely malleable, may be opened up to scrutiny, subject to various interpretations, and experienced or reacted to in different ways. This then is the domain of praxis, of effective choice, where each person realizes in his own way the possibilities given in his destiny. This is the domain of Sartre's project, in which present memories of a past relationship (*en-soi*) are surpassed by the countervailing force of the subject's purposeful actions (*pour-soi*).

In African thought, taking a decisive attitude towards existence depends on the acquisition of insight and know-how from elders. A corollary of this is that one should learn to use one's understanding and powers of action to bring about an adjustment of personal and social aspects of being. For instance, talents and dispositions which are unequally apportioned among different individuals as a result of prenatal decisions must be redistributed or used in ways which serve the commonweal. The attainment of personhood or maturity thus entails a passage from being a creature of impulse, ruled by a destiny of which one is only half aware, to becoming a conscious creator of a social world. This transformation does not involve the cultivation of a distinctive personality, but the practical use of intelligence to create a community of harmonious relationships.[8] African *praxis* is communal, not individual.

The manner in which socially acquired intelligence (*communis sententia*) can alter a person's prenatal destiny is nicely illustrated by the following examples. Among the Kalabari, diviners are able to "diagnose the words" which a person's teme spoke before coming to earth, and so confront a person with the words and help him repudiate them (Horton 1961:113). Among the Tallensi, diviners can also help a person revoke his prenatal destiny (*nuor-yin*), although a man's actual destiny always depends on a private cult of a particular configuration of destiny ancestors who have the power to override all other destinies (Fortes 1959). In Dahomey it was believed that a person could tap the antinomian energies of Legba, the trickster, and so change the direction of the fate he chose before his birth. Another "way out" lay in a man's "collective destiny" which included the destinies of others in his family or house and was associated with a kind of guardian soul (Fortes 1959:22–23). Among the Edo the cult of the hand made it sometimes possible for a person to change his luck. A man who consulted a diviner about his ill fortune might be advised to "serve his Hand" by making offerings at the cult shrine (Bradbury 1973:264).

The recurring references to divination in these examples remind us that in the African view understanding and action are inseparable. One's destiny is embodied in habits and intentions[9] as much as it is manifest in obsessive ideas or desires. To break the hold of one's given destiny always entails gaining a new awareness and a new way of doing things. In African parlance it requires both the head and the hands (or legs).[10] Divination provides the means as the diviner gives a person insight into unconscious and normally hidden forces of destiny as well as advising a course of action that should be undertaken. In Africa, this action is usually sacrifice, and involves collective activity (see Jackson 1977b; 1978). This pragmatic attitude to destiny is conveyed by the Igbo proverb: "The world is a marketplace and it is subject to bargain" (Uchendu 1965:15). Actual destiny is therefore not fixed but reflects a dynamic interplay[11] between prenatal dispositions and social praxis mediated by the head and the hands.

ACTION AND REACTION: KURANKO MORAL REASONING

The lack of a belief in Kuranko society of a prenatal choice of one's destiny may be the product of its turbulent history. It could be conjectured that the adoption of the Islamic high god (*Ala* or *Altala*) reflects a quest for a common centering symbol among people not united by descent or estate (Jackson 1977a:130–136). It could also be supposed that the adoption of the Islamic belief in the destiny of every individual being ultimately determined by Allah is a response to a history of social upheavals in which it has seemed that man is powerless to shape his own social world. For whatever the reason, the Kuranko regard a person's destiny (*sawura*) as a "gift from *Ala*," decided before birth. One plays no part in making this decision. Nor can it be reversed: *latege saraka saa* ("no sacrifice can avert [cut] it").

In practical discourse, however, it is said that most natural gifts and dispositions are partly innate, partly acquired. Although *yugi* ("temperament," "proclivity") is generally regarded as innate, *miran* ("bearing," "self-possession," "presence") is an inborn quality which can be undermined or bolstered by the use of acquired skills and magical medicines. *Hank-ilimaiye* ("gumption"; also *nous,* "intelligence") is sometimes said to be innate, sometimes said to be entirely acquired through socialization.

While the interplay between innate and acquired aspects of personhood, intelligence, and morality is always indeterminate, it is thought that every individual should learn to master innate dispositions and use inborn gifts in socially approved ways. Only if a person is utterly incorrigible will moral excuses be found in his native proclivities. Then it might be said: *a ka tala, a soron ta la bole* ("he is blameless, he was born with it"), or *a danye le wo la* ("that is how he is made").

Although a person's fate seems to be in the hands of Ala, the Kuranko only speak fatalistically when they are commenting retrospectively on someone's behavior. Kuranko do not actually *behave* fatalistically. This is partly because a person's destiny can never be known beforehand, and partly because the fortunes of the individual are inextricably bound up with relations with kinsmen, friends, mentors, neighbors, strangers, ancestors, and bush spirits, as well as with Ala. *Sabu* ("reason"/"cause") refers to the dynamic interactions within this field of relations. The word is often explained in terms of gift giving. For instance, if a person gives a voluntary gift (*bol'fan*) to someone else, the gift improves the fortunes of the receiver and makes the donor his *sabu nyuma* ("good cause," i.e., the reason for his good fortune). Or, if a person introduces someone to a friend who is the means by which the friend finds good fortune, then that someone will be known as sabu nyuma. Any agency of ill fortune is known as a bad cause (*sabu yuge*). Although people often speak of divine will or ancestral influence in terms of implacable fate (*sawura*), it is always human choice which, in practice, determines the particular course of a person's destiny.

Of all the powers acquired through social interaction none is more important than moral understanding (*hankili*). Moral understanding is common sense or social shrewdness. It is acquired by listening to elders, and it is thought that both social well-being and personal longevity depend on it: *sie tole l to* ("long life is in the listening," i.e., heed your elders and you will live long and prosperously); *si' ban to l sa* ("short life ear has not," i.e., if you do not heed your elders, you will not live long). Social intelligence is associated with the head (*kunye*) so that a fool (*yuwe*: "crazy" or "socially stupid") is someone "without salt in his head" (*kor' sa kunye ma*) or "without brains" (*kun' por' sa*), while a responsible person has "good thoughts in his head" (*miria nyime a kunye ro*); his "head is full."

The interplay between inborn disposition and acquired controls is illustrated by the following dialogue between myself and Keti Ferenke Koroma, a renowned storyteller and composer of stories:

MJ: What shapes a person's destiny?
KF: Sawura is a gift from Ala.
MJ: Is it decided before a person is born?
KF: Yes. My father consulted the diviners before I was born. They told my father that his child was wise (*hankili kolo*).
MJ: Can a person change his destiny?

KF: It is my destiny to compose and tell stories. I could never stop thinking of stories, yet I could stop myself telling them (laughter). When someone asks me for a story the idea comes into my head at once. I cannot stop that. But I could stop myself telling the story.

Clearly, the *action of* destiny cannot be avoided, but a person's *reaction to* his destiny is a matter to be decided. Here moral understanding is crucial. One must gain insight into one's native abilities or inclinations, and then decide how these potentialities are going to be realized in practice. It is important to stress that many innate resources are ethically neutral. Thus, cleverness, cunning, strength, and other inborn "gifts" can be used to gain personal advantage or to serve the commonweal. It is in this domain of action that human choice is of the utmost importance, for though the distribution of talents is god given, the social use of these talents is open to interpretation, as well as subject to individual judgment and control.[12]

A person acquires moral understanding and self-mastery during the rite of initiation. It is at puberty that a person learns to take a decisive attitude towards his or her existence. A child's behavior is seldom taken seriously: "a child is just as it was born; it has no common sense (*hankili sa la*)" say the Kuranko. Initiation provides "new understanding" (*hankili kura*), and the child becomes a "new person." This transformation is sometimes spoken of as a "taming" of the "unripe" emotional nature of the child, and in effecting this transformation attention is focused on *dime,* which connotes both emotional "hurt" and physical "pain." Isolated from the community in a bush house, and cut off from emotional ties (particularly with the mother), the pubescent child is subject to a series of ordeals. These ordeals are said to simulate the crises which inevitably attend adult life. The neophyte must learn to control his or her *reaction* to suffering. Mastery of one's reaction to pain—standing still, not blinking, not making a sound, not wincing when one is cut—is regarded as the paradigm of all self-mastery. In the Kuranko view it is only when a person learns to discriminate between the action of hurt and his reaction to it that he gains any measure of control or freedom.[13] *Yiri* ("steadiness of body/mind") connotes this detached attitude to inner states, whether pain, grief, anger, or love. *Kerenteye* ("bravery") and *kilanbelteye* ("fortitude") suggest moral fiber, an ability to withstand the tides of strong emotions. These virtues are all dependent upon the cultivation of an abstract attitude which produces consonance between intentions and actions. Various adages bring home the importance of this:

> *morge kume mir' la i konto i wo l fo le*—"whatever word a person thinks of, that will he speak," i.e., think before you speak lest you blurt out stupid ideas.

i mir' la koe mi ma, i wo l ke la—"you thought of that, you do that," i.e., think before you act lest your actions belie your intentions.

The very concept of personhood itself—*morgoye*—means mindfulness of others and a "true person" is one who has harmonized inner being (*nyere*) with social being. Unlike the English word "personality" which connotes personal identity, "a distinctive individual character especially when of a marked kind" (OED), morgoye connotes abstract moral qualities which ideally characterize social relations: altruism and magnanimity.

For the Kuranko the domain of human freedom is charted by first recognizing internal talents or dispositions (given by Ala) and external mores (laid down by the ancestors, "the first people"). The interplay between these areas of limitation is a matter of human judgment and human purpose. Each life is a unique instance of the possibilities present in this indeterminate relationship between innate dispositions and extrinsic social norms.[14] The Kuranko say that two birds may be the same, but there are many ways in which birds fly in the sky. Sartre's conception of human freedom is not dissimilar:

> In the end one is always responsible for what is made of one. Even if one can do nothing else besides assume this responsibility. For I believe that a man can always make something out of what is made of him. This is the limit I would today accord to freedom: the small movement which makes of a totally conditioned social being someone who does not render back completely what his conditioning has given him [1969:45].

Journeying: The Distinction Between Society and Wilderness

The Kuranko image of birds in the sky and Sartre's conception of freedom as marking out "certain routes which were not initially given" lead us to consider the metaphor of journeying in African moral discourse.

Throughout Africa the semantic opposition between town and bush signifies, among other things, the contrast between the domain of collective rules and the domain of individual powers. The interplay between the fields of association and of individuation is represented allegorically in terms of journeys to and fro between community and wilderness. The exercise of freedom thus takes the form of what Georg Simmel called an "adventure": "an eternal process playing back and forth between chance and necessity, between the fragmentary materials given us from the outside and the consistent meaning of the life developed from within" (1959:247). In this dialectic, harmony is created between social rules and the "wild" forces of individual being. The integration of the community is seen to depend upon each person knowing and mastering himself. Using the metaphor of town/bush, the Fulani say that freedom in society depends on each person "entering into a direction relation with the bush" (Riesman 1977:257).

A common scenario in Kuranko oral narratives involves a young hero who hazards his life on a journey into the wilderness in quest of an object such as a musical instrument or fetish which will be of advantage to his community. In his confrontations with wild beings and his struggles against the temptation to use his gains for selfish ends, the questing hero embodies recurring moral dilemmas in Kuranko social life. The narratives show that the resolution of these dilemmas depends on choices made by each individual. The life of the community rests on the concerted activity of all its members. A good example of this social praxis is the storytelling session itself where moral issues are thrown open to discussion and agreement reached only after vigorous debate (Jackson 1982).

In other African societies curing rites are concerned with the same kind of harmonization of "town" and "bush." Among the Bakongo, agitation or "wildness" within a person must be counteracted by the "calming" or "cooling" effects of medicines culled from the domestic domain (Janzen 1978:199–203). This entails an adjustment of the relationship between internal and external fields of being, conceptualized in terms of white ("self") versus black ("other") or town versus bush. The same ideas inform medical practice among the Songhay. Jeanne Bisilliat emphasizes that although disease is often an uncontrolled invasion of self or town by "the bush," the cure entails a comparable movement, but one in which the patient exercises conscious control (1976:590).

The metaphor of journeying reappears in these medical contexts as an image of pathways within the body as well as between self and society and society and wilderness (Bisilliat 1976:555; Willis 1978:143; Jackson 1982). The key to well-being lies in a person's ability to control traffic along these pathways. Health, in psychic, physical, and social senses, is a result of a person's ability to effect adjustments himself between inner dispositions and external rules. In Africa sickness always has moral, physical, psychic, and social aspects,[15] and it usually reflects a loss of balance or harmony, either because a person succumbs completely to his inner nature and becomes ruled by "wild" proclivities or because he becomes rigidly rule bound and unable to see beyond his own social role. In Kuranko narratives these extremes are represented by the cunning hare ("the youngster") and the stupid hyena ("the elder"). The struggles between them are allegories of the interplay between the fields of natural and social being.

Initiations, scenarios of folktales, and curing rites all entail consciously controlled movements which accomplish a mutual adjustment between the social world and the wilderness. Divination involves the same kind of movement. But before considering divination, we must be more specific about African notions of inner disposition, whether this is said to be decided by each individual prenatally as among the Yoruba and Edo or decided by Ala as among the Kuranko.

The African notions of inner disposition are not exactly comparable to psychoanalytic notions of the unconscious as some writers have suggested (Horton 1961). The crucial difference is that while psychoanlysts regard the unconscious as a deep recess of interior being, Africans regard the unconscious as a force field outside one's immediate awareness, e.g., the realm where one's prenatal destiny was decided, the realm of night, the bush outside one's village, the country beyond one's own, the inscrutable designs of one's enemies, and so forth. The understanding of strange occurrences, whether interior (like dreams) or exterior (like drought) does not, therefore, proceed through introspection but through divination. In divination external objects such as pebbles or cowry shells are manipulated or extrasocial beings are addressed. These objects and beings can, by virtue of their otherness, embody disinterested truths (Jackson 1978). Among the Dogon, diviners mark out sand diagrams at dusk on the edge of the village, hoping for the night imprint of *Yourougou,* "the pale fox," who represents extravagance and disorder as well as oracular truth (Calame-Griaule 1965). The Dogon contrast Yourougou with *Nommo* who represents reason and social order. Among the neighboring Bambara a similar contrast exists between Nyalé, who was created first and signifies "swarming life," uncontrolled power and exuberance, and *Faro* and *Ndomadyiri* who were created next and signify equilibrium and restraint. With the advent of human society a dialectic appeared in which Nyalé and Ndomadyiri form "antithetical impulses." According to the Bambara the harmonizing of extrasocial energies and social order depends on every person acquiring moral understanding and taking an active part in communal life (Zahan 1974:15).

Dominique Zahan emphasizes that in African thought the person is a moral agent located "at the intersection of ... terrestrial and celestial coordinates." The person "sees himself as the synthesis of the universe ... neither a toy nor a straw between the hands of the forces which would escape him. He is the arbiter of his own game with these forces; he is above them" (1979:156).

Taking African cosmologies as our point of departure, we have looked at several aspects of the interplay between individuation and association.[16] We have seen that the African view is that a person is neither a creature of prenatal choices nor of god-given dispositions. He is a governor in the cybernetic sense, effecting adjustments within a universe of forces, some

of which assume the form of social rules, others of which are manifest
as inner dispositions. These forces all impose limitations, but the interplay
of these forces is forever indeterminate. Human freedom is seen to lie
within this indeterminate domain. It has been possible to show that this
African perspective is similar to an existentialist view of man. In Sartre's
words, "men make their history on the basis of real, prior conditions . . .
but it is *the men* who make it and not the prior conditions. Otherwise
men would be merely the vehicles of inhuman forces which through them
would govern the social world" (1963b:87).

This brings us back to the comparison of traditional African and
existential notions of choice. Although there are parallels between these
notions, there are also important differences in the way they are expressed
and in the interests they serve. Traditional African thought is invariably
concrete. Ideas and precepts are embodied in metaphors and examples
which are not mere illustrations, since it is impossible to articulate the
concept independently of the case. The word *is* flesh.

The fusion of idea and example is affected through metaphor and
synecdoche, so that particular parts of the human body signify general
processes (head–thought; legs/hands–purposeful action) and vital correspondence appears to exist between personal, social, and cosmic
domains. This synecdochism[17] does not indicate an inability to abstract
on the part of African thinkers; rather, it reflects a particular ethical orientation. First, the metaphorical character of African discourse (adage,
parable, folktale, myth, and so forth) means that crucial precepts and ideas
are equally accessible to everyone and constitute a familiar fund of images
or scenarios which are as common and as concrete as pathways, houses,
or parts of the human body. Second, the synecdochic connections posited
between personal, social, and extrasocial realms mean that the universe
is seen as a unified field with no causal breaks between these realms. Not
only does this view make the universe coherent and comprehensible (on
an analogy with the microcosm of the person or the community); it enables
man to act upon himself in the conviction that such action will have
repercussions in social and even extrasocial realms. Conversely, this view
enables man to manipulate words and things (as in divination or in healing
and cursing rites) in the conviction that such actions will have repercussions on one's self or other people. Thus, mastery of the external world
is always linked reciprocally to mastery of self. Or we could say that by
reducing the scale of the world to the scale of the self, man is no longer
intimidated by the universe but acts in relation to it as if it were an extension
of himself and vice versa. Absolute schisms between self and society or
society and nature are thus avoided. Unity and community are the key
postulates underlying the aesthetic forms and moral purposes of African
discourse.

By contrast, Western philosophical discourse, while it may have recourse to metaphor, is never ruled by it. Intelligibility is often based on a denial of the sensible, an abstraction from the empirical rather than a fusion with it, and facts are often artificially separated from values. As Clifford Geertz has pointed out, anthropological understanding betrays this very tendency whenever it replaces the "experience-near" tropes of native discourse with the "experience-distant" concepts of academic discourse (1976:222–223). Thus, a figure or metaphor whose value in the native culture lies in its power to mediate community is translated by the anthropologist into a conceptual token which is used to define a specialty, to distinguish a career, and to divide science from common sense.

In as much as Sartrean notions of choice are articulated on the far side of metaphor, and situated within a tradition of ideas which are abstract and arcane, these notions belong to a different context of values and human interests than the African notions which at first sight seem to similar.

Thus, in my view, anthropological fieldwork places us within a field of opposing forces and thereby starts us upon a journey of discovery. But the discoveries we make about others are valid only to the extent that we recognize them as reflections on ourselves. We find ourselves between the limits imposed by our culture, our science, and our temperament on the one hand, and the limits imposed by the fieldwork situation on the other hand. Our freedom to understand, to interpret, and to evaluate lies in this indeterminate zone. It is only by becoming aware of these limits that we become free to make *informed* judgments.[18] As Hubert Benoit states, "In refusing to accept limitations man deprives himself of the impression of liberty which he feels when he is within accepted constraints" (1955:66).

African viewpoints remind us that our freedom is conditional on moral understanding: on grasping the inner determinants of our nature as well as recognizing the bounds of our cultural being. In a truly reflexive anthropology we learn about ourselves in the same measure that we learn about others. Since we abandon the illusory partitions between observer and observed, subject and object, we locate ourselves squarely within the field of action and place ourselves under an obligation to make moral and aesthetic choices on the strength of our understanding. As A. R. Louch has argued, explanation can never realistically divide fact from value, description from appraisal, and "explanation of human action is moral explanation" (1966:4).

So the question arises, how can we work within our own intellectual traditions, yet close the gap which has opened between ourselves and those we study? I see this closure as involving greater reflexivity, the use of more accessible styles of writing, the clarification of the relationship between knowledge and human values, and the application of understanding to social action.

Notes

1. See Jackson (1982, Chapter one).
2. Existence is from the Latin *ex-sistere*, "to stand out, to emerge." Thus existentialism emphasizes the human being "not as a collection of static substances or mechanisms or patterns but rather as emerging and becoming, that is to say, as existing" (May 1958:12).
3. Cf. Lévi-Strauss: "Every effort to understand destroys the object studied in favour of another object of a different nature" (1973:411). Niels Bohr referred to this as the *Abtötungsprinzip*; one can kill off the experimental subject by too deep a material probing of its behavior. Devereux notes that extreme reductionist models of behavior have the same fatal consequences (1967:288).
4. For accounts of the leg as a symbol of power and generative potency see Jackson (1979:122–125), Onians (1973), Bunker and Lewin (1965), Bradley (1970), and Freeman (1968).
5. Cybernetic models (Wilden 1972) and Taoist notions (Needham 1978:164–166) of causation seem to me to be more adequate. See also Gauld and Shotter (1977:171–179) on selfhood and agency.
6. This conflict assumes different forms in different societies. Among the Kalabari the key contrast is between competitiveness and noncompetitiveness (Horton 1961:114). Among the Tallensi the key opposition is between the father's destiny and his firstborn son's destiny (Fortes 1959:47). Among many Mande-speaking peoples there is a forceful contrast between the rivalry among sons of the same father but different mothers (*fadenye*) and the amicability among sons of the same mother (*badenya; nadenye*).
7. Cf. Bradbury: "It is perhaps not too fanciful to make a comparison between the Benin conception of the head and the ego of the psycho-analyst" (1973:272). For our purposes the unconscious is best defined as "the realm of intentionality" underlying the plane of our conscious wishing and willing (May 1972, Chapter nine).
8. See Jackson (1982, Chapter one) for a fuller account of Kuranko concepts of the person, selfhood, and relationship.
9. The word "intention" aptly conveys the nondualistic character of the African worldview. Intention is a "set" of the body as well as a "purpose" in the mind. The Latin stem *intendere* suggests "stretching" and "tension" so that intention is a "stretching towards something" (May 1972:228).
10. Among the Ufipa people of Tanzania, the hands also signify praxis, the active measures man takes to make his world. As Fipa see it, "it is through such action that he constitutes himself as a person. The significance Fipa symbolism and medicine attach to the human hands (*amakasa*) reflects a perception that these organs are the means by which consciously mediated intentions are realised in a transformation of the natural environment. Through their social praxis, mediated through the hands, human beings transform nature and in so doing create their society and culture" (Willis 1977:283).

11. Among the Akan, the *e-su* (*phusis*, or "fundamental biophysical nature of man") is complementary to *n'kara* or "chosen soul" (*nous*, or "intelligence"). As J. B. Danquah notes, destiny is not, however, "wooden or cast-iron, but something lively, full of feeling, desired and rational" (1944:205).

12. This theme is explored fully in my study of ethics and ambiguity in Kuranko oral narratives (Jackson 1982).

13. During his fieldwork among the Jelgobe Fulani, Paul Riesman notes that feelings of hurt or pain were rarely indulged or expressed to solicit sympathy. "It was the same with all pain, physical or mental: people talked about it freely and objectively, so to speak, but they did not *express* it by that language of intonation and gesture which is familiar to us" (1977:147). According to Riesman this equanimity was neither the result of repression or stoicism, but of control. "To name pain and suffering in a neutral tone is to master them, *because the words do not escape thoughtlessly but are spoken consciously*" (Riesman 1977:148, my emphasis).

14. Cf. Riesman: "Even if we supposed provisionally that it were possible to predict the actions of men on the basis of a knowledge of the forces acting on them, we would have to accept the fact that, with the Fulani, one of these forces, *pulaaku*, is impossible to determine, both as to its direction and as to its strength. It is crucial that we recognize this, for we are thus obliged to realize that the problem of freedom cannot be reduced to an opposition between man and the forces acting on him" (1977:140–141). Pulaaku is translated as "Fulani-ness," but it is comparable to the Kuranko concept morgoye—"personhood".

15. I have discussed elsewhere in detail the Kuranko concept of *kenteye* which means both physical well-being and social propriety. A breakdown in health is thus often related to a breach of a social rule or the breaking of trust (Jackson 1982).

16. Among Mande-speaking peoples the relationship of rivalry between half brothers (*fadenye*) is often a metaphor for the centrifugal forces of individuation. The mother is, by contrast, a centering symbol. For instance, the Kuranko word for kinship is *nakelinyorgoye* ("mother-one-association"). In Mande hero myths, the hero mediates between individuation (the wild) and association (the community) (Karp and Bird 1981:13).

17. In ethnography, synecdochism is the "belief or practice in which a part of an object or person is taken as equivalent to the whole, so that anything done to, or by means of, the part is held to take effect upon, or have the effect of, the whole" (SOED).

18. In cybernetic parlance, "without limitation, no advantage."

References

Abimbola, W.
1973 The Yoruba Concept of Human Personality. In *La notion de personne en Afrique noire*, edited by G. Dieterlen. Paris: Editions du Centre National de la Recherche Scientifique.

Achebe, C.
1975 *Morning Yet on Creation Day; Essays*. London: Heinemann.

Benoit, H.
1955 *The Supreme Doctrine*. London: Routledge & Kegan Paul.

Bisilliat, J.
1976 Village Diseases and Bush Diseases in Songhay: An Essay in Description and Classification with a View to a Typology. (Translated by J. B. Loudon.) In *Social Anthropology and Medicine*, edited by J. B. Loudon. ASA Monograph 13. London: Academic Press.

Bradbury, R. E.
1973 *Benin Studies* (edited by P. Morton-Williams). London: Oxford University Press.

Bradley, N.
1970 The Knees as Fantasied Genitals. *Psychoanalytic Quarterly* 57:65–94.

Bunker, H. A. and B. D. Lewin
1965 A Psychoanalytic Notation on the Root GN, KN, CN. In *Psychoanalysis and Culture*, edited by G. B. Wilbur and W. Muensterberger. New York: International Universities Press.

Calame-Griaule, G.
1965 *Ethnologie et langage; la parole chez les Dogon*. Paris: F. Gallimand.

Danquah, J. B.
1944 *The Akan Doctrine of God, a Fragment of Gold Coast Ethics and Religion*. London: Lutterworth Press.

Devereux, G.
1967 *From Anxiety to Method in the Behavioural Sciences*. The Hague: Mouton.

Fortes, M.
1959 *Oedipus and Job in West African Religion*. Cambridge: Cambridge University Press.

Freeman, J. D.
1968 Thunder, Blood, and the Nicknaming of God's Creatures. *Psychoanalytic Quarterly* 37:353–399.

Gauld, A. and J. Shotter
1977 *Human Action and Its Psychological Investigation*. London: Routledge & Kegan Paul.

Geertz, C.
1976 "From the Native's Point of View": On the Nature of Anthropological Understanding. In *Meaning in Anthropology*, edited by K. H. Basso and H. A. Selby. Albuquerque: University of New Mexico Press.

Horton, R.
1961 Destiny and the Unconscious in West Africa. *Africa* 31:110–116.

Jackson, M.
1977a *The Kuranko; Dimensions of Social Reality in a West African Society.* London: Hurst.

1977b Sacrifice and Social Structure Among the Kuranko. *Africa* 47:41–49, 123–139.

1978 An Approach to Kuranko Divination. *Human Relations* 31:117–138.

1979 Prevented Successions: A Commentary Upon a Kuranko Narrative. In *Fantasy and Symbol: Essays in Honour of George Devereux*, edited by R. Hook. London: Academic Press.

1982 *Allegories of the Wilderness; Ethics and Ambiguity in Kuranko Narratives.* Bloomington: Indiana University Press.

Janzen, J.
1978 *Quest for Therapy in Lower Zaire.* Berkeley: University of California Press.

Karp, I. and C. Bird (eds.)
1980 *Explorations in African Systems of Thought.* Bloomington: Indiana University Press.

Lévi-Strauss, C.
1973 *Tristes Tropiques.* (Translated by John and Doreen Weightman.) London: Jonathan Cape.

Louch, A. R.
1966 *Explanations and Human Action.* Oxford: Blackwell.

May, R.
1958 The Origins and Significance of the Existential Movement in Psychology. In *Existence: A New Dimension in Psychiatry*, edited by R. May, E. Angel, and H. F. Ellenberger. New York: Basic Books.

1972 *Love and Will.* London: Fontana.

Merleau-Ponty, M.
1962 *Phenomenology of Perception.* (Translated by Colin Smith.) London: Routledge & Kegan Paul.

1965 *The Structure of Behaviour.* (Translated by Alden L. Fisher.) London: Methuen.

Needham, J.
1978 *The Shorter Science and Civilization in China.* Vol. 1. (Abridgement by Colin Ronan.) Cambridge: Cambridge University Press.

Onians, R. B.
1973 *The Origins of European Thought.* New York: Arno Press.

Riesman, P.
1977 *Freedom in Fulani Social Life; an Introspective Ethnography.* (Translated by Martha Fuller.) Chicago: University of Chicago Press.

Sartre, Jean-Paul
1963a *Saint-Genet.* (Translated by B. Frechtman.) New York: George Braziller.

1963b *The Problem of Method.* (Translated by Hazel Barnes.) London: Methuen.

1969 Itinerary of a Thought. *New Left Review* 58:43–66.

Simmel, G.
1959 The Adventure. In *Georg Simmel 1858–1918; A Collection of Essays,* edited by K. H. Wolff. Columbus: Ohio State University Press.

Uchendu, V. C.
1965 *The Igbo of Southeast Nigeria.* New York: Holt, Rinehart & Winston.

Wild, J.
1965 Foreword. In *The Structure of Behaviour,* by M. Merleau-Ponty. London: Methuen.

Wilden, A.
1972 *System and Structure; Essays in Communication and Exchange.* London: Tavistock.

Willis, R.
1977 Pollution and Paradigms. In *Culture, Disease, and Healing: Studies in Medical Anthropology,* edited by D. Landy. New York: Macmillan.

1978 Magic and "Medicine" in Ufipa. In *Culture and Curing; Anthropological Perspectives on Traditional Medical Beliefs and Practices,* edited by P. Morley and R. Willis. London: Peter Owen.

Zahan, D.
1974 *The Bambara.* Leiden: E. J. Brill.

1979 *The Religion, Spirituality, and Thought of Traditional Africa.* (Translated by Kate Ezra Martin and Lawrence M. Martin.) Chicago: University of Chicago Press.

PART V

Biological Givens and Symbol Choice

9

The Fetal and Natal Origins of Circumcision and Other Rebirth Symbols[1]

MICHAEL A. H. B. WALTER

Robin Fox (1967:35) once asserted: "the facts of the physiology of parturition ... are of no concern to the anthropologist." He was stating this in the context of the study of kinship, which is not the context here. Nevertheless my present purpose is to demonstrate that some knowledge of the physiology of parturition, and indeed of human embryology, is essential for an understanding of much of the symbolic actions found cross-culturally in initiation rituals. I say initiation because I shall focus primarily on male initiation rites, but "passage" rituals is a more informative term since it emphasizes that initiation into one status is subsequent to departure from another.

This element of passage from one status to another was demonstrated long ago by Van Gennep (1960, orig. 1909). Since man for his own cultural purposes wishes to impose his categories on those of nature, he also has to establish the boundaries of those categories in order that the status changes are socially recognizable and confirmable. Van Gennep showed how this was done cross-culturally by ritual activity that focussed attention successively on the act of separation from old status, the state of liminality (a status limbo), and the act of incorporation into the new status. Thus by establishing discontinuity, the distinction between old and new status is highlighted.

Cross-culturally, the commonly found framework which organizes this ritual passage is the theme of death and rebirth. As Leach (1976:78–9) points out: "since every discontinuity in social time is the end of one period and the beginning of another, and since birth/death is a self-evident 'natural' representation of beginning/end, death and rebirth symbolism is appropriate to all rites of transition and is palpably manifest in a wide variety of cases." Eliade (1958:xii) makes a similar statement. He adds: "The majority of initiatory ordeals more or less clearly imply a ritual death followed by resurrection of a new birth." Indeed, Eliade subtitles his book: "The Mysteries of Birth and Rebirth."[2]

Often in initiation rites there is explicit reference in word or action to death and birth. Initiands may be "killed" in various ways, swallowed by "monsters," while the ensuing stage of liminality or transition is frequently likened to being in the womb (Turner 1974:81). The subsequent rebirth of the initiands may be called a "coming-out" or "emergence" (see, for example, White 1961:12).

The focus of this paper is upon some of the symbols and symbolic actions that are cross-culturally typical of male initiation rites—and in several instances for passage ritual in general. I refer here to such practices as haircutting, anointing with oil or fat, nail paring, genital mutilations, and the daubing of the face and/or body with ash or clay. I should make it clear that I am not trying to offer in the manner of such authors as Young (1962), Harrington (1968), Cohen (1964), Norbeck et al. (1962), or Brain (1977) sociological or psychological explanations of the incidence of male initiation rites, or of the presence or absence of a particular symbolic action, such as circumcision. I am also not endeavoring to analyze the elaborated significance of the cultural or psychological impact of specific ritual symbols or practices in a culture, such as Abrahams (1972) does for the use of ash and Turner (1962:140–147) for white clay, or cross-culturally what has been done notably for the cutting of head hair—thus Leach's (1958) "Magical Hair," Hallpike's (1969) "Social Hair," Derrett's (1973) "Religious Hair," Cooper's (1971) "Hair," and see also Berg (1951), Firth (1973), and Hershman (1974).

In a sense, my concern is the most basic one: I am looking at the origins, or rather the originals, upon which typical symbols and symbolic actions accompanying the rebirth theme of initiation rituals have been modelled or derived. Employing another quotation from Fox, though one depicting a considerable shift in the position of the one with which I began the paper, I can say the case I seek to make is a literal illustration of his assertion (1975:275): "the potential for culture lies in the biology of the species." I propose that the derivation for these typical rebirth symbols in male initiation rites (and I use "rebirth" in a broader sense to refer to both the liminal and incorporation [rebirth] stages) lies in the human biology, more specifically in the fetal and natal process. I wish to make it clear that I do not believe this focus upon the biological nature of man thereby precludes anthropological theorizing about the cultural significance attending the creation and use of rebirth symbols, nor for that matter do I think it prevents the psychoanalyst from theorizing about the impact of the symbols on the individual. I am simply asserting that for certain symbols in male initiation rites the original model lies in the body and not in the mind of man.

Yet, it is the mind of man which deliberates on the choice and use, or purpose, of such symbols to reinforce the values and beliefs which for a particular scheme of things—a culture—he holds dear. As Derek Freeman (1969:26) has pointed out: "This capacity to exercise preferences has gradually emerged in the course of human evolution in close conjunction with the capacity to symbolize ... We are here confronted with the phenomenon of human values, for values are a function of the capacity to exercise preferences, and so ineluctably, become a part of the subject matter of evolutionary anthropology."

Derek Freeman's statement came in the context of his determination to establish beyond all doubt the interrelation of phylogeny and environment as the basis of all anthropological study. While my own focus is a much narrower one and upon the cultural impact of ontogeny rather than phylogeny, it endorses the importance of understanding the determinisms of nature, especially of the determinisms of his own body and brain,[3] that Derek Freeman argues (see 1969:28) for man.

WHY SHOULD MEN CHOOSE TO BE MOTHERS, AND IF THEY DO, WHY SHOULD THEY NOT DO THE JOB PROPERLY?

There is a basic contradiction in human society. Culture is everywhere androcentric, and posterity is everywhere gynecocentric. In other words, while societies are organized from a male point of view which establishes the superiority of the male principle,[4] from that androcentric point of view posterity appears, biologically, gynecocentric—it is the female who carries and gives birth to the offspring. Mothers and daughters could organize their sons within a gynecocentric culture and still control posterity, or at least that is how it might seem to fathers conscious of their redundancy once they have provided sons. There is, of course, no way of establishing that scenario historically, but it provides an acceptable speculative background to the major theme in sex initiation rites for the male: that men wish to provide their sons with a status that identifies them with their father (adult males) and not their mothers (adult females); to "make men of them" if you like. The fathers' second defense against redundancy is that they have to give birth to these "new" men, and so become equally necessary to posterity.

I am not offering a "theory" to account for male initiation rites, I am simply using a device to highlight the three major themes of male mothers, boys reborn as men, and sexual antagonism (between adult men and adult women). With some reservation about the term envy, I broadly support the position taken long ago by Margaret Mead and more recently by Bettelheim (1954) and Brain (1977), that the cultural message tells us of the human male's envy and apprehension of the physiological capabilities of the female. For me, male initiation rites are exactly that: initiation into social maleness—the abandonment of social asexuality and the attainment of social sexuality. This is usually cast in the framework of a rite of passage (see Kennedy 1970) in which adult males are asserting at the same time both their physiological equivalence with females and the separation and common identity of male sexuals by socially (and so symbolically) conceiving, bearing, and giving birth to the new male sexuals.

I use the term "male mother" to refer to the widely found concern of the adult human male to present symbolically this possession of the physiological capability of giving birth. While my interest in this paper is focussed on the body symbolisms of the fetus and newborn, the symbolic representation in male initiation rituals commonly extends beyond this. The structure in which initiands may be lodged, for example, may be represented explicitly or implicitly as the parental body, perhaps specifically the womb. For instance, White's (1961) description of the *Mukanda*, the male initiation rites of the Luvale of Zambia, details how leftovers of food brought to the initiands within their lodge are thrown out by the food bringers through a small hole at the back of the lodge, a part of the lodge which the initiands must avoid at all costs. In the same ritual, the initiands rhythmically beat sticks inside the lodge, which suggests the heartbeat of the "mother" (on their own). However, while initiands in male initiation rites are usually tended by adult, initiated males, I am not asserting the latter persevere with this mother status outside the ritual situation of symbolized birth.

If men are so determined to act out motherhood (and oblige their sons to act out birth) and go to considerable measures to simulate physiological birth (see, for example, White 1961 and Turner 1962:124–173) why should they concentrate their symbolizing on the grosser fact of parturition and not, in their drive for authenticity, seek to replicate in rites of initiation other details of birth, details unlikely to be esoteric in the small-scale kinship society?

The question in my section title here is rhetorical. My premise is that in primitive society sufficient knowledge of the human fetus and birth would have been culturally available for this whole process of male motherhood to be symbolically represented in an extremely detailed way.

In the following section I take some of the common passage ritual symbols found cross-culturally and demonstrate how aptly they reflect the natal evidence.

THE NATAL FACTS OF REBIRTH SYMBOLS

The placing of ash or white clay on the face and body of the initiand and the ritual emphasis on the color white[5]

The human body at birth is a decidedly bluish color, the body being in a state known as cyanosis; that is, lacking oxygen. The blue fades rapidly as soon as the baby inflates its lungs with its first breath. The bluishness is partially masked by an oily white substance that in fact appears a dirty, greyish white as a result of the blue beneath. The substance is called *vernix caseosa*. Bourne (1975:72) aptly describes it as "a greasy adherent, cheese-like, material." It collects on the fetal skin from the fifth month onwards (Crouch and McClintic 1971:524–525).

Nilsson, Ingelman-Sunberg and Wirsen (1966:132) write:

> Next to each hair are one or more sebaceous glands which provide an oily substance called sebum to keep the hair lustrous and the skin soft. This is especially important during pregnancy, when the baby floats in water. The skin must not become sodden. The sebum from the sebaceous glands and cells shed from the epidermis form a protective ointment, called vernix caseosa. The lanugo hairs help the vernix cling to the surface of the skin. Hence large amounts are seen in hairy areas such as the eyebrows, scalp and upper lip. At delivery the fetal waters are usually muddy with loosened vernix, and the newborn baby looks greasy before it has been bathed and carried in again, neat and rosy.

Because large amounts may be dislodged during parturition, a considerable variation shows in the extent of vernix cover of newborn babies. Many have just a few small patches; some, however, are liberally covered as though they had been dipped in a bowl of it. Much less variation and a consistently higher coverage is found on the fetus (see Nilsson, Ingelman-Sunberg and Wirsen (1966:93, 122, and 133 for photographs of the vernix covering of the face and hand of a six-month-old fetus).

It is very difficult not to be impressed by the similarity in appearance of the vernix on the fetus or newborn baby with the ash smeared on candidates in initiation rituals. This is well demonstrated in Crawford's (1981:264–283) series of photographs of the male initiation ceremonies of the Gogodala of the Lower Fly in Papua New Guinea. Stylized patterns are evident in Schindlbeck's (1980: plates 63–65) photographs of female sex initiation ceremonies of the Sawos in the middle Sepik, Papua New Guinea. The association with the use of a white color on facial masks is also evidenced in, for example, Crawford (1981), and White (1961: Frontispiece).[6] Where the ash or clay is a symbolic representation of vernix, the ritual stage indicated can be either liminality (fetal) or incorporation (natal).

Anointing with oil or smearing with fat

The use of either oil (see, for example, Beidelman 1965:146) or fat (see, for example, Brain 1979:182) appear good enough representations of the greasiness of a baby at birth. In both the examples cited, African (Beidelman) and Australian (Brain), the use of the oil and fat are immediately prior to the initiands' re-entry into society. But as with ash, oil and fat can equally represent liminal or incorporation stages.

The cutting of head or body hair

A human baby at birth is growing its third set of hair. The first fetal hair appears in the third month "a kind of vibrissae or whiskers on the upper lip, the eyebrows, and—curiously enough—on the palms and soles. Gradually these coarse primordia disappear and a softer hair, called the lanugo, develops all over the body like a downy fell" (Nilsson, Ingelman-Sunberg and Wirsen 1966:126). This begins in the sixteenth week (Bourne 1975:70). The head hair starts to appear at twenty weeks when the fetus is ten inches (1975). Nilsson, Ingelman-Sunberg and Wirsen (1966:126) remark: "The hair of the head, eyebrows, and eyelashes grows rather slowly: the coiffure at this early stage looks nicely trimmed." While the head hair continues its very slow growth, the lanugo hair is eventually lost. Nilsson, Ingelman-Sunberg and Wirsen (1966:143) write that at birth the rest of "the lanugo hairs are shed together with the vernix. The baby swallows part of them together with fetal fluid and they come out on the first diapers."

The terminal head hair itself grows coarser and may change its "style" during the first year or so of a child's life. Europeans are aware that the curly-headed baby boy beauty may need to forego a haircut if he is to retain his glory. However, it is apparently less known or, more likely, less remarked upon that among curly-headed people a baby may start life with straight hair and his curls appear only later (up to a year). The spouses of a mixed Melanesian-European marriage, for instance, have no way of telling at their child's birth whether it will ultimately have straight, wavy or curly hair.

It may seem extremely simplistic, given the amount of literature on the ritual significance of hair to relate ritual haircutting to natal symbolism. But ritual shaving or cutting of head hair both point to the natal appearance of a "nicely trimmed coiffure." The newborn baby has relatively little head hair (usually concentrated in a patch or ridge); it is short (two to four centimeters according to Bourne 1975:80); and it gives way to a more vigorous, coarser, growth. Whether initiands' head hair is simply cropped or shaved completely varies cross-culturally in rites, but the message is the same. The depilation of body hair which accompanies some rituals, for example, in the treatment of the Iranian girl prior to marriage, has the same function of symbolizing the natal state.

Nail paring

Nilsson, Ingelman-Sunberg and Wirsen (1966:92) state that at the fetal age of five and a half months (when the fetus is twelve inches) the nails are about to reach the finger tips. Between seven months and term they continue to grow, eventually reaching just beyond the finger tips, so that often the fingernails have to be cut immediately after birth to avoid scratching (p. 143) and so avoid becoming liable to infection. (Though Bourne 1975:80 asserts the nails "are soft and will not damage the skin by scratching during the first twenty-four hours of life.") In the ritual context, nail paring is frequently carried out at the same time as haircutting and ash daubing.

Knocking-out of a tooth

Prenatal appearance of teeth is very rare and for many months after birth the baby has no teeth. The knocking-out of one or two front teeth, usually the central or lateral incisors which in the deciduous (milk) teeth are commonly the first to drop, could be seen as symbolic of a return to the "gummy," natal state.

Ritual emphasis on the color red

There is a "pool or lake of maternal blood lying immediately beneath the placenta" (Bourne 1975:82) and "into which the lobes of the placenta are immersed" (1975:82). Consequently there is a lot of maternal blood around at birth and the newborn is liberally covered with it. The flow of a thick, sticky bloody mucus from the vagina is a sure sign that the labor pains have begun in earnest (Nilsson, Ingelman-Sunberg and Wirsen 1966:140).

Ritual emphasis on a dark color (blue, black)

The cyanosed state of the baby's blood at birth gives it a distinctive blue appearance. The fairer-skinned the baby, the more vivid the coloring, but it is readily apparent in darker-skinned babies.

Use of water and purification

There are two referents for this symbol in the birth process. First, the fetus lives its life in the watery world of the amniotic sac. The bursting of this sac and subsequent flood of fetal fluid from the vagina is the first sign of imminent birth.[7] Bourne (1975:85) states that at ordinary term delivery (fortieth week), the amount is usually just over one liter. Secondly, birth is a very messy business. Apart from the blood and greasy slippery vernix, the mother freely defecates since control over these muscles is lost in the rhythm of the birth contractions. Hence, one of the baby's first experiences before being presented to the world is to be gently cleaned and bathed.

Heat and warmth (actual or reference to)

At birth the baby is leaving an environment of about 98 degrees Fahrenheit. Relative to the outside temperature it is warm, even hot, to touch. Initiands may be referred to as "hot," especially at the actual rebirth rites (see, for example, White 1961:10).

Hazing

Birth is a difficult and undoubtedly painful (traumatic?) experience for the baby. The forced passage is well represented in the Mukanda initiation ritual of the Luvale of Central Africa. "Here the novices take off their kilts, the thicket is set on fire, and the novices one by one with *sakambungu* [the leader of the novices] in front, leap through the flame and try to break through a row of men armed with switches, finally throwing themselves into the river" (White 1961:10).

Nakedness and the burying or destroying of the clothing of liminality

Nakedness of initiands is not commonplace in male initiation ritual. It may be stressed at different times in a ritual (see, for example, the quote from White immediately above), but it is unusual for initiands to remain naked throughout their seclusion period. Stress on nakedness seems more marked in passage rituals of rulers (see, for example, Gluckman 1963:118–126). The burying of the clothes of the seclusion period is a common occurrence, but it is perhaps too speculative to associate this with the burying of the placenta.

There are other symbolic actions found cross-culturally in male initiation rites—the burning of the "womb" of seclusion, initiands' inability to speak or to recognize persons, and so forth, the birth symbolism of which is generally acknowledged in the literature. That acknowledgment, I would say, is added support for the explanations which I have been giving here.

FETAL FACTS AND PENILE SURGERY

If we accept that these common symbolic actions in initiation rites do represent features of actual birth, what does this tell us of the widespread initiatory practice that traditionally has so attracted the attention of anthropologists: circumcision? Can this be related to the natal facts? Or should we recognize circumcision rites as a special category of their own (the kind of "collecting" which Leach—for example, 1976:96—is anxious to avoid)?

I find it impossible to relate circumcision to the *natal* facts. But given male determination to be mothers, why should the symboling in male sex initiation rites be restricted to the natal? What about the fetal facts?

Prima facie, the possibility of tribal men's knowledge of fetal facts is certainly going to arouse more objections than the idea of his familiarity with natal facts. Babies are being born continuously and there is little reason to suppose knowledge of the phenomena of birth would not be widespread and well-known in a community. But how often would fetuses be seen?

In answer to this major objection I would first emphasize that the context is not a particular set of men in a particular community at a particular time discussing the attributes of human fetuses around the campfire. What I am talking about is the culture memory, if I can for the present purpose divest the concept of its psychoanalytical connotations. The fact is that over a considerable period of time, knowledge on different subjects will continually be gathered, stored, and accumulated in succeeding generations. It may well be that this process in some areas of knowledge will be through the agency of specialists hoarding, or revealing, esoteric facts for their own or their community's purposes—the Gagools and their neophytes.

What, then, are the chances of a culture accumulating knowledge of fetal existence? I think they would be quite good. In every generation it is likely that miscarriages will occur. Pregnant women sometimes die and may then be open to inspection for signs of witchcraft or sorcery.[8] Pregnant women (among others) may indeed have been killed and "dressed" for the table in some societies, or simply opened up for their king's curiosity (shades of Shaka). It is true some scholars—notable among them Bettelheim (1954:104)—have assumed tribal peoples uniformly will have little knowledge of the internal form and functions of the human body. But is that an acceptable assumption? William Mariner, shipwrecked in the Tongan

Islands in 1806 (see Martin 1817) and obliged to turn native for four years, was astonished at the skill with which the wounded in battle were treated. And yet was there good reason for his surprise? Certainly in any society where bodies are being for some reason cut up, some knowledge of form and function, even if restricted to "specialists," is likely.

In my opinion, knowledge of the human fetal life over time, over generation after generation, over epochs, would filter into the culture memory and accumulate. It can surely be no coincidence, for example, that many of the monsters of myth so closely resemble the monsters of anomalous embryonic growth, even if, as with Cyclops, we name the latter after the former. If men choose to be "mothers," and if this is important enough for them to go to at times incredible lengths in organizing rituals of great complexity for this purpose, it seems unlikely such a rich source of knowledge would have not been utilized.

But granted this, a further caution can be made. What details to perhaps a tutored eye but nonscientific mind will a human fetus yield at what stages of growth? The question of size is important. A twelve-inch fetus aborted or in utero is easily locatable and large enough to provide considerable detail to the unaided eye. But a one-inch fetus? Clearly size at some stage comes into the reckoning. A text book for midwives (Myles 1972:43) in an opening statement to a chapter on fetal development makes the following warning: "It is essential that the midwife should have some idea how very small the embryo is during the early weeks so that, in cases of abortion, she may know what to look for. Very seldom is the embryo of less than six weeks seen as it is not readily detected in the blood clot." Bourne (1975:270) refers to "a clot of liver-like material." The embryo is, in fact, just visible to the naked eye at the end of four weeks.

At eight weeks and one inch, however, the embryo, or rather fetus now,[9] is much more visible or locatable than even its doubling in size would suggest. Though it is still very small, it is now contained within the roomy watery world of the amniotic sac and, moreover, the embedded chorionic villi start to grow profusely to form the attached placenta, which is well formed from the twelfth week. Myles (1972:43) gives the size of the sac as a hen's egg (presumably a 1971 hen's egg) at eight weeks and a goose's egg at twelve weeks, with the placenta now weighing more than the fetus. As the embryo/fetus itself grows, it becomes more readily locatable (aborted or in utero) by its growing sac and placenta. At term, the placenta is a dish shape seven inches in diameter, one and a half inches thick, and weighing about one and a quarter pounds (Bourne 1975:82).

Myles (1972:43) warns her student midwives: "It is not always easy to estimate the age of an embryo. Length and weight, the degree of development and the period of gestation are all taken into consideration." From the variations (at times considerable) in the correlations of age and size by different authorities, I would say her warning could apply equally to the fetus. Since it is important for my argument that the reader has a reasonable idea of the size, appearance, and detail of a fetus at a particular stage, and so the degree it might be a source of information to a person examining it, I illustrate this variation below. I have made length uniform in centimeters (because this is what most authorities use) and age in weeks.[10]

Crouch and McClintic (1971) and Hamilton and Mossman (1972) produce, or are on their way to producing, babies of less than fourteen inches at birth, while the other three produce twenty-inch babies. The ideal solution for the reader—and this applies to the entire argument of these last sections of the paper—is to examine a set of human fetus specimens for himself. Whatever the variation, one thing is clear: the very rapid growth of the fetus. Bourne (1975:71, 73–76, 78–79) represents this well in a series of illustrations that also gives the size of the growing fetus (at 12, 16, 20, 24, 28, 32 and 34–36 weeks respectively) relative to the mother's body.

By the twelfth week from ovulation, the fetus is recognizably human to the uninformed eye (Bourne 1975:68) and is properly formed. Bourne (1975:10) comments: "The remainder of the pregnancy is designed not only to allow the fetus to grow to a size at which it is capable of independent survival, but also to give all the vital organs in the body sufficient time to mature and to develop their highly complex processes which are essential for independent survival."

For the layman a most startling fact of this process of maturation is that in its early stages between twelve and sixteen weeks, when the fetus is easily recognizable as human and it is sufficiently large (up to a maximum of more than six inches) for it to be examined in detail, the sex is difficult to determine, but it appears to be male. Certainly the sex of the fetus can be diagnosed prior to the sixteenth week, for the development of the external genitalia begins to diverge from about the twelfth week, but my own experience as, to use Bourne's phrase, "an untrained observer,"

Table 1. Co-relation of Age and Size of Fetus by Different Authorities

Authority	Fetal Age (weeks)							
	4	8	12	16	20	24	28	40
Myles	.6	3.0	8.9	15.2	20.3	30.4	35.6	51
Bourne	ns	2.2	7.0	16.0	25.5	33.0	37.0	51
N.I.-S.W.	.6	3.0	6.5	16.0	25.0	31.0	34.0	51
Crouch/McClintic	.5	2.3	5.6	11.2	15.0	ns	ns	35
Hamilton/Mossman	.4	3.0	5.2	9.5	15.0	20.0	ns	ns

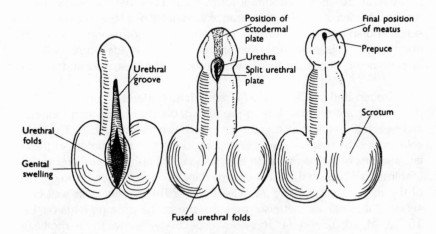

Figure 1. Development of the male external genitalia. Reprinted with permission from Beck, Moffat, and Lloyd, *Human Embryology and Genetics*, (Oxford: Basil Blackwell, 1973).

was to believe initially that all the specimens up to about sixteen weeks which I was looking at were male. "By the end of the sixteenth week," Bourne (1975:70) writes, "the limbs are properly formed and all the joints are moving . . . The fingers and toes are normal and fingernails and toenails are present. The head is still relatively large for the size of the body but fairly rapid growth continues to enlarge the body. Primary sex characteristics continue to develop and the sex of the infant is now obvious to the untrained observer." Myles (1972:43) tells her student midwives: "Sixteen weeks—The fetus measures 15.2 cm (6 inches) . . . sex can be distinguished." Hamilton and Mossman (1972:434) date "the definitive form of external genitalia" somewhat later (120–150 days) and reckon the fetus a little smaller (10–14 cms).

How do the male external genitalia develop? It was not feasible to paraphrase the textbook description, and so I have given a direct quotation (Beck, Moffat, and Lloyd 1973:257–258). Figure 1 should help in following the description.

> After the disappearance of the urogenital membrane the urethra is widely open in the perineum but the urethral folds soon begin to fuse with each other to close off the opening and form a floor to the posterior part of the urethra. This fusion takes place from behind forwards. When the process reaches the phallus the urethral

plate splits ventrally and forms an endodermal floor to a much deepened urethral groove. The ectoderm then fuses across the midline leaving the endoderm-lined urethra within the phallus, in a manner reminiscent of the closure of the neural tube. As a result of these changes the external urethral opening is carried forward towards the tip of the phallus although it still opens on the under surface. A plate of ectoderm then grows backwards from the top to meet the urethra. This becomes canalized and, with the closure of the previous opening, forms the terminal part of the urethra. A circumferential invagination of ectoderm invades the phallus (now known as the penis) for a short distance from its tip and when this breaks down it separates the prepuce from the glans penis. Finally the descent of the testis into the genital swellings, which thus form the scrotum, completes the development of the external genitalia.

The external urethral opening referred to is the urethral meatus. Beck, Moffat, and Lloyd do not give the age and size of the fetus at the different stages of the above development. Hamilton and Mossman (1972:434), however, give the following details for the progress of the meatus according to fetal age (they state from ovulation) and size:

Fetal age	Size
90 days	55 mm—meatus on under-surface of penis proximal to glans
90–105 days	60 mm—meatus encroaches on undersurface of glans penis
105–120 days	70 mm—meatus confined to glans penis
120–150 days	100–140 mm—definitive form of external genitalia

I have already indicated that Hamilton and Mossman seem to underestimate the size of the fetus. Their figures (90 days at 60 mm to 120 days at 70 mm) also depict a very slow growth of the fetus. Nilsson, Ingelman-Sunberg and Wirsen (1966), for example, see the fetus *doubling* in size between three and four months (in fact from three inches to six inches). But even with the lower figures, the shifting position of the meatus is observable to the naked eye.

The prepuce begins developing in the fifth month, subsequent to the final positioning of the meatus. As far as the appearance of the external genitalia is concerned, this is prior only to the descent of the testes which occurs in the eighth month.

FETAL SYMBOLS: CIRCUMCISION, SUBINCISION, AND SUPERINCISION

The fetal facts are there, but are tribal peoples or their specialists aware of them? I have to admit in my own fieldwork I have not pursued the subject, either because my theory had yet to be formed or because more recently my research has been on behalf of government and in far-removed applied fields. Furthermore, I am not acquainted with any literature that deals with what one might call "ethno-embryology," and even for anthropologists that is a fairly obscure subject. But given the circumstantial evidence of the fetal facts, given the resoluteness of adult males to become "mothers," given their ready employment of natal symbolism, the argument for fetal symbolism is strong.[11]

In the context of rebirth, the natal symbols once identified are self-explanatory. Thus the smearing of ash on the face represents the vernix covering that indicates birth. The baby at birth *has* a covering of vernix. But what about circumcision? The male baby at birth has a foreskin! Clearly we need an explanation.

One evident factor is that circumcision commonly takes place at the beginning of initiation ritual, that is before, often long before, the natal and parturitional symbolic actions occur. So this suggests the symbol represents the prenatal, that is fetal, form. This as we have seen bears with the facts. The penis has a most decidedly circumcised look up to the fifth month precisely because the prepuce has yet to appear.

More significant, though, is the common reference and association of the act of circumcision with killing and dying (see, for example, White 1961:4; Beidelman 1965:144), which may or may not be accompanied by the symbolic acting out of the death of initiands (for example, being swallowed by mythical monsters). The message now appears clear. Circumcision is a symbolic killing because it reduces the young, socially asexual boy to the status of a fetus, an unborn: he is being killed to be reborn. The circumcisional act demonstrates that he is, so to speak, being put back into the womb. Which symbolically, in fact, usually proceeds to happen, though of course it is a male womb in which he is now placed, and out of sight and out of sound of secular (profane) society.

Putting him back in the womb fits in well enough with adult males demonstrating their motherhood. But the further question remains: why the concern to symbolize a fetal rather than the natal state of the penis?

While sexuality is the motif of the male initiation rite, particular attention to the penis is not unexpected. Yet the male fetus at term has its prepuce. But then this is the point. The male fetus at term is being born of woman, subsequently to be given the status of child and asexual. The male initiand at term is being born of man, subsequently to attain the status of male sexual. The penis, in being circumcised, is being restored to an original fetal form existing prior to the growth of the prepuce that characterizes the social asexual at birth.[12] The young initiand has been "killed," resurrected as a fetus, and is now grown and matured to emerge at term as a male characterized by a penis that now has sexual functions and represents his new status.[13]

Circumcision, then, symbolizes a fetal stage prior to the development of the prepuce (and the reference here is to a fetus at least eight inches long). The male "mothers" are symbolizing not only that they are nurturing a fetus, but that a fetus born of them will be without the asexual mark of the infant boy; that is, it will be born a sexual. This argument, of course, supports the well-established assertion that circumcision is to bestow and demonstrate social maleness. But while I agree that its effect is that, I emphasize that my purpose here has been to establish the consistency of the act of circumcision within the general complex of rebirth symbolism.

If circumcision is consistent with the theme and symbols of rebirth, what of the other male genital mutilations: supercision and subincision? These are much rarer than circumcision, and subincision, which I shall look at first, seems confined to Australia.

A wide range of origins have been proposed for subincision. Some of these have been remarkable. Singer and Desole (1967), for example, propose its origin in kangaroo bifid penis envy. As far as kangaroos are concerned, I am in sympathy with Cawte's (1968:962) more cautious approach: "Our field studies incline us to agree with our Walbiri informants in attaching some significance to the 'marsupial' origins of subincision." But I think I am in large company when I observe that local exegetes do not necessarily expound structural explanations.

Easily the commonest explanation of subincision origin is female envy. The penis is operated upon to make it resemble the vagina. The operation is drastic enough to oblige the subject subsequently to squat to urinate. Periodically thereafter the subincised person causes himself to bleed from the operated area, hence the theme of male menstruation. Bettelheim (1954:204) puts this down to the "human beings' envy of the genital apparatus of the other sex [which] leads to the desire to acquire similar organs and to gain power and control over the genitals of the other sex." His insights are derived from clinical work with schizophrenic children, but he is not alone in perceiving subincision as a male attempt to reproduce the female form.

But is it necessarily the female form? The semblance of the subincised states to the condition of hypospadias has not gone unnoticed in the literature. Cawte (1968:962), for example, allows among other things a "folie communiquee induced by an innovator with penile hypospadias . . . could serve to reinforce the [subincision] practice." The drawings of penile and peno-scrotal hypospadias in Figure 2 certainly are impressive in their similarity with the appearance of the artificially mutilated penis (Cawte 1968:963 includes a photograph of a subincised Australian). But then if we ponder on that similarity we come up with another. For the condition of hypospadias represents an arrested stage in the fetal development of the male urogenital system (compare Figures 1 and 2).

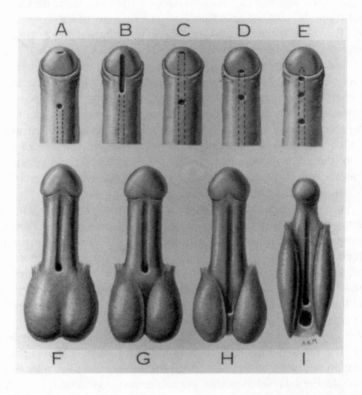

Figure 2. Drawings to show varieties of hypospadias. *A–E*: penile, with the urethral meatus situated on the ventral surface of the penis; *F–I*: varieties of peno-scrotal hypospadias. Reproduced with permission from Hamilton, Boyd, and Mossman, *Human Embryology* (London and Basingstoke: Macmillan, 1972).

Taking the detail in Figure 1 with the account I have already given of the development of the male external genitalia, including the encroaching movement of the meatus on the glans penis, it is evident enough that the genital operation of subincision could well symbolize the fetal facts. According to Hamilton and Mossman, the meatus does not reach its terminal position on the glans penis until the fourth month, at the end of which the fetus is (according to the authority you choose) anywhere between ten and sixteen cm long. It could be, in other words, that subincision represents an early (fetal) form of the male genitalia.

A new generation of female writers has highlighted the scientific findings of the female as "...nature's original and most durable model" (Nowak 1980:245). Nowak remarks (p. 27) that a "hormonal push" is essential for masculine development: "Here, once more, the female-base principle is operative. Unless 'something more' is added, this time hormones, fetal development is feminine. The principle is evident, too, in the development of the external genitals. Without any extra hormonal incentive,the genital tubercle and associated structures develop into the female clitoris and vagina ... The fetus can coast easily along the direct path toward feminine fulfillment." She cites various scientific authorities to the effect that "the 'resting state' is on the female side." Finally (1980:25) she quotes Lief (n.d.): "The primordial fetus is, then, female. If one wishes to be mythically symbolic, one might say that Eve preceded Adam and that the Biblical story is a reflection of ancient male chauvinism."

Embryologists, in fact, refer to the early growth of the fetus as the "indifferent stage" (see, for example, Hamilton and Mossman 1972:433). But the expert description is based on scientific knowledge of the developmental homologues of the male and female genital systems. The notable phenomenon of these early stages to the *untrained* eye of the modern layman, and I would suggest to the trained eye of a primitive nonscientific man, is not undifferentration of sex in fetuses, but the presence of a single sex: all fetuses up to about sixteen weeks appear to be male. For the untrained, the male (not the female) may be perceived as the basic human theme.

If we accept that in some societies men's resolve to present themselves as "mothers" leads them to the extremes of fetal symbolization of the young males they are nurturing and giving birth to, then the same question arises with subincision as with circumcision: why represent an early stage of fetal growth rather than the terminal stage?

Where practiced subincision usually follows circumcision, the fetal stage of the growing of the new male is then already established by the latter operation. Subincision, I believe, emphasizes belief in the original male prototype of the human being from which the female only later develops. It portrays the antithesis of modern scientific findings that the female is nature's basic theme: "She is the original upon which the male is later moulded, with appropriate modification. She is the alpha; he, but a beta." (Nowak 1980:20) But in the androcentric way of things it is essential that *he* is the alpha, that Eve is formed from Adam's rib, not vice versa. The question I leave unanswered here as beyond my present terms of reference is why subincision is limited to some Australians? What is it about their culture that has produced this practice but kept it uniquely their own? One has surely to return to the starting point: the basic fact that men exercise their choices from a range of possibilities to establish the values their cultures enshrine and start the search for correlations.

One prominent feature of subincision is that the site of the wound is subsequently used to induce periodic bleeding. Australian informants themselves say they make the boys bleed so that they become like women. Douglas (1975:65) writes of "initiation rites in which the genital organs of boys are cut so that they bleed with the explicit intention of making a parallel to female menstruation." In producing this effect subincision is similar to supercision (a far less drastic operation) where cuts are made on the glans penis to produce bleeding and this practice is carried on from initiation into adulthood.

The representation of menstrual flow in the males by supercision may be quite explicit in the culture as Hogbin (1970) well illustrates for the Wogeo of New Guinea in his book *The Island of Menstruating Men*. The Wogeo culture carries overtones of male envy of menstruation, for the latter is perceived in terms of a natural cleansing operation. Thus Hogbin (1970:91) observes:

> The salutary effects of penile surgery are said to be immediately observable. The man's body loses its tiredness, his muscles harden, his step quickens, his eyes grow bright, and his skin and hair develop a luster. He therefore feels lighthearted, strong, and confident. This belief provides a means whereby the success of all perilous or doubtful undertakings can be guaranteed. Warriors make sure to menstruate before setting out on a raid, traders before carving an overseas canoe or refurbishing its sails, hunters before weaving a new net for trapping pigs.

Apart from hacking at the glans penis, blood may even be induced to flow from the urethra itself. Thus Tuzin (1980:75) gives a rather heart-stopping, firsthand account of bloodletting by an Ilahita Arapesh adult:

> After stimulating an erection he inserted a green stem about eight centimeters long into his urethra and, with a shudder that ran visibly through his thighs and torso, yanked it out. Blood oozed from the urethral opening; within three or four repeats of this action, it was spurting a fine spray to a distance of about two meters. The stem, as I had been shown beforehand, was covered with small barbs pointing slightly downward along its length. This meant that, while the stem could be easily inserted, on pulling it out the barbs caught and tore at the urethral lining. In all, Kwambafum used eight stems, inserting each of them until the barbs wore down, that is to say, five to ten times.

But why should the males have envy of the menstrual flow? True, they certainly seem the better for menstruating as Hogbin (1970:91) and Tuzin (1980:76) point out, but it seems a rather drastic tonic. Do we simply have to rely upon the envy thesis of Bettelheim and others as an explanation? I suggest we might go one step further than this.

I can make out no fetal or natal symbolism for supercision, but the emphasis on bleeding does place the operation and practice securely within the rebirth theme which has been the context for such symbolism.

There is one aspect of menstrual blood, one complementary to menstrual flow, which has been passed over in the emphasis in the literature on male menstruation, envious or not. When the menstrual flow of a premenopausal woman does *not* appear, the indications are (and all cultures seem to recognize them) the woman is pregnant. Not surprisingly some cultures maintain that the blood which would otherwise have flowed now goes to make up or help make up the substance of the fetus. Of the Wogeo's conception belief, Hogbin (1946:207) states: "According to local theory conception takes place when the menstrual blood has been damned up in the womb by a considerable quantity of semen." Mountain Arapesh of the East Sepik, who include supercision in their male initiation ceremonies (Mead 1940:346), have a similar belief: "the child is product of father's semen and mother's blood, combined in equal amounts at the start, to form a new human being" (Mead 1935:31). But the blood contributed by the mother is seen specifically as the same as that of the menstrual flow—"her blood, no longer issuing forth as menstruation, becomes half of the material of the child's body, the other half of which is made of semen" (Mead 1940:350). Tuzin who describes (1980:66–78) a similar male initiation ceremony for the neighboring Ilahita Arapesh, also remarks (1976:151): "Foetal development, it is thought, occurs through the intermingling of sperm and menstrual blood in the womb." He footnotes this (1976:151): "The theory is that menstrual blood wells up from unspent periods during the pregnancy months."

The periodic bloodletting, the male menstrual flow, is in fact indicative of the potential and prowess of the male as mother. He can provide *both* the semen and the menstrual blood needed to form a fetus and give rise to the birth of a male. Thus man makes the firmest statement of the fiction of male reproductive self-sufficiency and independence.

CONCLUSION

Man is everywhere differentiated by his cultures. These cultures reflect the range of his ecologies and the variety of his histories. But taken together they also reflect a single evolutionary mode. The diversity of cultures comes as no surprise, but nor should the presence of unifying themes.

While scholars have to argue for common cognitive mechanisms in the mind of Man that can account for the existence of cross-cultural patterns of behavior, no one has to argue that the course of embryonic development is common to all men. It is a biological fact. Mankind constitutes a single species: irrefutable evidence to adduce for the assertion that all humans possess a common code of ontogenetical symboling.

Notes

1. I should like to acknowledge the following persons who have helped me in various ways to uncover the mysteries of the fetus and of birth: Dr. Eugene Tan, JoAnne Craig, and Professor Roland Sharma. I also thank Blackwell Scientific Publications, Oxford, for permission to reproduce Figure 1 from their publication *Human Embryology & Genetics* by F. Beck, D. B. Moffat, and J. B. Lloyd, and W. Heffer & Sons Ltd., Cambridge, for permission to reproduce Figure 2 from their publication *Human Embryology* by W. J. Hamilton and H. W. Mossman.

2. Man's appreciation of a death/rebirth model for arranging status changes in living society might be heightened by his desire for reassurance that life does follow death (see, for example, Romans VI).

3. With Derek Freeman's permission, I am citing from my own tatty but valued mimeo copy of his lecture, "Human Nature and Culture." The lecture was in the series of University Lectures of 1969, *Man and the New Biology*, given at the Australian National University. The University Press published the lectures in 1970 under the same title.

4. I am not denying cultural importance attached to complementarity of the sexes—the yin-yang connection. It is the existence of male dominance in a culture that makes anomalous the implications of female physiological capabilities, though cultures vary in their preoccupation with masking the fact. As Hrdy (1981:202n.9) points out: "Much of the controversy over male dominance revolves around the question of *inevitability*, rather than the issue of whether or not male dominance exists."

5. My evidence is based on what I have witnessed at human births supplemented by information from textbooks, including Nilsson, Ingelman-Sunberg and Wirsen (1966).

6. For textual reference to the smearing of white ash or clay on initiands see: White 1961:7, 10; Beidelman 1965:144; Brain 1979:182, to cite just a few examples.

7. The experience of David Copperfield who was born in an unruptured sac (or caul) is exceedingly rare according to Bourne (1975:84).

8. William Edel, Margaret Mead's co-resident in the Holt household on Ta'ū in Western Samoa "still vividly remembers an incident, described in *Coming of Age* [1968 edition, pages 105–106], when a post-mortem Caesarian section was performed with a bush-knife on a Samoan woman who had died in her eighth month of pregnancy. The fetus was cut from her belly as she lay in her shallow open grave so it could be buried in her arms instead of being reborn later as an avenging angel" (Howard 1983:70).

9. The embryo becomes a fetus at about the eighth week (Nilsson, Ingelman-Sunberg and Wirsen 1966:71) when all the primordia have been formed.

10. Average pregnancy, that is, from the first day of the last normal menstrual period, is 280 days or 40 weeks. Average age of the fetus at term counting from ovulation or conception is 266 days or 38 weeks. Unfortunately all the authorities I have consulted are confusing about which age scale they follow—even when they state explicitly their choice. On the question of size at a particular stage, it is noticeable in the table that the two "popular" books (Bourne and Nilsson, Ingelman-Sunberg and Wirsen) and the midwives' textbook are opposed to the two specialist texts. I add that they were all published within a period of ten years.

11. I would not restrict this to genital mutilations. The caul or amniotic sac which provides the bounds of the fetus' watery world evokes to a remarkable degree the shroud and veil, not uncommon clothing in some liminal states. See Nilsson, Ingelman-Sunberg and Wirsen 1966:116–117, 118–119, and 134 for photographs of fetuses between eight and twelve inches and four to four and a half months. On page 134, they write evocatively: "The baby sleeps inside its sheltering envelope." (Note: the eyes which close at ten weeks do not begin to open until the seventh month.)

12. The female characteristics of the uncircumcised thus lie not in any vulva-like appearance, sometimes commented upon in the literature, but derive from the asexual's association with the world of (female) mothers and women.

13. Even the scientific commentary is apt. Bourne (1975:70), writing of the properly formed fetus, observes "[but] if delivered it could not survive because although the organs are present they have not yet matured sufficiently to perform the duties for which they are designed."

References

Abrahams, R. G.
1972 Spirit, Twins and Ashes in Labwor, Northern Uganda. In *The Interpretation of Ritual: Essays in Honour of A. I. Richards*, edited by J. S. La Fontaine. London: Tavistock.

Beck, F., D. B. Moffat, and J. B. Lloyd
1973 *Human Embryology and Genetics*. Oxford: Blackwells.

Beidelman, T. O.
1965 Notes on Boys' Initiation Among the Ngulu of East Africa. *Man* 65:143–147.

Berg, Charles
1951 *The Unconscious Significance of Hair*. London. (Cited in Leach 1958.)

Bettelheim, Bruno
1954 *Symbolic Wounds: Puberty Rites and the Envious Male*. Glencoe: Free Press.

Bourne, Gordon
1975 *Pregnancy*. London: Pan.

Brain, James L.
1977 Sex, Incest and Death: Initiation Rites Reconsidered. *Current Anthropology* 18:191–208.

Brain, Robert
1979 *The Decorated Body*. London: Hutchinson.

Cawte, J. E.
1968 Further Comment on the Australian Subincision Ceremony. *American Anthropologist* 70:961–964.

Cohen, Yehudi A.
1964 The Establishment of Identity in a Social Nexus: The Special Case of Initiation Ceremonies and Their Relation to Value and Legal Systems. *American Anthropologist* 66:529–552.

Cooper, Wendy
1971 *Hair*. London: Aldus Books.

Crawford, A. L.
1981 *Aida: Life and Ceremony of the Gogodala*. Bathurst: Robert Brown.

Crouch, E. and Robert McClintic
1971 *Human Anatomy and Physiology*. New York: John Wiley.

Derrett, J. Duncan M.
1973 Religious Hair. *Man* 8:100–103.

Douglas, Mary
1975 *Implicit Meanings: Essays in Anthropology*. London: Routledge & Kegan Paul.

Eliade, Mircea
1958 *Rites and Symbols of Initiation: The Mysteries of Birth and Rebirth*. (Translated by Willard R. Trask.) New York: Harper and Row.

Firth, Raymond
1973 Hair as Private Asset and Public Symbol. In *Symbols, Public and Private*, by Raymond Firth. London: Allen & Unwin.

Fox, Robin
1967 *Kinship and Marriage*. London: Penguin.

1975 *Encounter with Anthropology*. New York: Delt.

Freeman, Derek
1969 Human Nature and Culture. Mimeographed. A lecture in the series Man and the New Biology, The University Lectures, 1969, The Australian National University, Canberra. (Published in 1970 in *Man and the New Biology*, edited by R. O. Slatyer et al. Canberra: Australian National University Press.)

1983 *Margaret Mead and Samoa: The Making and Unmaking of an Anthropological Myth*. Canberra: Australian National University Press.

Gennep, Arnold Van
1960 *The Rites of Passage*. (Translated by Monika B. Vizedom and Gabrielle L. Caffee.) London: Routledge & Kegal Paul. (Originally published in 1909.)

Gluckman, Max
1963 Rituals of Rebellion in South-East Africa. In *Order and Rebellion in Tribal Africa*, by Max Gluckman. London: Cohen & West.

Hallpike, C. R.
1969 Social Hair. *Man* 4:256–264.

Hamilton, W. J. and H. W. Mossman
1972 *Human Embryology*. Cambridge: Heffer.

Harrington, Charles
1968 Sexual Differentiation in Socialization and Some Male Genital Mutilations. *American Anthropologist* 70:951–956.

Hershman, P.
1974 Hair, Sex and Dirt. *Man* 9:274–298.

Hogbin, Ian
1946 Puberty to Marriage: A Study of Sexual Life of the Natives of Wogeo, New Guinea. *Oceania* 16:185–209.

1970 *The Island of Menstruating Men: Religion in Wogeo, New Guinea*. Scranton: Chandler.

Howard, Jane
1983 Angry Storm Over the South Seas. *Smithsonian* 14:66–75.

Hrdy, Sarah Blaffer
1981 *The Woman that Never Evolved*. Cambridge: Harvard University Press.

Kennedy, John G.
1970 Circumcision and Excision in Egyptian Nubia. *Man* 5:175–191.

Leach, Edmund
1958 Magical Hair. *Journal of the Royal Anthropological Institute* 88:147–164.

1976 *Culture and Communication*. Cambridge: Cambridge University Press.

Lief, Harold
n.d. Introduction to Sexuality. In *Comprehensive Textbook of Psychiatry*, edited by Alfred M. Freeman and Harold I. Kaplan. Baltimore: Williams & Wilkins. (Cited in Nowak 1980:27.)

Martin, John (ed.)
1817 An Account of the Natives of the Tonga Islands . . . Arranged from Exten-
      sive Communications of Mr. William Mariner . . . . Two volumes. London:
      Murray.

Mead, Margaret
1935 Sex and Temperament in Three Primitive Societies. London: Routledge
      & Kegan Paul.

1940 The Mountain Arapesh: II. Supernaturalism. New York: American Museum
      of Natural History.

1968 Coming of Age in Samoa. New York: Dell. (Originally published in 1928.)

Myles, Margaret F.
1972 A Textbook for Midwives. Edinburgh: Churchill Livingstone.

Nilsson, Lennard, Axel Ingelman-Sunberg, and Claes Wirsen
1966 A Child is Born. (Translated by Britt Wirsen, Claes Wirsen, and Annabelle
      MacMillan.) New York: Delacorte Press. (Originally published in 1965 as Ett
      barn Blirtill. Stockholm: Albert Bonniers Forlag.)

Norbeck, Edward, Donald E. Walker, and Mimi Cohen
1962 The Interpretation of Data: Puberty Rites. American Anthropologist 64:463–
      485.

Nowak, Mariette
1980 Eve's Rib: A Revolutionary New View of Female Sex Roles. New York: St.
      Martin's Press.

Schindlbeck, Markus
1980 Sago beiden Sawos (Mittel Sepik, Papua New Guinea). Basel: Ethnolo-
      gisches Seminar der Universitat und Museum fur Volkorkunde.

Singer, Philip and Daniel E. Desole
1967 The Australian Subincision Ceremony Reconsidered: Vaginal Envy or Kan-
      garoo Bifid Penis Envy. American Anthropologist 69:355–358.

Turner, Victor W.
1962 Three Symbols of Passage in Ndembu Circumcision Ritual: An Interpre-
      tation. In Essays on the Ritual of Social Relations, edited by Max Gluckman.
      Manchester: Manchester University Press.

1974 The Ritual Process. London: Penguin.

Tuzin, Donald F.
1976 The Ilahita Arapesh: Dimensions of Unity. Berkeley: University of California
      Press.

1980 The Voice of the Tambaran: Truth and Illusion in Ilahita Arapesh Reli-
      gion. Berkeley: University of California Press.

White, C. M. N.
1961 *Elements in Luvale Beliefs and Rituals*. Manchester: Manchester University Press.

Young, Frank W.
1962 The Function of Male Initiation Ceremonies: A Cross-Cultural Test of an Alternative Hypothesis. *American Journal of Sociology* 67:379–398.

Index

Abimbola, W. 195
Abrahams, R. G. 214
Abstract analytical system 49, 50
Academy of the Social Sciences
    in Australia 19
Achebe, C. 196
Actions 44, 48, 49, 93, 139, 152, 153,
    189, 197, 198, 200, 204-206
Action, Lord 85
Actor-centered approaches 43, 44
Adam's sin 75
Adaptation viii, 34, 138
Aeschylus 67, 138
Affines 71
Africa 48, 69, 92-94, 197, 198, 201, 202,
    203, 205, 206, 218, 220
African Segmentary Model 94
Agar, M. H. 185
Agaria 66
Age of Discovery 77
Agriculture, swidden 7, 8
Akan 207
Alahita Arapesh 116, 117
Alexander the Great 70, 73, 74
Alison, Sir A. 86
Altruism 151
Ambivalence 15, 35, 36, 70, 113, 114, 116
    132, 133, 139, 142, 151, 152; father-son
    ambivalence 114, 115, 118, 119, 128,
    130, 132, 134; fraternal ambivalence
    114, 118, 128, 133
Amis, K. 83
Amity 114, 129, 139, 151
Anglo-Australian social anthropology;
    see Anthropology
Anglo-Australian structuralism 71;
    see Structuralism
Anthropology 3-5, 8-17, 20, 22-24, 31, 33,
    35-37, 44, 48, 63, 66, 71, 72, 92, 93, 99,
    113, 133, 142, 143, 151, 159-161, 169,

175, 185, 187, 188, 190, 193, 194, 205,
213-215, 221, 226; and biology, relations
between 22; Anglo-Australian social 69,
70, 71, 91, 93, 94; Boasian 11, 17;
British social anthropology 8, 11, 13;
cultural 4, 17, 20; evolutionary 16;
of choice 43, 193; psychoanalytic vii;
reflexive 205; social 4, 31, 35, 44, 47,
69, 71, 91, 92, 124, 174; socio-
cultural 32, 36
Anthropology of choice, see Anthropology
Antistructure 57-58; see Contrastructure
Aphrodite 64
Appell, G. N. 8, 32-34, 36, 43-44, 46-48,
    50-52, 55-58, 153; and R. Harrison 55
Aranda 92
Aristotelianism 81
Aristotle 73, 74, 76, 77, 139
Asexuality 216, 226, 227, 233, see also
    Sexuality
Association of Social Anthropologists,
    Australian Branch 10, 18
Attachment behavior 19, 35, 114, 150
Augustus Caesar 76, 86
Australia, aboriginal 69, 71, 92, 218,
    227-230
Australian and New Zealand Association
    for the Advancement of Science 22, 138
Australian and New Zealand College of
    Psychiatrists 13
Australian Anthropological Society 10
Australian Institute of Aboriginal Studies 19
Australian National University vii, 57, 70,
    188, 232
Australian Society of Psychoanalysts 16

Bakongo 202
Bali 19
Ballanche, A. T. 87
Bambara 203

239

244   INDEX